# Ruby Ann's
# Down Home Trailer Park
# Holiday Cookbook

# Ruby Ann's
# Down Home Trailer Park
# Holiday Cookbook

## Ruby Ann Boxcar

**Foreword by Tammy Faye Bakker Messner**

CITADEL PRESS
Kensington Publishing Corp.
www.kensingtonbooks.com

CITADEL PRESS BOOKS are published by

Kensington Publishing Corp.
850 Third Avenue
New York, NY 10022

All Kensington titles, imprints, and distributed lines are available at special quantity discounts for bulk purchases for sales promotions, premiums, fund-raising, educational, or institutional use. Special book excerpts or customized printings can also be created to fit specific needs. For details, write or phone the office of the Kensington special sales manager: Kensington Publishing Corp., 850 Third Avenue, New York, NY 10022, attn: Special Sales Department, phone 1-800-221-2647.

Photos by Ruby Ann's husband Dew

First printing: October 2002

10  9  8  7  6  5  4  3  2

Printed in the United States of America

Library of Congress Control Number: 2002104520

ISBN 0-8065-2350-6

This book is dedicated to my husband, Dew,
to the Good Lord Above—the Baptist one,
of course—and to everybody at the
High Chaparral Trailer Park, and
to all my loyal fans.

# Contents

# *Foreword*

When Ruby Ann asked me to do the foreword for her newest book, you can't imagine how thrilled I was. After all, she and I are two peas in a pod! And I loved *Ruby Ann's Down Home Trailer Park Cookbook.* I laughed till I cried, which is what I'm known for. So when the invitation came, I told her that I'd be delighted to do it.

With that said, I was honored that the good folks at the High Chaparral Trailer Park had selected my birthday to be one of their celebrated days. The only thing I wish was that Ruby Ann had asked me for some of my makeup tips to include in that section since I've been doing makeup for years. I think my personal tips might have helped you readers to get even more into the holiday in the same way that birthday hats, or Santa caps, or even fun costumes do during other parts of the year. For example, think how much more you might enjoy my birthday if I'd been able to advise no matter what people say, less is *not* more! Smear it on, ladies! And DO NOT BLEND! Why rub it all off after just putting it on? And as Ruby Ann knows, blue eyeshadow is always in! Can you imagine what fun you can have in March if you listen to me when I say that an old barn looks a lot better with a good coat of paint? But that's OK—even without my added words, *Ruby Ann's Down Home Trailer Park Holiday Cookbook* is both wonderfully funny and helpful. And since I've had not one but TWO husbands in prison, I especially appreciate the extra visiting day that she mentions in each holiday section. And the food. I can't wait to try some of the recipes!

Ruby Ann is a dear. Just seeing her smiling face on the cover and reading the first book made me happy! And now there's more. We surely do need more laughter in this old world. And you'll find plenty of it in this book, too.

Love to you all,
*Tammy Faye*

# *Preface*

When it comes to everyday life in a trailer park, things can be somewhat ho-hum. A typical resident will get up, work like a dog for nine hours at minimum wage, come home, eat, maybe have a drink, watch some TV, and go to bed. Then you got the folks who get up, eat, get drunk, watch game shows or talk shows or soaps, pass out, cook somethin', get drunk, watch TV, and go to bed. Every once in a while the police show up and arrest a neighbor. As sad as it sounds, that's what the typical day is like. Or should I say used to be like.

Back in the 1990s, with my personal friend Bill Clinton in the White House, we at the High Chaparral Trailer Park decided it was time to make a change. We were all people who loved livin' but just couldn't afford to do it. We liked havin' a good time, but with our downtrodden lives, it was hard to find the sunshine in our everyday world, with the exception of a birthday, anniversary, or major holiday like Christmas or Halloween. Well, the trailer park council, which I happened to be on, came up with the idea of celebratin' all the major holidays plus a few others that meant a great deal to us, like the birthdays of Reba McEntire, Lorretta Lynn, Tammy Faye Bakker Messner, and Elvis. Well, the first year everyone loved it so much that they decided to go ahead and add some extra days like Tax Day or National Pig Day. In any case, it was as if our lives had been magically changed. Now at least once and often twice a month, we had a reason to get up and celebrate the special day that lay ahead. It was a miracle. People were bathin' daily, wakin' up before the noonday news, and even brushin' their teeth. And it was all because we'd decided to celebrate even more holidays than before. As time passed and I traveled around this fine country of ours, I spread our celebration idea from trailer park to trailer park, and now this way of life is taking place in almost *every* American trailer park. Now I know that findin' this much joy or fun by markin' special days every month is hard for some of you to believe.

For some folks the simple thought of a down home style holiday among people whose houses consist of thin layers of aluminum, insulation, and wood panelin' with nothin' but air and tires between them and the ground is nothin' less than mind-bogglin'. These people simply just don't know what they're missin'. They've never been blessed with the excitement, thrill, and tasteful decorations of a trailer celebration like me and my fellow residents at the High Chaparral Trailer Park have. They've never seen the smile that can come to a small child's face—or an out-of-work adult's face, for that matter—as he or she partakes in National Pig Day. But hope is near, thanks to this book that you're holdin' in your hand.

Because of *Ruby Ann's Down Home Trailer Park Holiday Cookbook,* everyone will be able to enjoy life and even pretend they were born on the wrong side of the tracks regardless of their geographical location, personal wealth, or social standin'. Regardless if your clothes are designed by Vera Wang in New York or Wang Chung in Taiwan, you'll be able to create the easy-to-make holiday food dishes, and with my decoratin' tips, you'll be able to give your abode the fantastically fun feelin' that can only be found in a trailer park holiday celebration. But wait, that's not all! Far be it from me to make this book all about myself. I've invited all the gang from my original cookbook, *Ruby Ann's Down Home Trailer Park Cookbook,* to share some of their favorite recipes as well.

My goal in this endeavor is to bring back the days when holidays meant somethin'. My trailer park holiday handbook will be somethin' that families can read and follow together, single people can share with their friends and loved ones, and everyone can buy for themselves or for others to brighten up their lives. *Ruby Ann's Down Home Trailer Park Holiday Cookbook* is sure to make the world that you live in even better than before. I'm no miracle worker (I will happily take your love offerin' in the form or a cashier's check or money order nonetheless), but the joy and positive nonchild-producin' type of love that will fill you, your home, your clan, and even your neighborhood if this book is followed to the letter will amaze and surprise you. I'm not jokin' when I tell y'all that even if you are the tightest-ass humbugger in the dang world, this book and its practices will make you see life in a far less mean-spirited way. Yes, dear reader, after just a few months of followin' the holiday celebrations that are printed on these pages, even a Republican would find his life so changed that he'd actually bend over and compassionately hug one of those single welfare mothers and her thirteen kids.

So are you ready to enjoy life again? Are you tired of watchin' the parade pass you by? Are you ready to move from the back seat of the bus by that bathroom with the door that won't stay shut up to the driver's seat? Are you ready to take control of this cheap roller coaster ride that you've called livin' and turn it into an All Park Pass at one of them big theme parks in Florida? If you've answered *yes* to all the above questions, then welcome aboard! My name is Ruby Ann Boxcar and I'm goin' to be your hostess! With all that out of the way, it's time for a few instructions.

I've tried to make this book easy for y'all to follow. At first I was tempted to simply list the holidays in alphabetical order since everyone already has a calendar. But after testin' this theory out on my niece Lulu Bell, my older sister Donna Sue, and my beloved Me-Ma, I found that the alphabetical thing was a bit tricky for those who are mentally challenged, drunk, or older than the wood Noah built his dang ark with. After tryin' a few other methods of layin' out the contents of this book on those I mentioned above, I finally hit paydirt when I simply listed the chapters in a calendar-type order. Once you know what month the holiday you're lookin' for is in, then all you have to do is go to that month's chapter, and you should find it. The only ones that y'all should have any trouble with are Easter and Passover. To help with those holidays, I've put 'em both in the month of April. Even if they fall in March this year, you'll find 'em in April. Trust me, it works out just fine. As far as the rest of the holidays go, they are in their traditional months. This uncomplicated book is simple and easy, and doesn't require much thought process, just like Lulu Bell, Donna Sue, and Me-Ma.

There are fourteen sections in this here book, and the first two are simply this one and an update on everyone in the trailer park. The next twelve are the chapters, which I've named after the 12 months of the Gregorian calendar. They include the guides to the holidays and some of my favorite recipes.

And bein' the history nut that I am, I've included some brief insight into each month at the start of its chapter. Speakin' of history, here are some tidbits about the Gregorian calendar that you might not know. We used to use the Julian Calendar until 1582, when Rome decided we needed less of a sissy-sounding name for measurin' our yearly times, thus the Gregorian calendar. Now the English, who are well known for both their sissy boys and their personal dislike of Rome, decided not to switch their monthly schedule at that time. It wasn't until the mid-eighteenth century that they and their colonies finally accepted the calendar change (it should be no surprise that Greece didn't give up the Julian Calendar until 1928). Currently every American-speakin' country in the world uses the Gregorian calendar, which, I might add, was not named after Gregory Peck, as many of us in the trailer park had thought, but after some fella named Pope Gregory XIII. You'll also notice that I list some of the month-long celebrations so y'all got things to celebrate on every day of the month. Me and the folks at the High Chaparral Trailer Park will help y'all with some of these thirty-one-day holidays by includin' recipes, but for the most part y'all are goin' to have use your own "wrong side of the track" imaginations.

In each chapter are the main holidays that we celebrate durin' that month, and they follow a simple format. At the top of the page, you'll find the name of that special day (Thanksgivin'), the date or day of the month that it usually falls on (the fourth Thursday of November), and if it's a day that conjugal visits are allowed. Now this last part is very important to most folks in a trailer park. As y'all have seen on TV shows like *Cops,* at some time in our life, somebody in the trailer park is goin' to jail for doin' somethin' stupid or sayin' somethin' stupid. Regardless, a holiday will come along and you'll need to know if your incarcerated loved one gets to celebrate it with a special gift or not, if you know what I mean. This information is also helpful for those of you out there who are doin' volunteer work, like my sister Donna Sue. My dear sister is more than just a fifty-six-year-old overweight drunken stripper. She happens to be a kind-hearted pillar of our community who, along with Little Linda and some of the other gals at the Blue Whale Strip Club in Searcy, Arkansas, spends her extra time goin' from prison to prison on conjugal visit days just to make sure that even the loneliest inmate has someone to call his own for at least five minutes of that day. When it comes to the penal system, my sister is right dab on it. And this information lets her and all you other kind souls know if you're goin' to be able to get any that holiday or not. God bless her and all you others out there who are helpin' those misguided men and women that fill our prisons in both this country and abroad.

Next come my comments on that holiday. I share some stories or history on that day in hopes to make this special time more meaningful for y'all. I follow this with four sections: "Things to Get You in the Holiday Mood," "Things to Do," "How to Decorate your Trailer for This Holiday," and "Trailer Park Tradition." All of these are pretty self-explanatory and I'm sure you'll have no problems followin' 'em. Just remember that these are simply ideas to help your enjoyment of these holidays. Feel free to come up with your own if you'd like, and if you do, please take the time to let me know. Send me an e-mail at rubylot18@aol.com or send those ideas to me via the fine folks who put my books out at Citadel Publishin'. Oh, and by the way, about the decorations: If you have problems pickin' any of 'em up, just do your best to sweep 'em over into some of your corners. At the end of the year, we'll vacuum those corners up and make the trailer home all nice and clean for next year's celebratin'!

"Somethin' to Bring to a Party" and "Dinner Menu" all revolve around the best part of a festive day, food. In each chapter, me and the folks at the High Chaparral Trailer Park have come up with some edible suggestions that are sure to make everyone in your trailer, house, apartment, or government-assisted livin' facility jump for joy. And trust me when I tell you that these recipes are good. Now, we by no means have created these recipes. We ain't got that kind of time on our hands. But what we've done is share some of our favorites. These dishes have been handed down from family members, clipped out of the newspaper, or just swiped from someone else's recipe box while they weren't lookin'. For you single folk out there, remember that you can always freeze those leftovers to enjoy at a later time. There are a couple of things I do want to mention to those of y'all who have not had the chance to pick up a copy of my first book, *Ruby Ann's Down Home Trailer Park Cookbook*. First off, some of the recipes call for government cheese, but you can use any cheese you like, includin' Velveeta, if you got that kind of money. Second, I've included some of my personal comments right below the dish's title. And last but not least, DO NOT ATTEMPT ANY OF MY ME-MA'S RECIPES! God bless her, I tried to leave hers out of this book, but the senile old thing insisted that I put her recipes in. Folks, I did my best, but I dare any of y'all out there to tell your dear old me-ma that you can't put her handwritten recipes in your book while she peers at you through those gigantic lenses that make her eyes look like two big Ping-Pong balls. I ask you, how do you say no to an elderly woman whose vivid fire-red wig is bein' held halfway on her head by three bobby pins and a prayer? Just remember to skip those dishes.

That's it! The intro is finished! Now we can move on! So let's go, and let me be the first to welcome you to the wonderful world of tires on your roof, propane tanks, two steps up to your front door, and three steps down on the social ladder, which all make up what we call trailer park livin'!

# *Update*

Pastor Hickey proudly welcomes all sinners to the
First Baptist Church of Pangburn on
this billboard out by the highway.

# The Residents of the High Chaparral Trailer Park, Lot by Lot

Since my first book, *Ruby Ann's Down Home Trailer Park Cookbook*, came out, I can't tell y'all how many people have asked me how everybody at the High Chaparral Trailer Park is doin'. I mean, it's amazin' all the love and care y'all have shown for my neighbors and family members. With all that in mind, I've decided to update y'all on all the changes and happenin's that have taken place. Now, let me start off by tellin' y'all that I do not believe in gossipin' like some folks. As a matter of fact, the only reason I'm even tellin' y'all this stuff is so you'll know what specifics to mention when you remember 'em in your prayers.

Before we can get into the happenin's in the trailer park, I've got to share the nightmare that most of us around here have been goin' through at the First Baptist Church of Pangburn. I'm surprised it hasn't made CNN, MSNBC, or even *Extra* for that matter. It hasn't been easy, but we've been makin' it through. Anyways, as y'all might recall, I mentioned our pastor, Pastor Hickey, in my last book and even showed a picture of his new son, little Dick Hickey, at the start of Chapter 8. Thanks to Pastor Hickey and his modern way of thinkin', just this last year we were able to proudly put up a billboard out along the highway that read "The First Baptist Church of Pangburn welcomes you . . . now acceptin' Visa, Master Card, Discover, and American Express." Yes, dear reader, it was totally Pastor Hickey's idea to wheel up in front of the altar, the only big-screen TV in town on Monday evenin's. And right after that our Monday-night service attendance went from just a few to double digits. Durin' the first part of the church services he'd hold an early offerin', and once he'd gotten what he thought was a fair dollar amount in the plate, he'd turn on Monday Night Football (muted, of course) for the menfolk to watch durin' his service. It was also his idea to install a gated pool for all members of the church to use durin' the summer. Our membership rose like there was a war on. Pastor Hickey was so thoughtful that he even offered seasonal memberships to those who didn't want to quit the church they were attendin' already. So for just $35 a year, a good Episcopalian could temporarily become a Baptist and enjoy the swimmin' pool. What Pastor Hickey didn't tell these Episcopalians, Lutherans, Methodists, Presbyterians, and Catholics was that he'd say a few words when they jumped into the pool so that when they came back up for air, they were comin' up as rebaptized-by-submersion Baptist. All in all, Pastor Hickey did a lot for our little country church. That's why it was such a shame that we had to kick his butt out of town.

The last thing all of us ever expected from Pastor Hickey was a scandal. He was happily married with a new son, and he didn't drink, smoke, play cards, or dance. He was well loved by every member of his flock. But all of that would be meaningless when he was rushed to the emergency room of the hospital in nearby Searcy, Arkansas, on that hot August night. At first the reason behind his visit to the ER was kept hushed up by both the hospital and Pastor Hickey. As a matter of fact, it wasn't until our own Sister Bertha of lot #12 started investigatin' several days after the fact that the truth, which would set this town on its ear, finally came out. Thanks to her many years of pryin' into other people's business, Sister Bertha was able to stir up enough trouble to make Pastor Hickey stand up in front of his congregation and address his visit for medical attention.

Accordin' to Pastor Hickey, every Saturday night around 10 in the evenin', he likes to bare his soul to the Lord by holdin' a self-purification service with just him and God attendin' in the church. He bases these services on those that King David used to hold in the Bible. He basically walks around the entire church, includin' the basement, sanctuary, offices, classrooms, coatroom, bathrooms, and even the kitchen, prayin' out loud. This whole service goes on for around an hour, and Pastor Hickey says that it helps put him in tune with God for Sunday. Well, of course, all that is fine and well with those of us who attend the First Baptist Church of Pangburn, although we did wonder why it only took him an hour to conduct his service when on Sunday it takes him at least three hours. But anyways, Pastor Hickey went on to tell us that durin' his last church sweep talk with God, he unexpectedly was involved in a freak accident in the kitchen that was both painful and embarrassin'. He explained that while in the kitchen, he noticed a roach up on a shelf so he grabbed somethin' to hit it with and climbed up on the kitchen counter. Well, of course he missed when he swung, but managed to kick the lid off the communion tray that rested on the counter. As he began to make his way off the counter, he ran into the uncovered communion tray. Now for those of you who ain't never seen a Baptist communion tray, they're usually about three-inch-tall silver or brass trays that are about the diameter of a record and hold 40 small tiny glasses. Typically they've got a metal cover with an upright cross that's used for decoration and also as a handle. We've got three of these trays at the First Baptist Church of Pangburn, which are stacked on top of each other to form one unit with a single cover on top. Now that you got an idea, let me continue with my story. It seems that Pastor Hickey unwittingly got one of the glasses from the tray stuck to a portion of his body. It had to have been a finger that got stuck since those glasses are so tiny (my sister Donna Sue says they're about half the size of a shot glass). Well, we were wrong. As you've probably guessed by now, the part that got stuck as Pastor Hickey descended off the counter was his penis. When he admitted this, there wasn't a dry eye in the church on account of all the laughter that rang out. I felt sorry for the man as he stood up there in front of the whole church, red-faced with embarrassment. That is to say, I felt sorry for him until he landed his bombshell. It seems that he conducted these private weekly sessions with God wearin' nothin' but a smile. At first there was total silence as people sat stunned in their pews. But then gaggin' and vomitin' started to set in as we all realized that his nakedness had been all over the church. Who knew what else he'd rubbed his body up against, and was this the first time his genitalia had gotten that close to the communion cups? Long story short, as Christians we could forgive him, but as Baptists we were too proud to have a pastor that could fit his penis into a communion glass, so we voted to let him go immediately. We gave him our best wishes, and us ladies of the church told his wife that she'd always be in our prayers. Last we heard he was tryin' to start up a church in some small town in Alva, Oklahoma.

Now the only reason I'm airin' our dirty clothes or lack thereof in public like this is because of the shake-up that it's caused at the High Chaparral Trailer Park. Pastor Hickey had lived in a nice four-bedroom home between Pangburn and Searcy that he had the church rent for him and his family while he made our Associate Pastor, Ida May Bee, live in an old trailer next to the church. Well, with his departin', we at the church decided it was time to break with tradition and voted Associate Pastor, Ida May Bee, in as our first woman pastor in the history of our small church. We felt she had all the credentials and the qualities that we were lookin' for in a new leader (plus we knew she'd keep her clothes on at all times). Pastor Ida May Bee decided the big old home Pastor Hickey was livin' in was just too large for her and her husband, but the trailer at the church was fallin' apart. For reasons we'll get into later in this chapter, our prayers were answered and a trailer was provided for our new pastor right in the High Chaparral Trailer Park. So for the first time ever, we got a true-blue member of the Baptist clergy livin' amongst us (Sister Bertha ain't been ordained). I'm thrilled! My sister's frightened.

Now let's meet and learn what's been up with all the residents of the High Chaparral Trailer Park.

# LOT #1

Lot #1, as most of y'all will recall, was the trailer home of Tammy Cantrell (age 24) and her six bastard kids: Tammy (7), Dolly (6), Patsy (5), Conway (4), Reba (3), and Oakridge (2). Her on-again off-again trucker boyfriend and father of all her babies, Hank Householder (28), had also been stayin' there every so often. Well, things sure have changed since we last spoke. Hank decided to give up truckin' and asked Tammy to marry him. Not only was she excited about the proposal (with those hips of hers as well as her addiction to Susie Qs, she knew there was no way she was gettin' married unless it was Hank who asked her), but she was also thrilled that her bastard babies would finally have a real last name. Shortly after the weddin', which, even though it was held out by the trailer park swimmin' pool, really wasn't much to talk about with all those screamin' children of hers runnin' around like a dang pack of wild dogs, Hank came up with an idea that'd let the whole family work together as well as travel the country. Before we knew it, Hank, Tammy, and the clan were tourin' this great land of ours as the Singing Houses (Householder was too long for the signs), performin' their act at Flying Js and other large truck stops. Tammy had sewn 'em cute little costumes out of some old curtains the funeral home was goin' to throw away, and they did selections from *The Sound of Music*. Even though they all sang pretty well, everyone couldn't help but notice that they only had six kids whereas the movie had seven. Since Tammy's tubes were tied, there was only one thing that Hank could do to correct this noticeable mistake. He went out and got an old empty coffee can, painted on two eyes and a mouth, added a mop for hair, and called it Hank Jr. Then he turned around and became a ventriloquist, which, regardless of what Kitty Chitwood of lot #11 tells you, has got nothin' to do with not bein' able to eat meat. Well, with the little outfit that Tammy pieced together from the curtain scraps attached to the rim of Hank Jr., he was ready for his debut. I tell y'all, when I saw Hank movin' Hank Jr. around just so and the rest of 'em standin' up there between the pay phones and the books-on-tape rack singin' their little hearts out, well, they were almost lifelike! And believe me when I tell y'all that their rendition of "Edelweiss" would make even the hardest trucker cry. With their newfound success, Hank and Tammy decided to sell their trailer to some friends of his in Joplin, Missouri, and also put lot #1 up for sale. They bought one of them big RVs, loaded up their belongin's along with their formaldehyde-smellin' costumes, and hit the road with the kids and Hank Jr. (Lord, I can't imagine spendin' more than two minutes in that RV with those little heathens.) Every once in a while I'll get a call or a postcard from Tammy tellin' me how they're all doin' just fine. I am truly happy for her even though we don't get discounts at the day old Dolley Madison store in Searcy since she don't work there anymore.

Well, dear reader, lot #1 didn't lay vacant for very long. As a matter of fact, before you could put a car up on cinderblocks, some newlyweds had up and moved their brand-new trailer home into that lot. Now, let me warn y'all that you're goin' to be shocked when you find out who the bride is, 'cause I was just knocked off my feet by the news. This past September, Dottie Lamb of lot #14 gave her dirt-ugly daughter away in what has to be the weddin' of the millennium. I don't say that on account of the weddin' bein' all fancy and beautiful, which is was, but simply because Opal was actually able to land a man who could wake up next to her godawful ugliness in the mornin'. It was just a few weeks ago that Pangburn lawyer Dick Inman moved back into town from California where he'd been livin' the past twelve years. Well, as fate would have it, he stopped by Lamb Department Store to pick up his International Male catalog, which had been delivered there by mistake, when he ran into Opal. Well, one thing led to another and before we knew it, just days later Pastor Ida May Bee was performin' her first weddin'. I'd love to say that the bride was a vision in white, but even a Republican would be hard-pressed to tell a lie like that. After a short honeymoon in Mexico City, Opal, Dick, and their new live-in maid that they brought back with 'em, Fernando somethin' or other, moved into their new trailer in lot #1. You should see this trailer! Dick has really made it beautiful. And I tell y'all it is just amazin' the magic that man can do with flowers and a vase!

All of us at the High Chaparral were just pleased as punch to see Opal marry, well, that is all of us except for Donny and Kenny in lot #15. They were against the weddin' from the start. I think they didn't like Dick, which just surprised us all. Actually they told Opal that Dick was not the kind of man she should be with and that she'll get hurt in the end. Well Opal told 'em thanks for their concern, but she was goin' to marry Dick regardless of the kind of man he was. And you know, dear reader, I've got to admit that I had my doubts about Dick and Opal takin' the plunge. And I agree with Kenny and Donny, I don't like his kind either, but just that shouldn't keep Opal from bein' happy. So what if he's a lawyer? I changed my mind in favor of the weddin' after I'd asked Opal what made her fall in love with Dick so quickly. She looked me straight in the eye and said that it was because of two things: He never tried to touch her inappropriately on their dates even when he was rip-roarin' drunk, and he was able to eat a whole meal with her at the table without gaggin'. If that's not love, what is? And besides, most of us have a soft side for Dick. It was terrible what he'd been forced to go through in that crazy state of California. They actually allowed this fella who'd been livin' with Dick for the past nine years to up and sue him for "palimony." That kind of stuff just doesn't go over here. Regardless of how close or tight two pals might be, when that friendship is over, it's over and nobody sues somebody for it around here.

# LOT #2

Anita Biggon is still occupyin' lot #2, but usually you'll find her down at her bar, Three Cigarettes in the Ashtray Bar, with the newly added grill. And boy, let me tell y'all, her business has really picked up since they opened the kitchen! Now, don't get me wrong, you still get lowlife scum-of-the-earth skanks who couldn't tell you what day it was hangin' out there, but now people like my folks or Ben Beaver and Dottie Lamb have been spendin' time there on account of the grill. They got a fried pickle that will make you jump up and yell "glory." I mean it's good-good-good eatin'! When I asked this old girlfriend of mine, Anita, where she'd gotten all her recipes for the bar and grill, she told me they all belonged to her dear momma, who y'all might recall passed way not too long ago, leavin' her daughter lot #2 and the trailer that was on it. Well, I love Anita like a sister, but I don't ever remember her momma's food tastin' anything like what's comin' through that bar's kitchen doors. As I recall, when she was a youngun' she used to get up in the middle of the night and bury the dinner leftovers, claimin' that she'd gotten hungry and ate 'em just so she wouldn't actually have to. Her momma's food was so bad the roaches would order out. (That last one was a joke; there never was a phone in that trailer till after her momma passed.) Well, it seems that my suspicions about the bar's food were right. Kyle Chitwood, who happens to bartend at Anita's bar, and his wife, Kitty, of lot # 11 came over one evenin' for cards. Well, a few of my mother-in-law's Fall Frenzies and he was ready to spill the beans. Her momma's recipes, my big bottom! It turns out that the recipes belong to the fella she's got cookin' in the back named Darnell Dingsnabel. But don't worry, dear readers. Thanks to my sister and a bottle of wine, I managed to get that pickle recipe!

## LOT #3

Lois and Hubert Bunch of lot #3 still own and run the half Tex-Mex restaurant–half tackle shop called the Taco Tackle Shack. It's doin' so good, they've bought the Dream Cream and turned it into the Taco Tackle Shack North, even though it's only a block away from the original store. They also opened up a little drive-through hut that served fresh coffee and mornin' pastries like donuts, cinnamon rolls, and the like along with bait, fishhooks, and assorted fisherman needs. It opened at 2 in the mornin' and ran until around noon. It was close to the highway so folks who'd pass by on their way to fish could stop by and get their last-minute fishin' needs as well as a good cup of coffee and a roll. At first business was a bit slow. It seemed like most people would just drive by it real slow takin' pictures. For some reason, the Master Baiter's Buddy just wasn't attractin' the right kind of business. And the phone calls they were gettin' were just terrible. Finally, after gettin' a phone call from some New York newspaper, they quickly changed the name to the Fisherman's Friend, and it was all downhill from then on. When I asked Hubert and Lois what the reporter from the paper said that made 'em go with a new name, they both just turned red and said that the new name captured the essence of the place a lot more than the first name. I don't get it, but maybe that's why I'm an entertainer/advisor and not an ad person.

## LOT #4

Nellie has started a new business where she travels around the state tunin' organs. She tunes your organ, blows the pipes, and polishes the whole thing by hand. Nellie says that when she's done, your organ will swell with pride. Nellie's motto is simply that if it's not the best blow and hand job you've ever gotten, then it's free. Needless to say, no one's asked for their money back yet. Nellie knows her organs, all right.

C.M. and Nellie have also added a new resident to their home. Eighty-nine-year-old Wendy Bottom has moved in so she can study the organ with Nellie. She's always wanted to learn how to play the organ and since the death of her husband, Harry Bottom (he was a plumber), she decided to follow that dream. Nellie, who's been thinkin' about cuttin' back to a few

Sundays a month, welcomes Wendy's desire to learn how to play the organ. She's cut out pieces of colored paper and put 'em on the keys of the church organ. She went through the Baptist hymnal and changed the notes to colors so Wendy can read the music. So when Wendy plays the organ, instead of playin' C, C, A, F, F, G notes, she plays red, red, blue, yellow, yellow, green. It's simple, but hey, so is she, God bless her.

## LOT #5

Momma and Daddy went to Mississippi for a visit with an old friend of theirs and won an Audi TT Roadster playin' dollar slots. Actually, Momma won it. She'd been doin' so well on the nickel slots that she decided to try her luck and hit the jackpot on a dollar progressive slot machine. At first they were goin' to take the money rather than the car, but while they were waitin' for the casino people to come and help 'em collect on their winnin' machine, Momma reached behind her and played the five dollar slot. Well, lo and behold she hit a combination that paid off $30,000. That gave 'em more than enough to pay the taxes, tags, and insurance on the car. Needless to say, the casino quickly paid off and gave them tickets to go and eat at a really nice restaurant that was on the other side of town. Anyways, Momma and Daddy just love their Audi. Daddy says that thanks to their new TT Roadster, they can get to all the gospel singin's in the state and at half the time, which is good since it takes both of 'em almost 20 minutes each to work their way out of the sports car. Momma kids Daddy about how now that he drives that car, he thinks he's Mr. Tom Cruise in *Mission Impossible II*. Of course she goes on to add that thanks to that Audi and Viagra, he acts like a movie star as well. Momma's only complaint on her vehicular winnin' is that she has to put her seat as far back as possible and lean way down just so she don't squash her hair.

## LOT #6

This past June my sister, Donna Sue, of lot #6 met and instantly fell head over heels in love with this fella she met in Little Rock. For Donna Sue it was love at first sight, or at least as soon as she found out he was a big-time liquor distributor. And old Moe had the hots for her as well. Actually his name was Muammer Ibn Majah and he was originally from Libya. Anyways, they hit it off like gangbusters, and come the end of June they were already talkin' marriage. Before you could say "free booze for life," the date had been set. The only problem was that Donna Sue was a Baptist and her new husband-to-be was a Shi'ite Muslim. Finally they decided on a simple justice-of-the-peace weddin' that would take place in the Taco Tackle Shack South on July 3. Well, needless to say, Arkansas in July can be downright ungodly on account of the heat, so we was all afraid that Moe or Donna Sue would end up passin' out while they took their vows. In an attempt to help with this problem, Lois and Hubert added a few box fans right next to where the happy couple would be standin'. Sure enough, the third of July was just awful. I don't recall the exact temperature, but trust me, Satan himself would've been hard pressed not to break a sweat in Pangburn that day. But we were all in good spirits and ready for Donna Sue to finally tie the knot even if her betrothed wasn't a good Baptist boy. Mind you, Momma and Daddy were a bit upset that Donna Sue was havin' a non-Baptist service, but Pastor Hickey told 'em that for $30 he'd sit up front and conduct the approved Baptist weddin' ceremony under his breath, assurin' 'em that their daughter wouldn't be livin' in sin.

Donna Sue looked lovely as she came down the makeshift aisle all dressed in taupe, which was about as close to white as she dared to get. Daddy walked Donna Sue down to Moe, and Judge Perkins conducted the ceremony. Now, God bless him, Judge Perkins, who retired back in 1973, but is still allowed to perform weddin's, is just two years shy of hittin' 100. At four foot three inches, he also happens to be the shortest man I've ever met in my life. Because of his height, we had to stand him up on one of the restaurant tables. Durin' the rehearsal the poor thing lost his balance and almost fell right off the dang table, so we clamped down a baby's crib to the tabletop and filled it with them round soft colored balls like they got in the play area at McDonald's. It worked like a charm and Judge Perkins did just fine. Well, as fine as a tiny little ninety-eight-year-old man in a child's crib can be expected to do. Oh, I forgot to mention that he's got something like Tourette's syndrome, didn't I? It wasn't that bad, really, except for the fact that he kept callin' Donna Sue a "fat ass" and "cow whore." There were a few other words that he uttered, which you can find in *Lady Chatterley's Lover* if you care to look. But for the most part he did just fine, considerin'.

My sister wrote her own vows, and they were just lovely. She told Moe how her life had been empty without him, and how he was her Alpha and her Omega, whatever the hell that is. Anyways, it was just beautiful. And then it was Moe's turn. He started off tellin' her how special she made him feel, and how their love was undyin', but just in case some unforeseen death of their eternal feelin's should take place, he wanted her to sign a prenuptial, which he pulled out of his pocket. Donna Sue told him that she would happily do anything for love—that was until she read the clause about how she wouldn't get a drop of liquor if they ever divorced. Well, my sister turned a shade of red that I've never seen before. Needless to say, the Shi'ite hit the fan! She cold-cocked Moe so hard he was out for almost an hour and a half, which, thanks to the Jaws of Life, gave us plenty of time to get him out of the box fan.

None of us have heard from Moe since, but Donna Sue seems to be doin' all right. Every time she opens a bottle of scotch, she curses his name, which basically means she talks about him all the time.

## LOT #7

It breaks my heart to tell y'all about the untimely passin' of Dora Beaver after a tragic accident in the liquor store. She was hangin' up decorations in her and Ben's liquor store, Beaver Liquor and Wines, when the ladder gave out from the weight and she came crashin' down along with the fully stocked liquor case she grabbed hold of. The vodka that she so loved ended up crushing her to death.

All us gals made dinners and pies and cakes for Ben to eat. Well, somethin' happened with Dottie Lamb and Ben. They've fallen for each other, and since Opal moved out, Ben moved in with Dottie. He lives in Opal's old bedroom, but we all think that just as soon as the 2002–2003 memorial sale in honor of Dora is over at Beaver Liquors, they might just be tying the knot.

Ben donated his trailer and lot #7 to the First Baptist Church of Pangburn in Dora's name. Well, they accepted the donation and moved Pastor Ida May Bee and her husband Woody into the pledged trailer home. Needless to say, Pastor Ida Mae and her husband are just tickled pink!

## LOT #8

Poor dear Lulu Bell. As I'd mentioned in my last book, she was tryin' to start up a Kathy Lee Gifford fan club. But unfortunately, she wasn't able to find anyone who'd join. Her downed spirits were lifted when a bit of land that she'd originally bought with some of the money my late brother had left her finally sold. And the good part was that the land was bought at the price she was askin' for it. My dear dim-witted niece made a mint off the deal, but later regretted it after it turned out to be the property that now houses Faye Faye LaRue's Danglin' Tassel Strip Club. Well, she did reinvest the money into a new business. She bought the old Pangburn Pool Hall between Lamb's Department Store and the Pangburn Diner and turned it into Lulu Bell's Pool Hall. What's amazed me, dear reader, is that she hasn't let her retardation get the best of her. Even though she can't count higher than a hundred, she is quite the businesswoman. As a matter of fact, she has worked out a deal with the Last Stop Nursing Home, which happens to be where we keep Me-Ma, who is doin' just fine, thank you. Every day around noon, the nursin' home drops off a vanload of seniors who do nothin' but rack up the pool balls and make sure that the pool sticks ain't crooked. And it allows the nursin' home to hose down the senior's rooms without havin' to find a place to put the residents meanwhile. Plus it gives the seniors a chance to get out and enjoy themselves even though the Last Stop Nursing Home insists that they be chained to a table. It's a win/win situation for everybody.

## LOT #9

Who would have guessed it? Harland has been moved up from pin boy to shoe boy at the Great Big Balls Bowling Alley. That's an additional 15 cents an hour that he and Juanita can count on, plus he can take any pair of bowlin' shoes home with him if he wants. Talk about your luck.

Juanita has also gotten a promotion from cashier at the Piggly Wiggly to customer service rep, which means she cashes payroll checks, gives out rolls of change, and takes payments for utility bills. She now makes an extra quarter an hour, but don't worry, she'll still be drivin' the bookmobile durin' the weekends.

Juanita asked me to let everyone know that the girls are doin' just fine. We all were worried after what happened in August when poor little Harlinda went with Harland to the Great Big Balls Bowling Alley and got her head stuck in the ball return. They finally got her out, but no one had thought to shut the dang thing off. Heck, the folks on the lane bowled two more frames before they got her little banged-up head dislodged.

## LOT #10

Poor Ollie White has had nothin' but heartache recently. It seems she was once again up for the prestigious Miss White County Hairnet Award with her scrumptious Fudge-RC Cola Cake, when her world was rocked with scandal. Accordin' to the *Pangburn Bugle,* an anonymous tip came into the school superintendent's office in regard to a web page that contained nude photos of one of his employees. Well, before you could whistle "Someone's in the Kitchen with Dinah," Ollie had been suspended until further notice. Of course the news got around town faster than a case of mono that Ollie White had been suspended from her job in the school cafeteria on account of nude pictures of her on the Internet. Well it didn't take anytime for the Miss White County Hairnet Award committee to disqualify Ollie's entry on the grounds of it's bein' made by a sexual pervert. The award went to Vineta Chumley and her ravioli casserole from White County Central. Needless to say, Ollie was just broken hearted about the whole thing. The worst part about it was that the pictures turned out to be the work of some kid who was upset about not gettin' as much "corn" with his pizza as everybody else. He'd gotten Ollie's head by scannin' her photo in the yearbook, and then simply put it on top of what turned out to be a few nude pictures of Pamela Lee Anderson. Well, as soon as we all saw the supposed pictures of our beloved Ollie, we knew it wasn't her. First off, the nude body was tanned, second there wasn't a wrinkle on it, and third, well, like my sister said, that gal had a fully stocked bar whereas Ollie barely has enough to fill a shot glass. According to the *Bugle,* just before the judge sentenced the boy who had openly admitted his guilt, he allowed Ollie to say few words. Ollie rose to her tired feet and began to remind his honor that "this dear little boy is just that, your honor, a child. Yes he's simply a babe who didn't realize that his practical joke could possibly hurt another human bein'. I hold no personal contempt for this small little ill-guided child. That's why I'm not askin' for the death penalty in this case, but all I simply want is for you to lock him up in the deepest darkest hole you can find in this great state of Arkansas and let him spend the rest of his miserable life thinkin' about all the sufferin' he's put me through!" The *Bugle* goes on to say that it took three grown men to drag her out of that courtroom while she went on about how the Hairnet Award should have been hers. The award committee agreed with Ollie and even tried to take it back from Vineta Chumley, but the ACLU wouldn't have it. As a matter of fact, the ACLU (All Cafeteria Ladies United) said that since the awards committee had disqualified Ollie's entry before the judgin' had actually started, then she didn't have a support-hose-wearin' leg to stand on. To make up for their rush to judgment, the awards committee gave her an honorary Hairnet and promised to present her with next year's lifetime achievement award. Needless to say, Ollie was happy. Oh, and as far as that little boy went, well he got a much lighter sentence than the one Ollie had requested. Ollie's still fightin' that one.

## LOT #11

Not much has happened with Kitty and Kyle Chitwood since we last talked, with the exception of Kitty winnin' a bunch of money from a frozen ice drink pullin' contest. When the owner of the Gas and Smokes, thanks to an anonymous tip, was arrested for sellin' Viagra out of the trunk of his car, Kitty was able to buy up her place of employment for a song. It really was a stroke of luck in her favor.

As far as Kyle goes, he's still pourin' drinks at Anita Biggon's bar. With the addin' of food, you'd have thought he'd have put on at least 20 pounds, but I guess that's not somethin' he has to worry about. Oh, the benefits of havin' worms. If only I could be so lucky.

## LOT #12

Since outin' Pastor Hickey's penis in the communion cup drama, Sister Bertha has been on a mission to drag out sin wherever it might be hidin'. She led a rally to burn the public library's copies of *Peyton Place* and *Valley of the Dolls*. Unfortunately, when her and her group of God-fearin' women stormed the library, both the aforementioned books were checked out. So instead, they just ripped out the index cards for those two books and burnt them. And Pastor Ida May Bee put Sister Bertha in charge of drivin' the Sunday school bus. So early every Sunday mornin' Sister Bertha pulls up in front of each house in Pangburn, parks the bus, honks its horn, and yells out over the PA system, "Are you goin' to church or are you goin' to Hell?" The attendance has amazingly risen for both Sunday school and Sunday mornin' services.

## LOT #13

Mickey Ray is still holdin' down the fort at the Dr Pepper Bottling Plant. He loves it and they love him.

Mickey Ray's momma, Wanda, didn't stay at the Dream Cream when the Bunches took it over and turned it into the new Taco Tackle Shack North. Instead, Wanda is now our Schwan's Route Sales Manager, which is a fancy way of sayin' that she drives the Schwan's truck. She drives it all right; sometimes she drives it right past my trailer and I got to chase her down. I'm not built for runnin', but trust me, when it comes to my food, you wouldn't believe the speeds I can hit.

Connie, Mickey Ray's wife, has kept busy as our local Amway rep, which y'all might recall from the first book. Since then she's added Shaklee products to her line of wares, and with the recent announcement from Lovie

Birch that she was retirin', Connie has taken on her old Avon, Mary Kay, and Tupperware routes to boot. I hate to admit it, but if I see Connie comin' toward my trailer, I mute the TV, lie on the floor, and grab some snacks (Connie can be persistent).

## LOT #14

Dottie has added some new handicap features to her trailer home for Ben's comfort, includin' a larger bathtub so he can easily get in and out. Mind you, all of us think it is so they both can get in, if you catch my drift, and I ain't talkin' for swimmin' lessons neither.

Tragedy did hit Dottie and her daughter Opal just recently. Lamb's Department Store, a fixture in the Pangburn skyline, caught on fire and burnt to the ground. It was terrible. Thank goodness, they'd been doin' some remodelin' and had moved the entire store inventory over to the new warehouse they'd recently built just days before the blaze. We all thought that the fire must have been due to the old wirin' in that buildin', but we were wrong. Accordin' to Sheriff Gentry, the fire was on account of someone accidentally leavin' a can of gasoline by the heater in the basement. Isn't that terrible? Of course, why they had the heater runnin' in early August is beyond me.

## LOT #15

Since my last book, *Ruby Ann's Down Home Trailer Park Cookbook*, came out, we ain't seen lots from Kenny and Donny. It seems that my book made their antique store, As Time Goes By Antiques Store, very popular. As a matter of fact, they was clean sold out of everything by June! Because of this, they've been spendin' five days out of the week travelin' around the country searchin' for new items for the store. While they been gone, they've had Momma waterin' their plants for 'em. After *The Price Is Right* is over, Momma's got nothin' else to do with her day till Oprah comes on, so she volunteered her time. Of course she was kind of embarrassed after the last trip Kenny and Donny went on. It seems that when she went into Kenny's bedroom to water his hibiscus, she knocked into a chest that was in front of the bed. Well, the dang thing started to make a buzzin' sound. Momma figured it was an expensive electric razor or somethin' that cost a pretty penny since Kenny had it locked up in that chest. Not knowin' what to do, she gave it a good kick, thinkin' that maybe it'd shut it off. Needless to say, it didn't. As a matter of fact, it had the opposite effect, and before Momma could say "shake, rattle, and roll," she had a bunch of stuff runnin' in that chest. That thing started vibratin' across the bedroom floor and headed down the hall toward Kenny and Donny's glass curio cabinet filled with their collection of Franklin Mint dishes. Well, Momma jumped on top of that vibratin' footlocker and braced her legs against the wood-paneled walls. Without takin' a breath she did what any seventy-two-year-old woman would do. She pressed the button on her medic alert necklace and told the operator on the other end, "I'm vibratin' and I can't get up." Well, they called Daddy at home and he came over with some cinderblocks, which he put on the chest to hold it down. They duct-taped some pillows all around the edges, and pushed it into the bathroom where it couldn't do any damage while all the batteries ran down. When Kenny and Donny arrived back home, Momma told 'em what she'd done. I don't know who was more red-faced, Momma or Kenny and Donny. Accordin' to the boys, they had found some great deals on battery-operated tie racks, change counters, and electric toothbrushes so they bought a bunch of 'em for this year's Christmas presents. Personally, if they were able to propel a big old chest across a trailer, I don't know if I'd want to put one of those electric toothbrushes in my mouth.

## LOT #16

Momma Ballzak of lot #16 is still ringin' up meals at the Pangburn Diner durin' the day, and spendin' her wages on Lucky Strikes and alcohol durin' the rest of the time. (I know that ain't what the doctor ordered, but if that's what makes her happy, what can me and my husband, Dew, say about it?) My husband's momma, Momma Ballzak, has taken on a part-time job. She's sellin' what we all affectionately call "trailer park Tupperware."

Momma Ballzak is a pack rack who has kept everything that she might be able to use a second time. But after a dream where she was bein' chased by a Cool Whip bowl, Momma Ballzak got the idea to sell off some of her collection. So two or three times a month she packs up her empty cottage cheese containers, sour cream containers, margarine containers, pint-size ice cream containers, and, yes, Cool Whip containers, and holds trailer park Tupperware parties all around the surroundin' area. Needless to say, this ticked off Lovie Birch so much that she threw her arms in the air and sold her Tupperware route to Connie Kay. Momma Ballzak has done real good, which is nice, but I've got to admit, me and my husband, Dew, were kind of disappointed. We'd hoped that maybe she would've left those to us in her will. Oh well, a person can dream can't she?

# LOT #17

Tragedy has once again struck lot #17 with the untimely death of Marty Scaggs. His wife found his body in the bathtub along with the toaster, the waffle iron, an electric skillet, the electric knife, and the coffee maker. Sheriff Gentry believes it was a terrible accident. Accordin' to the sheriff, he thinks Marty was runnin' late for work so he tried to take a bath and make breakfast all at the same time. Sheriff Gentry also adds that he doesn't think Marty died right away. He believes that even after the first few kitchen appliances hit the water, Marty, in a desperate attempt at survival, tried to save his life by switchin' the coffee maker settin' from brew to warm. "Alas," adds the sheriff, "it was too late."

His young widow, Mable, after sellin' off Marty's business and collectin' her inheritance and insurance, took the trailer and moved to Rockwell, Texas, with her old high school sweetheart, Buddy Dixon. They hadn't seen each other since he left town right after Eula's passin'. As a matter of fact, the first time they'd laid eyes on each other was the day before Marty's tragic death. Well, all I can say is, thank goodness someone was there to comfort her durin' this terrible time in her life.

When the new neighbors moved in to lot #17, we were all shocked, 'cause it was like a ghost from the past had done come back to haunt us. About 30 years ago my sister, Donna Sue, had a rival in the strippin' world by the name of Faye Faye LaRue (her real name was Jeanie Faye Stopenblotter), who resided in lot #3. You wouldn't believe the bloody hell that would go on when they'd run into each other while one of 'em was drunk, which basically meant any time of the day or night. Well, long story short, Faye Faye got pregnant, and eight months later when she finally stopped workin' so she could have the baby, she started badmouthin' my sister to all the strip joints. This gossip lost Donna Sue jobs, and she wasn't happy. Fed up to her eyeballs, my sister went over to Faye Faye's trailer, and when she wouldn't answer the door, Donna Sue kicked it in. Now, my sister has done a lot of things, but hittin' a cheap 2-dollar pregnant stripper is not one of 'em. In any case, the police got called out and Faye Faye claimed Donna Sue had hit her. Judging by the massive scratches all over Faye Faye's body, it looked like there had been a terrible fight, and since Donna Sue didn't have a mark on her, the police took Faye Faye's word on what'd happened and took my sister off to jail. Late that night, while my sister sat in jail, Faye Faye hitched up her trailer to the VW Beetle and snuck out of town. Mind you, with the weight of the trailer, she kind of crawled out of town and down the highway at five miles an hour. My sister was released from jail and all charges were dropped when new evidence was discovered. It seemed that C. M. Tinkle, while collectin' the trash that day, had found an empty tube of calamine lotion in the garbage that Faye had left behind. Those scratches that the police had seen were actually self-inflicted due to a bad case of scabies. We'd all long forgotten Faye Faye until she showed back up this last month, towin' a trailer into the recently vacated lot #17. But this time she's got her daughter, Tina Faye Stopenblotter, and a checkin' account full of money with her. If her movin' back into town hasn't ticked Donna Sue off enough, Faye Faye has opened a new strip club up in Searcy. That's right, Donna Sue at the Blue Whale Strip Club and Faye Faye LaRue at the Danglin' Tassel Strip Club are at it again.

## LOT #18

Me and my husband, Dew, have been talkin' about makin' a few changes to our pink two-story double-wide. Even though the park has its own pool, I've always dreamed of ownin' a pool myself that was larger than one of them turtle pools. But on account of the amount of space, lack of privacy, and yearly floodin' problems, a pool in my yard is definitely out. So instead me and my husband, Dew, are thinkin' about addin' a pool to the top of our second story. The first problem we came across was the tire situation. As y'all know, us trailer folks have our roofs loaded down with tires in an attempt to weigh down our homes durin' high winds or even a possible twister. So what do we do if we put a pool up there? Well, after weeks of thinkin' this through, I came up with the brilliant idea of takin' those tires and turnin' 'em into pool furniture. You could stack up three of 'em, nail a board to the top tire, and presto, you've got a table for your drinks. Nail a piece of steel to the bottom of a tire and then fill it with sand for a stationary poolside ashtray. Stack up four or five tires, stuff the inside all the way up with old couch cushions, and before you know it you've got the perfect seat for us big-boned gals. Do the same thing with tractor tires to make those wider seats for gals like my sister, Donna Sue. Anyways, that's what we're debatin' right now. Heck, we might just add a third story. Who knows?

# LOT #19

Death has just hung over us this year like stench at a stockyard. Dear old Jimmy Janssen went on to meet his Maker just this past September. As those of you who've read *Ruby Ann's Down Home Trailer Park Cookbook* will recall, Jimmy and Jeanie Janssen had retired early and were travelin' the U.S. on the money that their two preacher boys, Jack and Josh, gave 'em each month. Well, it seems that they'd gone to Salmon, Idaho, in their little camper that they'd purchased to experience a cornfield maze. Jimmy just had this thing about mazes. He just loved 'em. Anyways, I guess that night after doin' the maze, Jimmy decided to surprise his wife, so while she was out lookin' in the campground's gift shop, he put little candles everywhere. Well, Jeannie had come back a bit soon and walked in on him. Frantically, he told her to close her eyes and get out. He'd call her when he was done. The police believe that there was a small propane leak, so when he lit his lighter so he could light the candles, the whole thing exploded, killin' him instantly. Of course the boys flew up there and got Jeannie as well as made arrangements for Jimmy's ashes to be flown back to Arkansas. Well, long story short, poor Jimmy got lost for a month and a half. By the time he finally arrived in Pangburn, accordin' to the airport stamps on the box that held his ashes, he'd been to every state on the East Coast. Jeannie said that Jimmy had always wanted to go to the East Coast. So they buried Jimmy's ashes in that box over in the cemetery. Jimmy will be missed. I got to tell you, I don't know which was worse, goin' like that or dyin' in Utah.

## LOT #20

I don't know if it was the success of my book or the fact that a Republican is in the White House, but Lovie Birch has flipped her lid. She's sold off all her makeup and Tupperware routes, and has been spendin' most of her time talkin' to both the state and national Democratic Party headquarters. They've got something cookin', and I think it's goin' to be big. Of course her husband, Elmer, is still active with the local branch of the party, but here lately he's turned all of that political stuff over to his wife so he can get more involved with his work at the local newspaper he owns, the *Pangburn Bugle*. He's been real busy with all the scandal that the paper unveiled in the Ollie White situation as well as the recent coverin' of the Pastor Hickey debacle. Now that all that is over, maybe the *Bugle* can get back to doin' the real news stories that people find interestin'. You know, the ones about me.

# *Chapter 1*

Faye Faye LaRue and her daughter, Tina Faye Stopenblotter, of lot #17 show off their Elvis shrine.

# *January*

As most folks know, January is the first month of the year unless you follow one of them non-American calendars. The month of January was named after Janus, the non-Baptist Roman god of beginnin's. Originally January only had 30 days, but back in 46 B.C. Julius Caesar, who'd sworn he'd start his diet on the first of February, added an additional day to the end of the month (most of y'all will recall that Julius Caesar was the fella who, when stabbed in the back by his friend, said "Et tu, Brutus," which when translated means "Acupuncture my ass!"). Over 2,000 years and a cheesecake later, the first month of the year has held on to its extra day.

The Anglo-Saxons called the first month of the year Wolfmonth on account of the wolf was comin' into the villages in winter, searchin' for food. Now at the High Chaparral Trailer Park, we've nicknamed January Tramp Month on account of the tramps, hobos, and drifters spendin' the night with my older stripper sister, Donna Sue, in her trailer durin' the winter, searchin' for a warm place to rest and for some food. Some of the local churches in the surroundin' areas are goin' to try and find another option for these poor men so they don't have to suffer this way every year, especially right after Christmas.

There are only three big holidays that we trailer folks actually go all out on and celebrate durin' the month of January. The reason for this is simple. We're just plumb tired and tuckered out after all the festivities we partook in durin' October, November, and December! We need a little break, so we only do three real special days this month. But one of those days is very sacred and somewhat holy to us trailer folk. We'll get into that later on. But what do you do for the rest of the days in January? Well, actually January has several month-long holidays that you can follow when plannin' your family meals and events.

January is:
*National Egg Month*

# OH HAPPY DAY EGG CASSEROLE

*You know, with great recipes like this, you'd have
thought Sister Bertha would've found some wimpy
little man she could have pussy-whipped by now.*

*Makes 4 to 6 servin's*

1½ pounds sausage meat

½ cup seasoned croutons

2 cups grated Cheddar cheese

4 eggs

2½ cups milk

½ teaspoon salt

1 can cream of mushroom soup, diluted with ½ cup milk

¾ teaspoon dry mustard

Pepper

Grease a casserole dish and preheat your oven to 300 degrees F.

Cook the sausage meat in a skillet and drain it. Set aside. Line the bottom of the casserole dish with the croutons. Sprinkle a little more than half the cheese on top of your crouton layer, then add the cooked sausage meat on top of that. Beat your eggs, then add the milk and salt, and beat that all together. Once it's well beaten, pour it over the sausage. Cover and put in the fridge overnight to set.

The next mornin', pull out the casserole dish from the fridge. Mix the mustard and pepper into the diluted soup. Top that with the rest of the cheese and pop it in the oven for about an hour and ½ to an hour and 45 minutes. Serve with biscuits.

*—SISTER BERTHA, LOT #12*

*National Wheat Bread Month*

# WHEAT BISCUITS

*These go real good with Sister Bertha's egg dish.*

*Makes a couple dozen*

2 cups whole-wheat flour

2 teaspoons bakin' powder

1 tablespoon sugar

½ teaspoon honey

¾ teaspoon salt

¼ cup margarine, softened

⅔ cup milk

Take a big bowl and mix everything together. Make sure you mix well, but don't overblend. Put the dough on a floured surface and roll out to ½-inch thickness. Use a biscuit cutter or the floured rim of a drinkin' glass to cut your biscuits. Place these rounds on a lightly greased bakin' sheet and bake at 450 degrees F. for 15 to 18 minutes. Brush the tops with margarine when you pull 'em out.

*—OLLIE WHITE, LOT #10*

*National Oatmeal Month*

# OATMEAL PIE

*This'd make Wilford Brimley climb off that poor*
*horse's back and head to the dinner table.*

*Makes 1 pie*

¼ cup margarine, softened

½ cup sugar

½ teaspoon ground cinnamon

½ teaspoon ground cloves

¼ teaspoon salt

1 cup dark corn syrup

3 eggs

1 cup instant oatmeal

1 9-inch piecrust

Cream the margarine and the sugar in a bowl until it's nice and fluffy. Add the next 4 items. Add one egg, stir, and repeat until all 3 eggs are in. Make sure everything is mixed well. Add the oatmeal and stir. Pour into the piecrust and bake for an hour at 350 degrees F. Serve hot.

*—JEANNIE JANSSEN, LOT #19*

# NEW YEAR'S DAY
## January 1
### (A prison holiday)

New Year's Day is the shortest trailer park holiday in the entire calendar year. Now I don't say that cause of some kind of freakish time-warp thing, but rather on account of it bein' the one holiday that most of us celebrate by sleepin' in. That's right, we don't get up until noon or later since we were up so dang late bringin' in the New Year the night before. Even our elderly sleep much later than usual. Of course, that's on account of the fact that we slip 'em some heavy tranquilizers before they go off to bed on New Year's Eve. There is a code of conduct in the trailer-park community that says if for some reason or another you did get up early, you are not allowed to call or visit anyone until after noon. And if you try to do some kind of crazy loud madness outside, then you will be reported to the sheriff after one o'clock when he gets into his office. So basically nothin' happens until after 12 in the afternoon on New Year's Day.

New Year's Day is celebrated pretty much the same way in the trailer park community as it is in the rest of the world. For example, we make resolutions just like everybody else does. Of course, ours are a little different. You see, while most folks are resolvin' to stop smokin' or lose weight, we're personally promisin' to not sleep with the last person at the bar when it closes, to actually find and buy some tires and remainin' parts for that 72 Ford LTD that we've been workin' on since 1994, or that we'll think up some good comebacks for that dang carnie dunk tank clown when he makes fun of us at next year's fair. We've pretty much given up on the impossible things like quittin' smokin', losin' weight, learnin' new words, or findin' out who our real father might be. No, we use this special day to publicly and privately announce our goals for this New Year in our lives. We've learned not to set our hopes too high (we will buy only one tube of Avon lipstick at a time, we will return library books within the same decade that they were checked out, we won't buy new towels every time we get a new mailer from Fingerhut, or we will use the brain and smarts that God gave us and finish at least one dang *TV Guide* crossword puzzle this year).

But just like the rest of the human race, we tend to break those resolutions or, in a week or two we forget about 'em until next December 31.

Food plays a small part in a trailer park New Year's Day tradition. It's said that if you eat black-eyed peas on the first day of the New Year you'll have good luck all year long. Even though I don't personally care for 'em, I manage to eat at least one. Here lately I brought back from one of my trips to Holland their tradition of eatin' somethin' in the shape of a ring. This symbolizes "comin' full circle" and good luck. So we eat donuts on January 1. Unlike the black-eyed peas, I have no problems eatin' these. And if this old Dutch tradition is true, my good luck should be set for life! With the idea of lookin' forward into a better year, another Dutch tradition is that you never eat chicken on account of how it scratches backwards. You can eat pork since pigs are considered good luck 'cause they can't look backwards.

The first of January also means the Tournament of Roses Parade, which gives us yet another reason to sit in front of the television. It also just boggles the mind when you see what those folks can do with chicken wire, glue, and a bunch of flowers. We tried to do a parade like that in Pangburn, but it didn't turn out quite like the one in California. Instead of roses, we used crepe paper, which we'd formed into great big flowers like they sell at amusement parks around the world. Old hay wagons served as our basic structures for the floats. The menfolk attached the chicken wire and formed it into shapes, while the womenfolk, under the direction of Kenny and Donny, carefully and strategically placed the crepe-paper flowers in the right holes. Kenny and Donny are so creative when it comes to visualizin' just where to stick things like this. And even though it may not seem right, if you put it where they tell you to stick it, it comes out fantastically beautiful. After a good day's work on the 29th, we had four nice size floats that'd be pulled down Main Street on New Year's Day. On the afternoon of January first, we woke up to unseasonable weather. Most of the snow had melted and the sun was out. It looked as though the good Lord up above had smiled his approval for our first annual Tournament of Crepe Paper Parade. That approval would only last until around one P.M., when the wind picked up and the temperature took a drastic nosedive. By the start of our parade at three o'clock the snow had started fallin' and the wind-chill factor was at 15 degrees. It was dang cold! But we were committed. So some of the menfolk hooked the handmade floats up to the tractors and right at 3:00 on the dot our parade began down Main Street. Needless to say, there was no one out on the street to cheer for us. Those who had come out were inside the buildin's that had opened specially for this event. Well, for those of y'all who don't know it, colored crepe paper and snowflakes don't mix. Actually crepe paper and any kind of moisture don't mix. As each float was slowly pulled out from the barn, it instantly began to disintegrate. By the time the floats had started down the parade route, they were nothin' more than hay wagons of chicken wire and wilted wet crepe paper, whose colors were all over the place. The snow had made the ink in the crepe paper run, and everyone on the float was covered with it. You can only imagine what those poor gals who'd worn crepe-paper flowers in their hair looked like with the dye flowin' all down their faces onto their clothin'. It was tragic, but not as tragic as what was soon to follow. When Ms. Pangburn Suzie Pinkerton's specially designed Tournament of Crepe Paper Parade purple crepe-paper dress dissolved in the snow, leavin' her in nothin' but a bra and panties, the driver of the tractor that was pullin' the float decided to gun it. Well, since he was the last float, his speedin' twenty-mile-an-hour tractor and float came racin' up behind the other participants, which in turn made them put the pedal to the metal. This was all good and well since the parade was already a bomb, but what nobody took into consideration was that the water from the thawed-out snow had refrozen. Before you could say "Disney on Ice," the parade had turned into a dang Ice Capades show. Those trailers and floats started doin' donuts and twirls like there was no tomorrow, leavin' streams of loose wet crepe paper all over the streets. The spectacle finally came to a halt as each tractor and float and their riders came crashin' into the old dilapidated buildin's that had once been known as the Pangburn Arms Motel. Thank the good Lord no one was seriously hurt, with the exception of the mayor, who slipped on the ice while tryin' to get a better look at seminude Suzie Pinkerton as she was laid passed out on one of the hay wagons. Needless to say, that was the first and last parade we had on New Year's Day. Several years later, the mayor is fine, the Pangburn Arms Motel as you well know has been reopened under a new name, and rumor has it that there are some parts of Suzie Pinkerton's body that are still a shade of purple.

*Things to Get You in the Holiday Mood*

Watch and rent the movie *Ice Castles*. It ain't got nothin' to do with New Year's, but the scenes of them skatin' reminds me of that dang parade.

Stop by a Krispy Kreme, Dunkin Donuts, or Winchelle's.

Visit the official Tournament of Roses Parade web page at www.tournament ofroses.com

Visit the Pasadena live cam at www.oldpasadena.com/oldpas/parade2002.asp

*Things to Do*

Watch the Tournament of Roses Parade.

Watch the Rose Bowl football game.

Try to remember where you left your right shoe last night.

Take a nap.

Call those who gave you gifts and see if they've found the receipts yet.

Bail your loved ones that got arrested last night out of jail.

*How to Decorate Your Trailer for This Holiday*

There are no special decorations for this holiday. Just rest and take it easy.

*Trailer Park Tradition*

The ancient Babylonians used to return borrowed farm equipment on this day. We trailer folk follow this tradition by returnin' borrowed items (guns, videotapes, cigarettes, cookin' oil, pots, pans, Gold Bond, etc.) to our neighbors without any questions asked. My sister returns items of clothin', wallets, watches, or other trinkets that were left in her trailer by last year's one-night stands.

*Somethin' to Bring to a Party*

## "OH THE PAIN" NUTMEG COOKIES

*Since these are great for upset stomachs after a night of drinkin', my sister highly recommends these for the day after New Year's Eve. Of course she also recommends a fifth of scotch with every meal!*

*Makes 2 to 2½ dozen*

1 cup margarine

2 cups sugar

¾ cup milk

5 cups flour

1 teaspoon bakin' powder

Grated numeg to taste

Mix the margarine and sugar together in a bowl. Add the milk and mix thoroughly.

In a different bowl, mix the flour, bakin' powder, and nutmeg together. Slowly add it to the wet mixture. Mix well and shape into golf-ball-size balls. Put 'em on a cookie sheet and flatten each one of those little devils. Bake at 375 degrees F. for 20 minutes. These cookies are good even when you don't feel bad.

*—DONNA SUE BOXCAR, LOT #6*

*Dinner Menu*

# HOWDY NEW YEAR DRINK

*My husband, Dew, says that these have always been a New Year's Day staple in the Ballzak household. I could be wrong, but I think that Momma Ballzak celebrates the New Year on a weekly basis.*

*Makes 2 drinks*

1 cup milk

2 ounces light rum

1 teaspoon sugar

2 drops almond extract

Dash of bitters

Dash of grated nutmeg

1 cup crushed ice

Put everything in a blender and hit the high speed button for 3 seconds. Strain into glasses and serve.

*—MOMMA BALLZAK, LOT #16*

# HOPPIN' JOHN

*Every good Southern gal who's worth her weight
has a variation of this recipe! Trust me, with the
weight that's on old Wanda, this is one of the best
ones out there.*

*About 10 servin's*
8 bacon strips
¼ cup diced onion
½ green bell pepper, diced
½ red bell pepper, diced
2 (10-ounce) packages frozen black-eyed peas
½ cup uncooked white rice
2 cups water
Salt and pepper
Hot sauce
1½ cups grated Cheddar cheese

Chop up your bacon and put it in a skillet with onion and peppers. Cook until the bacon is crisp (save that bacon grease for the GOOD LUCK COLLARD GREENS on page 12). Add the peas and rice, then stir in the water. Cover and let simmer for 20 minutes over low heat. If the rice is not tender at that time, cook a little longer. Add salt, pepper, and hot sauce to taste. Then put in the cheese. Pastor Ida May Bee says her husband, Woody, likes to add a little bit of soy sauce as well.

*—WANDA KAY, LOT #13*

# MOMMA BOXCAR'S ROT-YOUR-TEETH-OUT SWEET CORNBREAD

*Oh, this here is real good! What a way to start
your New Year off right!*

*Makes a 9-inch panful*
1 cup flour
1 cup yellow cornmeal
⅔ cup sugar

1 teaspoon salt

2 teaspoons bakin' powder

1 tablespoon honey

1 cup milk

1 egg

⅓ cup vegetable oil

Start off by givin' your pan a light greasin' (be careful not to overgrease or you'll burn your bread). Get out a large bowl and put in the flour, cornmeal, sugar, salt, and bakin' powder. Mix 'em all together real good. Set aside.

In a smaller bowl, put the milk and the honey. Grab your mixer and mix real well. This will give you a sweet milk mixture. Now add the egg and vegetable oil. Mix well. Add this mixture to the big bowl of dry ingredients that you had set aside earlier. This needs to be mixed real good. Pour it into your pan. If you beat your pan just a bit against the countertop, most of the air bubbles will come to the top of your batter. Turn your oven up to 400 degrees F. and after lettin' it preheat for just a bit, pop that pan in and cook for 25 to 30 minutes, or until nice and golden brown.

*—MOMMA BOXCAR, LOT #5*

## GOOD LUCK COLLARD GREENS

*I must admit that we never ate collard greens in the Boxcar trailer home, but of course we weren't as low-life or trashy as Faye, God bless her.*

*Serves 4 to 6*

2 boxes of frozen collard greens

2 tablespoons bacon grease

Salt and pepper

Ketchup or hot sauce

Follow the directions on the box when it comes to cookin' the greens, but first add the bacon grease to the water that's called for. Once they are done, make sure you drain off all the water. Add the salt and pepper to taste, and pour on the ketchup or hot sauce if you like.

*—FAYE FAYE LARUE, LOT #17*

# HAM BALLS

*No, no, they ain't them kind! These are the balls*
*that you put in your mouth.*

*Makes around 3 dozen*

1¼ pounds ground ham, a sweet ham like honey baked works best

1 pound ground pork

½ pound ground beef

2 eggs

1 cup milk

1½ cups crumbled butter crackers

Put everything in a big bowl and mix it up real good. Usin' your hands, shape into good-size balls (about 2½ inches across). Place in a large bakin' dish, and set aside briefly.

In a pan, combine the followin':

1 can of tomato soup

2 tablespoons vinegar

1 cup brown sugar

1 teaspoon dry mustard

¼ cup maple syrup or apricot jam, whichever your family prefers

Cook over low heat until everything is melted and smooth. Pour the sauce over your balls, the ones you set aside earlier. Stick 'em in the oven at 350 F. degrees and bake for an hour. Serve hot or warm. If you have to cart these somewhere, either cook 'em, freeze 'em, and then heat 'em back up at your destination, or simply get 'em hot in a Crock-Pot and take 'em with you that way.

*—ANITA BIGGON, LOT #2*

# COCONUT BLENDER PIE

*We just love Bisquick at the High Chaparral*
*Trailer Park, and this here recipe shows you why.*

*Makes 1 pie*

½ cup Bisquick mix

½ cup sugar

4 eggs

2 cups milk

3½ ounces flaked coconut

1 teaspoon vanilla extract

3 tablespoons margarine, melted

Put everything in a blender and blend for 1 minute. Pour the mixture into greased 9-inch pie pan. Bake at 400 degrees F. for 20–25 minutes until the pie is set. The crust will make itself while it bakes.

*—NELLIE TINKLE, LOT #4*

# ELVIS'S BIRTHDAY
## January 8
### (Unless it falls on a weekend, this is not a prison holiday.)

Never did one man who was not a religious leader touch the hearts and souls of so many people durin' his lifetime and even after his death like Elvis Aron Presley did. The King, who was born in Tupelo, Mississippi, on this day in 1935, won many a fan with his music, personality, good looks, and gyratin' hips. He was an inspiration for those of us who weren't born with a silver, copper, or, for that matter, plastic spoon in our mouths. Many of us folks hold dear the idea and belief that things will be much better when we get to Heaven, but Elvis showed us that we didn't have to wait that long. He was that light in a rather dark world, that brown chip in the Lays bag, the good station on the AM radio, the real tooth in your girlfriend's mouth, the last nut in the Cracker Jacks box, or the safe step on the front porch. (Mind you, with my recent success, lots of the simple people around the world have put me up there in that void that he left with his untimely passin'.)

Elvis was more than the King of rock 'n' roll for the gentler sex. He was also their perfect idea of Mister Right. Every woman worldwide with an unattractive husband or boyfriend slept with Elvis more times than dear Priscilla did, if you know what I mean. Thanks to the King and a vivid imagination, many a relationship between two ugly people has lasted the sands of time. As a matter of fact, that's one of the reasons why there are so many children named Elvis in the southern states. (When it comes to the bedroom for men, Angie Dickinson is the equivalent of Elvis, unless they're sleepin' with my sister, Donna Sue, and in that case it's Angie Dickinson, Shelley Winters, Granny Clampett, or anyone other than their mother or wife.)

Elvis and I had a very close and personal relationship after he and Priscilla had divorced, which I won't get into right here and now; let's just say that one of the things he liked about me was that he could balance a box of donuts and a gallon of milk on my behind when it was needed. Period. Enough said.

I did start the official Sweat Scarves of Elvis Fan Club in my hometown of Pangburn, Arkansas. We even have our own bowlin' team and meet regularly throughout the year. But this day of all days is one that we hold dear. We gather together at one of our trailers for a nice dinner, which is listed below, and everyone brings a dessert, which is also listed below. After dinner we all get tipsy on Blue Hawaiians while listenin' to Elvis music. Finally we play an Elvis-related game called "What the Maid Didn't Get," which is basically a version of Dirty Santa. We all bring a gift that we've wrapped in newspaper (this represents the poverty that Elvis was born into) and topped with a black bow (a representation of the black hair his dear mother and he had). We place our gifts next to a pair of army boots (this represents his short military service), and then we all pull out a piece of paper from the boots usin' tongs (we may still worship a man who died back in 1977, but we ain't crazy enough to put our hands in there). On each piece of paper is one of Elvis's hit songs, and the person with the earliest hit picks a gift and opens it; then the next person can either take the open gift or choose a wrapped one. It's great fun for all, plus it allows us to pass on last year's lost-receipt Christmas gifts in a hope of gettin' somethin' else halfway decent.

### Things to Get You in the Holiday Mood
Rent and watch one of the King's movies.
Listen to his music.
Tape his picture to your ceilin' so he's the first thing you see when you wake up.
Vacuum your velvet Elvis paintin's.
Visit the live Graceland web cam at www.elvis.com/graceland/vtour/gracecam.asp

### Things to Do
Throw an Elvis Birthday Party.
Play "What the Maid Didn't Get."
Make a holy pilgrimage to Graceland.

### How to Decorate Your Trailer for This Holiday
Typically this marks the first actual holiday of the year that we decorate for, but since it's so dang close to Christmas, we're most likely livin' on change, so we do it cheaply. I like to sprinkle loose gold sequins all over the trailer floor the night before as well as pull out all the shaggy fake-fur pillows. Then the next day when you get up, the noonday sun comes shinin' through your window hittin' the sequins,

and your carpet glitters brighter than Elvis's white-stoned Vegas jumpsuit. Replace your Christmas wreath with one that you've spray painted blue. And last but not least, print out a picture of Elvis, cut out his face, and tape it to the infant in your Nativity scene.

### Trailer Park Tradition

Once again, seein' how we're cash-poor at this time of year, our trailer tradition is very simple. We exchange amongst each other in the trailer park Tums or Rolaids wrapped in toilet paper. That may seem kind of gypy, but with the food we're about to eat, trust me when I say a little old antacid is worth its weight in gold!

### Somethin' to Bring to a Party

# JELLY-FILLED DONUTS

*A dozen of these, a jug of milk, and a soft place to lay his head used to make the King extremely happy. Of course, so did I in a wet T-shirt.*

*Makes about a dozen*

¾ cup milk

¼ cup margarine

2 (¼-ounce) packages of active dry yeast

½ cup warm water

½ cup brown sugar, packed

4¼ cups all-purpose flour

2 eggs

1 teaspoon salt

1 teaspoon ground cinnamon

1 teaspoon grated nutmeg

½ cup raspberry jelly

2 egg whites, beaten

Vegetable oil

Confectioners' sugar, for sprinklin'

In a pan, bring the milk to a boil. Take it off the heat and stir in the margarine. Allow it to cool down a bit.

In large bowl dissolve the yeast in the warm water. Add the milk mixture, the sugar, and 2½ cups of the flour. Beat this until it gets nice and smooth. Stir in the eggs, the salt, cinnamon and the nutmeg. Add more flour, just enough to make a soft dough. Put it on a floured surface and knead lightly for about 2 minutes. Put it in a greased bowl and cover. Let it alone for an hour. Punch the dough down and put it on a floured surface. Roll it out to about ¼-inch thickness. Flour the rim of a glass and use it to cut out dough rounds. Take half the dough rounds that you cut out and put ½ teaspoon of raspberry jelly in the center of 'em. Brush the edges with the egg white and put the remain' nonjelly rounds on top of the others, sealin' the edges well. Place on a greased cookie sheet. Cover and let rise for 45 minutes.

Heat up your oil in a deep fryer to 370 degrees F. Put in a couple of your risen donuts at a time, turnin' once, until golden. Drain well on paper towels. Sprinkle with confectioners' sugar and serve.

—*LOIS BUNCH, LOT #3*

*Dinner Menu*

## RETURN TO SENDER FRIED CHEESE BALLS

> *Anita says that these are almost as big as the fried pickles at Three Cigarettes in the Ashtray Bar and Grill.*

*Makes about 20 balls*

1 cup grated American cheese
2 teaspoons flour
¼ teaspoon salt
2 egg whites
½ cup bread crumbs
Vegetable oil

Combine cheese, flour, and salt in a large bowl.

In a separate bowl, beat the egg whites till they get stiff. Mix 'em in with the cheese mixture, and roll 'em into balls. Take these balls and roll 'em in the bread crumbs (make sure they are completely covered with crumbs), and then carefully place 'em in the oil, heated in a frying pan, to fry. Brown all sides. Put on a paper towel to dry. Serve with your favorite sauce.

*—ANITA BIGGON, LOT #2*

## HOUND DOG HOT DOGS

*This will have you cryin' all the time!*

*Serves 8*
8 hot dogs
Oil
8 hot dog buns
Ketchup
¼ cup chopped onions
½ cup crushed potato chips
1 cup coleslaw

Take the hot dogs and split 'em lengthways down the middle, makin' sure that you don't cut 'em all the way through. Fry each hot dog by carefully placin' it into hot oil in deep fryer. When the hot dog gets to the doneness that you like, pull it out and put it on a paper towel to drain. Take a bun, open it up, and put a little ketchup in it. Now sprinkle some onions and crushed potato chips over the ketchup. Place the hot dog on top of this. Put some ketchup on top of the hot dog, followed by a big scoop of coleslaw. Sprinkle some more onions and crushed potato chips on top of the slaw. Serve with lots of napkins.

*—RUBY ANN BOXCAR, LOT #18*

## DON'T BE CRUEL FRIED PICKLES

*Just the dill smell alone brings back fond memories of the King for me. (By the way, these are the ones I was tellin' y'all about earlier that they have down at Anita's bar.)*

*Makes 6 to 8 servin's*
1 quart sliced dill pickles
1 egg, beaten

3½ cups flour

1 cup milk

1 tablespoon Worcestershire sauce

6 drops of hot sauce

1 teaspoon salt

¾ teaspoon pepper

Fryin' oil

Take your pickles and put 'em on a paper towel to drain off all the extra pickle juice.

Take a bowl and mix together the egg, just 1 tablespoon of the flour, the milk, Worcestershire sauce, and hot sauce. Set aside.

In a separate bowl, add the rest of the flour, the salt, and pepper. Mix well. Take each pickle and dip it first into the milk mixture, then dredge it in the flour mixture. Deep fry at 350 degrees F. until the pickles float to the surface. Drain 'em on a fresh paper towel.

*—ANITA BIGGON, LOT #2*


## ALL SHOOK UP FRIED CHICKEN

*One bite of this and you'll be gyratin' too!*

*6 to 8 servin's*

1 egg

1 cup canned milk or light cream

1 cup fine bread crumbs

1 cup flour

1 teaspoon poultry seasoning

A good dash of onion salt

2 teaspoons parsley flakes

Salt and pepper to taste

A good-size chicken, cut up

Oil for fryin'

Beat the egg and milk together in a large bowl. Set aside.

In a separate bowl, combine the bread crumbs, flour, poultry seasoning, onion salt, parsley flakes and salt and pepper. Dip the chicken parts into egg-milk mixure then into the dry mixture. Fry in oil in a deep fryer at 375 degrees F. till the chicken is tender and brown (15 to 20 minutes). When one side is done, turn on the other side. Place on newspaper or paper towel to drain off the grease.

*—RUBY ANN BOXCAR, LOT #18*

## LOVE ME TENDER PEANUT BUTTER BANANA FRIED ICE CREAM BALLS

*I can't eat one of these without thinkin' about the King.*

*Makes 5 to 6 servin's*

2 egg yolks

1 14½-ounce can of evaporated milk

½ cup peanut butter

⅔ cup sugar

⅛ teaspoon salt

½ banana, chopped up real good into tiny pieces

Beat the egg yolks well in a bowl. Blend in the milk, peanut butter, sugar, and salt and pour into ice cube trays. Freeze until almost hard, then pour into a bowl and beat until smooth. Add the banana pieces and mix. Return to the freezer tray or molds and freeze covered overnight.

Get out the followin' items:

½ cup crushed cornflakes

1 teaspoon ground cinnamon

2 teaspoons sugar

1 egg

Oil for deep frying

Honey

1 can of whipped cream

In a bowl, mix the cornflake crumbs, cinnamon, and sugar. Take out your frozen balls. Roll them in half of the crumb mixture and freeze again.

Beat the egg and dip the coated balls in the beaten egg, then roll again in the remainin' crumbs. Freeze until ready to use. (For a thicker coatin', repeat the dippin' in egg and rolling in crumbs.)

When ready to serve, in a deep fryer, heat the oil to 350 degrees F. Place one frozen ice cream ball in a fryer basket or on a perforated spoon and lower into the hot oil 30 seconds to 1 minute. Immediately remove and place in a dessert dish. Drizzle with honey and top with a squirt of whipped cream. Continue to fry the balls one at a time. The balls will be crunchy outside and just beginnin' to melt inside.

*—JEANNIE JANSSEN, LOT #19*

# SUPER BOWL SUNDAY
**Traditionally it falls on the last Sunday of January, but just like we all know, it can be changed to a later date if needed.**
(A prison holiday since it falls on a Sunday)

Now, most of us trailer park folks ain't real big on football unless, of course, it's college football (GO RAZORBACKS). For the most part, we tend to follow the more classic time-honored skills of sportsmanship like championship wrestlin' (male, female, and midget divisions), roller derby, professional fishin', huntin', bow and arrow shootin', pool, pinball, monster trucks, NASCAR motor racin', and putt-putt golf. But who can say no to the Academy Awards of football playin'? And as any person who's ever attended one of these shindigs will tell you, you don't even have to like football to have a good time. Most of the folks at my Super Bowl parties don't even know who the heck is playin' before the game starts. As a matter of fact, I'm sure if you polled last year's guests, less than 5 percent would even be able to tell you who won the dang thing let alone what the score was. But if you ask how many of 'em had a good time, I'm sure you'd get almost 100 percent (some people you just can't please). Anyways, don't let the fact that you don't know nothin' about football stop you from havin' one heck of a great Super Bowl Sunday.

Before you decide to throw a Super Bowl Party, you'll need to make sure you have four things:

1. Good television reception (everybody loves watchin' those fun commercials and the wonderful top-notch half-time entertainment that the Super Bowl is known for);
2. a workin' color TV with a workin' remote control so you can just mute the sound durin' the actual game and back up durin' the commercials and half-time show;
3. enough seatin' for all your guests; and
4. food, food, food, and more food!

I've found in the past that you get three gatherin's of people at a Super Bowl Party. There are those who gather in the livin' room to watch the telecast, those who gather in the kitchen to chit chat and gossip, and those who gather out on the lawn to vomit and pass out from drinkin' way too much. So a good trailer park Super Bowl will have a buffet-style food arrangement so that all your groups of gathered people can help themselves when they please (just keep an eye on the third group to ensure that they make it to the lawn before it's too late). This also allows you, the hostess, to enjoy all the celebratin' as well. Just remember that these folks are like dogs—if you run out of food, they're gonna go for your jugular!

### Things to Get You in the Holiday Mood

Rent and watch *Brian's Song* (a football movie a woman can enjoy).
Have a beer.
Go to the nearest buffet and practice eatin'.
Buy loose-fittin' pants or slacks so you can eat and drink without havin' to un-
button that top button.

### Things to Do

Place small bets on the game (the Bud Bowl game that is).
Watch the commercials and vote on which one was the best.
Take a poll on which player has the best-lookin' butt.
Place bets on who will be the first at your party to pass out or get sick.
EAT and DRINK!

### How to Decorate Your Trailer for This Holiday

Go to www.superbowl.com to find out the colors of the two teams that are playin', and then grab some glitter in those colors from your local hobby shop. Sprinkle the glitter in your house. The glitter along with the sequins you should still have in your carpet from Elvis's Birthday should really turn your home into a festive shiny party nerve center. Feel free to hang up a few streamers if you want, but the real area of decoratin' is the food table. My sister, Donna Sue, to make up for the fiasco of '97, has come up with the table centerpiece, and I must say, it is somethin'. What she does is she goes out dumpster-divin' back by the school. Usually way down in the bottom under all that garbage she's able to find an old football that's been discarded by the Pangburn athletic department. She'll take it home, cut the laces, and open the top right up. She then puts a piece of duct tape inside over the valve area, stuffs that thing with a half block of Velveeta cheese, and then fills it up with Lois Bunch's chili. She'll bring that over to whoever's trailer happens to be hostin' the party along with a couple bags of stale no-name brand tortilla chips that she picked up at Big Lots. Not only does it look good, but it's also a taste sensation. Back in '98 when she first attempted this tantalizin' taste-bud temptin' centerpiece, she took an old pair of shoestrings out of a pair of tennis shoes she was throwin' away and ran 'em in the holes on the football where the old laces had been. Once she'd filled the football up with the cheese and chili, she'd close it back up by tyin' up those old shoestrings. It looked real good, and helped hold the heat in. She'd pop it in the oven for 10 to 15 minutes, and with the exception of the burnt-rubber smell and smoke that'd temporarily fill the trailer, it'd come out tastin' just fine. But she only did that once on account of Hubert gettin' ill after he accidentally ate the dang shoestrings.

### Trailer Park Tradition
For this day and this day only, if the host trailer ain't got cable, the closest trailer that does let's em' run a coaxial cable between 'em while the Super Bowl is on.

### Somethin' to Bring to a Party

## DONNA SUE'S CREAM CHEESE PIE

*If while eatin' this wonderful pie you taste corn chips, spit it out pronto!*

Makes 1 pie
12 ounces cream cheese, softened
2 eggs, beaten
1 teaspoon lemon juice
¾ cup sugar
2 teaspoons vanilla extract

Toppin':
1 cup sour cream
3½ tablespoons sugar
1 teaspoon vanilla extract

Combine the pie ingredients and beat until light. Pour into a graham cracker crust (made by finely crumblin' up 14 graham crackers and mixin' 'em with ¼ cup melted margarine). Bake for 30 minutes at 350 degrees F. Remove from the oven and let cool while you make the toppin'.

Blend the toppin' ingredients in a small bowl. Pour over the pie and bake for 10 more minutes. Cover tightly and put in the fridge for at least 5 hours.

—*DONNA SUE BOXCAR, LOT #6*

*Dinner Menu*

## LOIS BUNCH'S ALL BEEF CHILI

*Accordin' to Lois, she got this recipe from an old friend who took it off a Mexican fella that he caught while workin' as a border patrol guard in Texas.*

Serves 6

3 pounds ground beef

1 onion, chopped

4 tablespoons minced garlic that you buy at the store

2 (15 ounce) cans tomato sauce

1 (6 ounce) can tomato paste

1 (15 ounce) can of tomatoes, peeled

1 teaspoon cumin

1 teaspoon paprika

2 teaspoons chili powder

1 teaspoon dried oregano

1 teaspoon salt

½ teaspoon pepper

1 teaspoon Worcestershire sauce

Grab a big skillet and throw in your beef, onion, and garlic. Cook until the meat is well done. Take a big pot and put all the remainin' ingredients in it. Drain your beef mixture and add it to the pot. Mix it all together and simmer for 2 to 2½ hours. If you like a thick chili, simmer for 3 to 3½ hours.

If you happen to like beans in your chili, Lois says to add a can when you simmer. Serve with crackers or corn chips.

—*LOIS BUNCH, LOT #3*

## CHEESY BACON DIP

*We make Dick bring two bowls of this when he visits!*

*Serves 8 to 12*

1 (8 ounce) package cream cheese, softened

2 cups sour cream

1 pound bacon, cooked until crispy, crumbled

3 green onions, chopped

2 cups grated Cheddar cheese

French bread, cut into chunks

Mix the cream cheese, sour cream, bacon bits, green onions, and Cheddar cheese together in a bowl. Put in a pan and bake in the oven at 375 degrees F. for 45 minutes to 1 hour. Serve with the French bread and beer.

—*DICK INMAN, LOT #1*

## PASTOR IDA MAY BEE'S BALLS

*If God attended potluck suppers and brought balls, I'm sure this is what they'd taste like.*

*Makes enough for 8 to 10 people*

1 pound ground beef

½ cup dry bread crumbs

⅓ cup minced onion

¼ cup milk

1 egg

1 tablespoon parsley flakes

1 teaspoon salt

⅛ teaspoon pepper

½ teaspoon Worcestershire sauce

¼ cup shortenin'

1 (12 ounce) bottle of chili sauce

1 (10 ounce) jar of grape jelly

In a bowl, mix the first 9 ingredients together. Shape 'em into little balls. In a skillet that you've already melted the shortenin' in, fry up the balls until cooked well. Drain off the fat, take the meatballs out, and add the remainin' ingredients. Stir constantly over medium heat until the jelly melts and mixes with the chili sauce. Put the meatballs and sauce in a Crock-Pot and stir. Say a blessin' over 'em, simmer for 30 minutes, and serve in the pot. Allow your guests to spoon 'em onto a plate and eat 'em with a toothpick. Serve with root beer.

*—PASTOR IDA MAY BEE, LOT #7*

## KAY IS SO DIPPY

*Kay is this new blonde waitress that works with Kitty's husband, Kyle, at Three Cigarettes in the Ashtray Bar and Grill.*

*Feeds 10 real easy*

1 pound block Velveeta cheese

2 cups grated Cheddar cheese

2 cans RO*TEL

1 (4 ounce) can green chilies

Beer

Put the Velveeta, Cheddar, and RO*TEL together in a Crock-Pot.

Turn it on high for 20 minutes, then switch to low. After all has melted, put in a splash of beer to thin it. Add green chilies and mix well. Add more beer if needed. Serve with chips and beer.

*—KITTY CHITWOOD, LOT #11*

## KITTY'S LEMON BEER CAKE

*This poor cake didn't stand a chance! It was gone in minutes!*

*Makes 6 to 8 servin's, if cut just right*

1 package of lemon cake mix

1 package of instant lemon puddin' mix

1 cup beer

¼ cup vegetable oil

4 eggs

Grease up and flour a Bundt pan (a 10-incher is fine). Turn your oven on to preheat it to 350 degrees F.

In a large bowl, mix the dry cake mix and the dry puddin' mix together well. Add the beer and oil, mixin' until all is moist. Add the eggs and beat the contents of the bowl with an electric mixer set on high. The batter should be smooth and thick. Once you've got it to that consistency, put it in the Bundt pan. Bake for 50 to 55 minutes. Let it cool for around 15 minutes or so and then turn it out. Let it continue to cool.

In the meantime, we can make the frostin'. You'll need the followin':

½ cup margarine, softened but not melted

1 large egg yolk

Pinch of salt

1 teaspoon grated lemon zest

2 tablespoons fresh lemon juice

4½ cups sifted confectioners' sugar

5 tablespoons heavy cream

Usin' an electric mixer, cream the margarine until it gets soft. Add the egg yolk, salt, lemon zest, and lemon juice and beat it all together. Add ¼ cup of sugar and with your electric mixer set on low, mix it in until it's smooth. Alternately add the cream and the remainin' sugar. Make sure you blend till it's smooth before addin' the next alternatin' ingredient. Feel free to add more cream if the frostin' is too stiff. If your frostin' is soft, chill it in the fridge.

Put the cake on a nice plate or cake server and frost it. Take an empty beer can or bottle and wash it both on the inside and the outside. Place the beer can or bottle as far down in the middle of the Bundt pan as possible without destroyin' the cake. If you feel creative, you can also place washed beer caps around the cake. Serve with coffee, milk, or beer.

*—KITTY CHITWOOD, LOT #11*

# Chapter 2

Opal Lamb-Inman of lot #1 enjoys a beignet durin'
Mardi Gras in the streets of New Orleans.

# *February*

February is the second month of the year, but in olden times "Februare" was the last month of the year. Durin' this last month, the Romans would purify themselves for the start of the New Year in March. Today we kind of do the same thing by purifyin' our intestines with massive amounts of beer consumption durin' Mardi Gras.

Our old friend Julius Caesar, who's orange-drink invention can still be found even today in malls across this great land of ours, decided to add another day to the month (shock surprise) durin' a standard year. He also decreed that every four years, a 30th day would show up at the end of the month. Well, later down the road, the Roman emperor Augustus decided he wanted an extra day for the month that was named after him, August, so he stole that extra day that his great-uncle had attached to February.

Currently there are 28 days in the month of February unless of course it's a leap year and then, in that case, there are 29.

Now, February is one of those tricky months when it comes to holidays. You see, you got things like the Chinese New Year, Mardi Gras, and Ash Wednesday that keep jumpin' from date to date and occasionally from month to month each year. Sometimes keepin' up with when these special days are celebrated is harder than lookin' at Opal Lamb's face for more than a few seconds. To simplify things, I'm includin' only one of those tricky holidays, Mardi Gras. But you've got to check your calendar each year to find out just what day it falls on, and if it even falls in February that year.

And another good thing about the month of February is that you get one of Sister Bertha's wonderful dessert recipes!

February is:
*Potato Lover's Month*

# HASH BROWN CASSEROLE

*It just amazes me how talented in the kitchen a*
*gal as utterly unattractive as Opal can be.*

*Makes 4 to 6 servin's*

1½ pounds hamburger meat

1 onion, sliced

Large package of frozen mixed vegetables

1 can of cream of mushroom soup

1 can of cream of chicken soup

Bag of frozen hashbrowns

In a long pan, press out the uncooked hamburger meat. Put the onion slices on top of that and cover with the raw frozen vegetables.

In a bowl, add the soups and mix 'em up. Pour 'em over the frozen veggies. Top this with the frozen hashbrowns, cover with foil, and bake for an hour at 325 degrees F. Uncover and bake for an additional 45 minutes.

*—OPAL LAMB, LOT #1*

*National Cherry Month*

# CHERRY BLENDER PIE

*Thank Heaven for Bisquick!*

*Makes 1 pie*

1 cup Bisquick

½ cup packed brown sugar

½ teaspoon ground cinnamon

2 teaspoons margarine, softened

Grease a 10-inch pie plate and turn your oven up to 400 degrees F.

In a bowl, put in the Bisquick, brown sugar, and cinnamon. Cut in the margarine. It should be crumbly. Set aside.

In a blender, put the followin' ingredients:

1 cup milk

2 tablespoons margarine, softened

½ teaspoon almond extract

2 eggs

½ cup Bisquick

¼ cup granulated sugar

Blend for 15 seconds on high. Pour it into the pie plate and evenly spoon on 1 can cherry pie fillin'. Now take the Bisquick/sugar mixture that you had set aside, and place that on top of the pie fillin'. Bake for 15 minutes.

*—NELLIE TINKLE, LOT #4*

*Great American Pies Month*

# SAINT PAUL'S PEANUT BUTTER PIE

*Accordin' to Sister Bertha, Saint Paul was talkin'*
*about his addiction to this dessert treat when he*
*spoke of his "thorn in the side." Pastor Ida May*
*Bee just shakes her head and keeps on eatin'.*

*Makes 2 pies*

1 cup powdered milk

⅓ cup granulated sugar

½ cup cornstarch

5 egg yolks (save egg whites for another use)

4 cups water

1 tablespoon margarine

2 teaspoons vanilla extract

2 cups confectioners' sugar

1 cup creamy peanut butter

2 baked 9-inch pie shells

Whipped cream

In a saucepan, mix together the first 5 ingredients and cook over medium heat, stirrin' constantly, until the mixture thickens. Remove from the heat; add the margarine and vanilla extract.

In a small bowl, crumble together the confectioners' sugar and peanut butter. Spread all but ½ cup of this mixture into the bottom of the pie shells. Pour the hot fillin' into the shells over the crumb mixture. Bake for 15 minutes at 350 degress F. When the pies have cooled, top with the remainin' crumb mixture. Add the whipped cream on top of the crumbs and serve.

*—SISTER BERTHA, LOT #12*

*Celebration of Chocolate Month*

# WALKIN' WITH JESUS BROWNIES

*One of these and you'd swear you were with the*
*Master on the streets of gold.*

*Makes between 20 and 25 brownies*

1 package brownie mix, to be prepared according to package directions

16 ounces chocolate chips, divided into a group of 6 ounces and one of 10 ounces

4 ounces semisweet chocolate

2 tablespoons margarine

8 ounces white chocolate

2 tablespoons heavy cream

Take a 9-inch pan and grease it up real good. Take a look at the brownie mix directions and preheat the oven to the suggested temperature. Take the 6 ounces of chocolate chips and spread 'em around the bottom of the greased pan. Put the pan in the oven so the chips can melt. Watch 'em carefully, since they will burn if they stay in there too long. While you're doing that, go ahead and make the brownie mix just like the instructions on the box tell you to. As soon as the chips have melted, pull 'em out of the oven. Spread the melted chocolate out evenly across the bottom of the pan. Set aside for just a minute. Add the remainin' 10 ounces of chocolate chips into the brownie mix. Mix real well and scrape the mix on top of the melted chocolate. Bake accordin' to the directions on the box. When done, pull out of the oven and let set.

In a pan put the white chocolate and the cream. Melt the chocolate and stir until it and the cream mix and become smooth. Spread this over your brownies. Set aside to cool. Melt the 4 ounces of semisweet chocolate in a pan. Add the margarine and mix well. Pour this mixture over the frosted brownies. Cover tightly and put in the fridge till the top layer of chocolate gets nice and firm.

*—SISTER BERTHA FAYE, LOT #12*

# GYPSY ROSE LEE'S BIRTHDAY
## February 9
### (Unless it falls on a weekend, this is not a prison holiday)

My 56-year-old stripper sister, Donna Sue, got us all celebratin' this special day. It seems that Gypsy Rose Lee is a role model/idol for all the Blue Whale Girls up at the Blue Whale Strip Club in Searcy where my sister works. To my surprise, even Kenny and Donny in lot #15 know all about Gypsy Rose Lee, and they just love both the musical and the movie version of her life story. Accordin' to Donna Sue, Gypsy was the queen mother of the burlesque dancers. She put the tease in striptease, barely takin' off her clothes, which unfortunately can't be said for my sister and her fellow dancers down at the Blue Whale (I don't understand how in the heck they stay open). Anyways, Gypsy, who's real name was Rose Louise Hovick, along with her sister, Ellen Evangeline Hovick, who became a famous actress better known as June Havoc many years later, performed together when they were little girls on the vaudeville circuit under the watchful and domineerin' eye of their mother, Rose. At the tender age of 13, June married a fella in the chorus and ran off, leavin' Gypsy to entertain on her own. Well, one thing led to another and Gypsy Rose Lee was born. She went on to do a few movies and television shows, including hostessin' two talk shows. She even wrote an autobiography simply titled *Gypsy*, which was turned into a Broadway musical that highlighted her mother, Rose, as the main character. Gypsy Rose Lee met her maker in 1970 at age 56.

Every year the Blue Whale holds a strip-a-thon in honor of Gypsy Rose Lee, givin' all the tips they make to Bunnie's Shed of Dance in Pangburn. Bunnie's Shed of Dance is just that, a shed were Bunnie Taps, who just last year retired at 93 from a career in the art of exotic dance, teaches young girls both ballet and, as you might have guessed, tap dancin'. Bunnie uses the money raised durin' the "Gypsy Rose Lee's Birthday Strip-A-Thon" to pay for lessons for all the poor little girls who have no funds to pay for them themselves. "Who knows," Bunnie says with a glimmer in her good eye, "maybe one day one of these trashy little lowlife girls who receive these lessons thanks to the strip-a-thon will someday grow up to be a sex kitten just like me." Yeah, that's all we need in this world, more gals who strip all the way to the cemetery.

### Things to Get You in the Holiday Mood

Go to the library and check out the book *Gypsy: A Memoir of Gypsy Rose Lee.*

Rent and watch the video *Gypsy* (Kenny and Donny tell me that both Rosalind Russell and Bette Midler's versions are now available).

Buy the soundtrack to *Gypsy* (personally I love Ethel Merman's the best) and play it all day long in your trailer. (Sorry, I searched the internet and ain't been able to find the 8-track versions.)

Visit www.rubylot18.homestead.com/bluewhale.html and say "Hi" to my sister, Donna Sue, and the other Blue Whale gals.

### Things to Do

Go to a strip show.

Do a strip show for your husband, boyfriend, or significant other.

### How to Decorate Your Trailer for This Holiday

This is another one of them easy ones. Simply take bras and panties and hang 'em up around your house. I've found that addin' a few tassels and some fake dollar bills to the Christmas tree helps to set just the right mood for the holiday celebration.

### Trailer Park Tradition

At the High Chaparral Trailer Park, we knock on the trailer doors of those who we don't want to see naked, and when they answer the door we tuck a dollar bill in their shirt or blouse. Lord you should see the money Opal Lamb-Inman makes on Gypsy Rose Lee's birthday. I swear she could buy a new car!

*Somethin' to Bring to a Party*

## DONNA SUE'S WHITE CHOCOLATE-COVERED CHERRY CHI-CHI'S

*Now these are some Chi Chi's I'm always happy to
put my lips around.*

*Make about 9 pairs of chi-chi's*
1 (8-ounce) jar of maraschino cherries
Rum
6 ounces white chocolate chips
4 ounces white chocolate candy coatin'

Drain the cherries and fill the cherry jar up with rum, makin' sure that all the cherries are covered. Put the top back on the jar and put in the fridge. Let the little red devils soak for 4 to 6 days. Drain the cherries, but keep the rum. Carefully place the cherries on a paper towel or paper plate, makin' sure not to squeeze them. Melt the white chocolate chips in the microwave and stir completely. Add about a quarter of the rum and stir until smooth. Allow this to set for a few minutes, then slowly add the cherries. Stir gently. As the mixture thickens, spoon the cherries onto wax paper. Put these in the freezer and let 'em set till they get firm. Melt the white chocolate candy coatin' in the microwave. Take a firm cherry and the jelly that should be around it and dip into the melted coatin'. Put each one on waxed paper so it can set. When they've hardened, you can carefully take 'em off the wax paper and place 'em in paper candy cups. Store in the fridge.

*—DONNA SUE BOXCAR, LOT #6*

*Dinner Menu*

## THE GYPSY ROSE STRIPPER

*Heck, after a few of these, I'd even look good naked!*

*Makes 2 quarts*

6 cans of beer

1 (12 ounce) can of lemonade concentrate

2 pints of whiskey

In a punch bowl, combine the beer, lemonade concentrate, and whiskey. Stir it up and serve in glasses with ice.

—*MOMMA BALLZAK, LOT # 16*

## SAUTÉED NIBLETS

*This dish is so easy to make, Lulu Bell's new boyfriend could make it without burnin' down her trailer. Lord knows sometimes he's one spark plug short of an ignition.*

*Serves 4 to 5*

4 ears of corn

Margarine

Salt

Cut the kernels off the cob, tryin' not to break 'em. Melt the margarine in a skillet, add the kernels, and simmer gently for 4 minutes, stirring constantly. Season with salt to taste.

—*KITTY CHITWOOD, LOT #11*

## CHICKEN BREAST WITH A CHAMPAGNE SAUCE

*My husband, Dew, said that I could strip for him any time if I make this for dinner, just as long as I keep the lights off and the light from the moon ain't bright.*

*Serves 4*

¼ cup all-purpose flour

2 teaspoons salt
1 teaspoon black pepper
1 teaspoon ground onion
4 chicken breasts
2 tablespoons olive oil
4 cups sliced fresh mushrooms
1 cup sweet champagne
1 teaspoon sugar
1 cup heavy cream

In a cereal-size bowl, combine the flour, salt, pepper, and ground onion. Dip each breast in the mixture, dustin' both sides, and place in a skillet with the hot olive oil (325 degrees F). Brown lightly on both sides. Take out the chicken. Add the mushrooms, champagne, and sugar to the skillet. Mix well. Place the chicken back in the skillet and cook over medium heat for 30 minutes. Take the chicken out again and add the cream to the pan. Stir and simmer for 6 or 7 minutes. Pour the champagne-cream sauce over the chicken and serve.

*—DONNY OWENS, LOT #15*

## SPOTTED DICK

*Donna Sue got some Spotted Dick when she went
to London with me.*

8 ounces self-raising flour
Pinch of salt
4 ounces margarine, softened
2 ounces castor sugar (if you can't find castor sugar, use superfine or confectioners'), plus more for sprinklin'
6 ounces raisins
6 tablespoons water

Sift the flour and salt together in a bowl. Add the margarine and mix with your hands. Add the sugar and raisins and mix well. Add the water to make a soft dough. Put it on a floured surface and form into a roll. Wrap a sheet of wax paper loosely around it and seal the ends with a string. Place it a microwave and cook on Medium for 11 minutes. Sprinkle with castor sugar and serve hot with puddin' (recipe follows).

For the puddin', you will need the followin':

3 egg yolks

1 tablespoon castor sugar, plus more to taste

½ pint milk

¼ teaspoon vanilla extract

In a large bowl, whisk the yolks and sugar together. Heat up the milk in a saucepan until it's just about ready to boil. Take the milk off the stove and gradually whisk it into the egg mixture. Rinse out the pan and add water to it. Put it back on the stove and heat it to a boil. Turn off the heat. Put the bowl over the pan and stir the mixture until it thickens. Add the vanilla extract and more sugar till you get a taste that you like.

*—DONNA SUE BOXCAR, LOT #6*

# DONNA SUE BOXCAR'S BIRTHDAY
## February 12
(Not a prison holiday yet, but the gals at the Blue Whale Strip Club
are lobbying to get this date added in Arkansas)

Now, as many of y'all know, President Lincoln's birthday falls on the 12th
of February also. So who's birthday do we celebrate? Well, let's see, old honest Abe lived in a log cabin and old trampy Donna Sue lives in a trailer and
is related to me. Shock surprise, we're goin' with Donna Sue! Abe Lincoln
was the only great Republican that ever held the office of President of the
United States, but my sister has managed to sleep with more men in her 56
years on this earth than voted Abe Lincoln into office (I won't be surprised
if some of those men were one and the same either). Anyways, at the High
Chaparral Trailer Park and in households across North America and many
third-world countries, February 12th will always belong to my sister,
Donna Sue Boxcar.

I'd give y'all a brief bio about my sister, but seein' how she's workin' on her
own book in between bottles, I don't want to steal her thunder. For those of
y'all who haven't had the chance to meet her or read about her in my first
book, *Ruby Ann's Down Home Trailer Park Cookbook,* let me fill you in just a
bit. There are two things that my sister loves to do: drink and dance. I can
boldly state that my sister has drunk every adult beverage know to man at
least once in her life. And I can also add that my sister has not been totally
sober since 1964. Now, don't get me wrong, she's not an alcoholic—she ain't
got time for the meetin's. Plus, doggone it, Momma and Daddy never raised
us kids to be quitters. Donna Sue doesn't drink 'cause she has to. Oh, no, she
drinks 'cause she likes to. It's just that plain and simple.

Donna Sue began exotic dancin' a short time after she started drinkin'.
At first she tried her hand at bartendin', but as you can guess, her behind
a bar didn't tend to be that profitable for the bar owner. So she decided
to mix her love of drinkin' with her love of dancin'. She soon found that
drunken men like to tip a gal who strips with both money and drinks.
Well, that was it. Donna Sue had found her niche in life. That was 30
some odd years ago. Since then, her talents have taken her to many a strip
joint in the South as well as the smaller countries in the world. She's

danced for kings, politicians, movie actors, and men of wealth (all of whom had lost most of their vision or were either near death and were hopin' this would push 'em over). She's been the play toy for many a man who was just as drunk if not drunker than she was at the time. But most important, she's been on a mission, unconsciously of course, to make sure that every single man on this planet, regardless of how unattractive or lowlife he might be, could stand up after an all-nighter and proudly say, "Hey world, at least once in my life, I slept with another human bein'—I think."

Twelve years ago, Donna Sue decided it was time to give up the road. As she'd enjoyed all the lights and glamour that headlinin' in dives around the world had to offer, she was ready to hang her tassels in one place. So my sister became the headliner at the Blue Whale Strip Club over in Searcy, Arkansas. Yes, now she and the other Blue Whale girls might have gotten on in years, and the portions of the famed fish basket at the Blue Whale might have increased (6 pounds of catfish) while the price has decreased (99 cents not includin' beverages), but as long as the drinks keep comin', so will my sister's dancin' routine.

Happy birthday to you, my dearest sister!

### Things to Get You in the Holiday Mood
Go into a bar and buy somebody a drink.

It ain't the Blue Whale, but you just might see a whale via a web cam at www. orcacam.com/cwrcam.html.

Visit a couple of Donna Sue's favorite web pages like www.geocities.com/living largecreations/mypage.html and www.bll.com

### Things to Do
Play put the lid on the bottle.

Divide up into two or more teams with at least three people on each team and play "Pass the Fruit" (members of each team must place their hands behind their backs and pass a fruit by usin' only their chin and neck from the first player all the way to the last player and then back). Another fun version of this game can be played if you have enough men and women. In this case, you pass a cherry rather than a large piece of fruit, but the men must use their mouths and the women use their cleavage. Now if you got a small-chested gal, she can use duct tape in an attempt to create cleavage. If that don't work, then she can take on the role of a man.

### How to Decorate Your Trailer for This Holiday

To capture that just-right feelin', I hang up a Happy Birthday banner backwards. I also go and make each picture in my trailer crooked. Place empty liquor bottles, cocktail glasses, and ice trays around your home. Full ashtrays also tend to add the perfect touch (if no one in your house smokes, just take a coffee can down to your nearest bar and ask them if they'd mind fillin it up with butts and ashes for you). Make sure you put out bowls of pretzels or beer nuts for your guests.

### Trailer Park Tradition

At 6:43 P.M. in your time zone, everyone yells "Ouch" in honor of Donna Sue's birth, and then we pass out to each other presents like a jar of olives, a set of cocktail glasses, a pack of fun novelty swizzle sticks, a bottle of booze, a bra, or anything else that would pertain to a bar/strip club. We follow this with a traditional birthday cake with Donna Sue's name on it, and a nice little dinner (which is listed below).

### Somethin' to Bring to a Party

# CRAB SPREAD

*I can't eat this 'cause it makes me itch.*

*Makes enough for 10*

2 (8 ounce) packages cream cheese, softened
½ pound crabmeat, flaked
1 teaspoon lemon juice
1 tablespoon chopped dill

Turn your oven up to 350 degrees F.

In a bowl, combine all the ingredients and mix 'em well. Spoon the mixture into a 9-inch pie pan and bake for 30 minutes. It should be nice and bubbly. Pull it out and serve with crackers.

*—DONNY OWENS, LOT #15*

# TASTY TEQUILA DIP

*Makes 6 to 8 servin's*

3 cups crunchy peanut butter

½ teaspoon dried crushed red chili

2 tablespoons lemon juice

½ teaspoon soy sauce

1 teaspoon yellow mustard

1½ cups tequila

Put everything in a blender and blend till it's well mixed. Put in a bowl and serve with chips, veggie slices, or a glass of tequila.

—*MOMMA BALLZAK, LOT #16*

# HAPPY BEANS

*These babies will blow you away.*

*Serves 4 to 6*

1¼ pounds dried navy beans

8 cups water

1¾ cups bourbon

½ teaspoon salt

1 teaspoon dry mustard

½ teaspoon pepper

½ cup packed brown sugar

⅓ cup molasses

½ teaspoon ground cinnamon

½ teaspoon grated nutmeg

2 yellow onions, chopped

1½ pounds salt pork

Rinse off your beans under some warm water and put 'em in a large pot. Add 4 cups of water and ½ cup of the bourbon. Cover the pot and allow to soak overnight. On the next day, go ahead and drain the beans. (Drink the water if you want. If not, just throw it away.) Add 4 cups of fresh water to the pot along with the salt, mustard, pepper, brown sugar, molasses, cinnamon, nutmeg, onions, and the beans. Mix well and bring to a boil. Once you've reached the boil, stir, cover, and allow it to cook for 45 to 50 minutes. Remove from heat, uncover, and add ⅓ cup of the bourbon to the mixture. Stir. Set aside.

Take a casserole dish and add ⅓ cup of the bourbon. Score your salt pork and place the scored sides down in the casserole dish. Add the beans and another ⅓ cup of bourbon. Cover the dish and bake for 5 hours at 275 degrees F. When it is finished, shut off your oven and take out your beans. Add the rest of the bourbon, re-cover the casserole dish, put it in the oven (which is shut off), and let stand for 45 minutes. Serve warm.

*—WENDY BOTTOM, LOT #4*

## I'LL DRINK TO THAT DESSERT

*Don't tell Donna Sue that this is her archenemy's recipe, 'cause she'll just suck the rum out and throw the rest in the trash.*

*4 to 6 servin's*

2 cups packed brown sugar

2 eggs

⅔ cup flour

1 teaspoon bakin' soda

1 cup chopped pecans

1 tub of Cool Whip

½ cup spiced rum

Mix the first 5 ingredients in a bowl, then pour into a greased 9-inch pan. Bake for 25 minutes at 350 degrees F. When done, let it cool completely.

While you are waitin' for it to cool, take the container of Cool Whip, dump it into a large bowl, and add the spiced rum. Take your cooled cake and crumble it into the Cool Whip mixture. Pour it back into the pan that the cake was baked in, cover tightly, and put in the freezer for 2 hours. Serve it in bowls.

*—FAYE FAYE LARUE, LOT #17*

# MARDI GRAS
## It falls on a Tuesday in February or March.
### (Not a prison holiday)

Personally I've never had the chance to actually go to New Orleans for Mardi Gras, but I hear it's just a blast. I sent my sister to New Orleans for her 45th birthday and she just had a ball. When she saw that her hotel was on Bourbon Street and they were callin' it Fat Tuesday, she thought the whole dang thing was for her birthday (I told y'all she ain't been sober since 1964). She really enjoyed herself. As a matter of fact, she had to buy another suitcase just to carry home the beads that people had thrown at her for showin' 'em her breasts. I have no idea why the heck she even bothered to wear a dang blouse while she was there.

When Opal from lot #1 was single, she attended the festivities in New Orleans and just downright hated it. She said it was loud, it was rowdy, and that when she lifted her top in an attempt to get some beads she was pelted with rocks and garbage. That, of course, just goes to show that there are times when there's just not enough liquor in the world for some folks, if you know what I mean. Poor thing! She didn't come back with one dang bead—a concussion, yes, but not one dang bead.

### Things to Get You in the Holiday Mood
Can't make it to Mardi Gras this year? See it online at www.nolalive.com/
   bourbocam/
Rent and watch a movie set in New Orleans like *Undercover Blues* or *The Big Easy*.
Practice liftin' your shirt up and down.
Take an old necklace and lightly toss it at the couch.

### Things to Do
Tell your female guests to wear their swim suits under their clothes. Then as the party goes on, y'all can start raisin' your blouses (the men folks can drop their pants) without upsettin' anybody there. After all, who can holler if a person lifts or drops an item of clothes to reveal their bathin' suit? Just make sure you set up a house rule that only beads can be thrown at those who partake in this tradition.

### How to Decorate Your Trailer for This Holiday

Go out and get some purple, green, and gold or yellow streamers. String these up all over your home. You could also throw around glitter that's the same color. Make sure that you play Dixie Land music in the background to get the right effect.

### Trailer Park Tradition

To add reality to your party, you can do what my sister, Donna Sue, does for her Mardi Gras get together. She puts out big white buckets that she's halfway filled with sand all over inside her trailer. When your guests have to pee, they just use those buckets. This adds that flair of peein' in the New Orleans streets that has become so common durin' the Mardi Gras holiday. Just make sure that everyone is fully aware that the buckets are for number one only! You let just one person forget, and you can kiss that party good-bye.

### Somethin' to Bring to a Party

## JUST LIKE BEIN' THERE BEIGNETS

*This is the only good thing Opal brought back from New Orleans.*

*Makes about 5 dozen*

1½ cups warm water
1 package of active dry yeast
½ cup granulated sugar
1 teaspoon salt
2 eggs, beaten
1 cup evaporated milk
7 cups all-purpose flour
¼ cup shortenin', softened
Oil for deep frying
Confectioners' sugar

In a large bowl, pour in your warm water and sprinkle in the yeast. Stir to dissolve. Add the granulated sugar, salt, eggs, and milk. Blend and add 4 cups of the flour; beat until smooth. Add the shortenin' and beat in remainin' 3 cups flour. Cover and chill overnight. Roll out on a floured board to ⅛-inch thickness. Cut into 2½-inch squares. In a deep fryer, fry at 360 degrees for 2 to 3 minutes until lightly browned on both sides. Drain on a paper towel and sprinkle with confectioners' sugar. Serve hot with milk or coffee.

*—OPAL LAMB INMAN, LOT #1*

*Dinner Menu*

# CHICKEN AND SAUSAGE JAMBALAYA

*Now, this is a dish I'd raise my shirt for!*

*Makes 8 to 12 servin's*

1 tablespoon oil
7 pounds chicken, cut into pieces
3 pounds smoked sausage, sliced up
2 pounds onions, chopped
½ pound bell pepper, chopped
½ pound celery, chopped
1½ tablespoons minced garlic
½ teaspoon dried thyme
1 tablespoon dried basil
1½ tablespoons hot sauce, plus more for servin'
½ tablespoon pepper
3 quarts chicken stock
2 quarts long-grain rice

Put the oil in a Dutch oven followed by the chicken. Brown for 10 minutes, turn the chicken, and add the sausage. Cook for an additional 20 to 25 minutes. Make sure that the chicken has browned on both sides. Add your onions, pepper, and celery. Reduce the heat and simmer for 20 more minutes. Add everything else but the stock and rice and let simmer for 10 more minutes. Pour the stock in and give it another 20 minutes of simmerin'. Put the rice in and increase the heat so you can get the mixture to come to a boil. Make sure you stir constantly. Reduce the heat to low, cover the Dutch oven with a lid, and let simmer for 20 more minutes. Take off the cover and gently stir a few times. Let the jambalaya set for another 10 minutes. Shut off the stove and serve with hot sauce.

*—TINA FAYE STOPENBLOTTER, LOT #17*

# RED BEANS AND RICE

*I hear that by the end of Mardi Gras, the streets
are covered with this stuff.*

*Makes 8 servin's*

1 pound dried red kidney beans

1 meaty ham bone

2 onions, chopped

1 bell pepper, chopped

2 celery ribs, chopped

2 garlic cloves, chopped

Salt

Pepper

Pinch of sugar

2 pounds spicy sausage links

Cooked rice

¼ cup parsley flakes

Rinse your beans and put 'em in a pot. Add enough water to the pot so that the beans are completely covered and let 'em soak overnight. The next day, simply dump out the water, rinse, and put in fresh water (about 4 cups) and the ham bone, onions, bell pepper, celery, garlic and salt, pepper, and sugar to taste. Cook over medium heat for 1½ hours.

In a skillet, fry up the sausage until it's crisp. Drain and set it aside until the beans have finished their 1½ hours cookin'. When the beans are done, add the sausage and stir well. Let everything simmer on low heat for another 20 minutes. Pour over the cooked rice and sprinkle the parsley over just before servin'.

*—FAYE FAYE LARUE, LOT #17*

# TRADITIONAL KING CAKE

*Normally the person who finds the baby in the cake
has to throw next year's party. Of course, back
when Me-Ma used to make this cake, the person
who didn't find somethin' like a Band-Aid, button,
chunk of gray hair, or other items had to throw the
party. Thank the good Lord her cookin' days are
long gone.*

*Makes 1 cake*

2 tablespoons yeast

½ cup sugar

½ cup warm water

3½ cups flour

1 teaspoon grated nutmeg

1 teaspoon grated lemon zest

2 teaspoons salt

½ cup warm milk

5 egg yolks

½ cup margarine, softened

2 teaspoons ground cinnamon

In a large bowl, sprinkle the yeast and 2 teaspoons of the sugar over the warm water. Wait 4 minutes, then mix thoroughly. Set the bowl in a warm place for 10 minutes.

In another large bowl, combine the flour, remaining sugar, nutmeg, lemon zest, and salt. Set aside.

Using an electric mixer, add the yeast/water mixture to the milk and egg yolks and mix well.

Gradually add the dry ingredients and softened margarine until it all comes together in a dough. Knead the dough for 10 minutes, addin' a bit more flour if necessary.

Place the dough in a covered, buttered bowl in a warm place for 1½ hours.

When the dough has risen, remove and punch down. Sprinkle with the cinnamon and form into a long French-bread-lookin' cylinder, then twist this cylinder and bend it into a circle or big ring. Pinch the ends together to complete the circle. Once again, cover and let rise for 45 minutes.

Preheat the oven to 375 degrees F.
In a small bowl, combine the followin':

1 egg, beaten
1 tablespoon milk
Brush the tops and sides of the ring with this egg wash. Put in the oven and bake for 30 to 35 minutes until golden brown. Put it on a cake rack and let it cool completely.

Take a little baby doll that you've picked up at a craft store and push it into one of the twisted folds of the cake so it's hidden real good.

Next you will need to mix together the followin' ingredients to make a frostin';

3 cups confectioner's sugar
¼ cup lemon juice
6 tablespoons water
Make sure that the mixture is smooth. Add more water if you need to. Ice the entire cake and immediately sprinkle on colored sugar (green, purple, and gold colors) in alternatin' rows. Serve as is, but make sure to warn everyone about the baby. Lord knows you don't want the person who finds the baby to die. Who in the heck would throw next year's party or provide the king cake?

*—LOVIE BIRCH, LOT #20*

# ST. VALENTINE'S DAY
## February 14
### (A prison holiday)

The Romans had originally claimed this time of the year their own over 800 years before the fifth century. They held a pagan celebration commemoratin' the young men's rite of passage to the god Lupercus (not to be confused with the mid-March Celtic celebration commemoratin' the short young men's rite of passage to the god Luperconus). In the Lupercus festivity, a young man would partake in a lottery by drawin' out the name of a young woman from a box. This gal would be his sexual mate for the rest of the year. Well, when the Roman church took over, they changed it a bit so that the names that came out of the box would be of saints, and the young men, or women, who were now drawin' as well, would have to take on the ways of that saint. Needless to say, nobody liked this new game at all, with the exception of the person that drew the name of St. Bernard, which meant they got to run around with a small barrel of rum around their neck.

The church also replaced the god Lupercus with a saint that would become the patron saint of love. They chose St. Valentine on account of how he'd secretly married soldiers to women even though Emperor Claudius ruled such marriages a crime. So Claudius had St. Valentine thrown in jail, which is where he fell in love with the jailer's daughter. Just before they took St. Valentine away to be stoned and beheaded, he wrote a love note to the girl, signin' it "From Your Valentine." Even with the changes that the church had made, Roman men still used this special day for St. Valentine to attract a girl's attention, which leads us to today's practices.

This year the Last Stop Nursin' Home over at the last stop on the old Lake Road ran a little special for all the folks in Pangburn. For just $14 a couple, you could rent a vacant room for an hour and get a nice holiday meal. Also included was a romantic canoe ride around the moat that surrounds the guard towers, barbed wire fence, and buildin' complex. Me and my husband, Dew, signed up for the whole package, but weren't able to use it since the resident in the room we'd rented didn't pass on until much later that night. Our good neighbor Mickey Ray Kay and his wife, Connie Kay, in lot #13 said it was one of the best times they'd had in a while. Accordin' to old Mickey Ray, once you'd gotten used to that strong urine smell, and knew which areas on the bed to avoid puttin' your hand on, it was pure romance to say the least. Connie thought the puréed Salisbury steak was very tasty once she'd added a few packets of salt that she'd brought along in her purse. As far as the canoe ride went, both Mickey Ray and Connie agreed that battlin' the snakes that kept tryin' to get into their canoe just showed 'em how much they really depended on each other. After hearin' them speak, I almost wished that old lady would've up and died a bit earlier so me and my husband, Dew, could've used our package.

### Things to Get You in the Holiday Mood

Hot-glue some rose petals to your private areas and wait for your loved one to come home. Before openin' the door, make sure that it's your loved one and not the fella from the propane gas company who's come to refill your tank.

Rent and watch a romantic movie like *Smokey and the Bandit* with your loved one.

### Things to Do

Try to make love to your husband, boyfriend, wife, or girlfriend without pretendin' that they're somebody else.

Since some florists mark their flowers way up at this time of year, stop by the cemetery and pick out a lovely arrangement for that special Valentine of yours.

Call your local nursin' homes and see if they happen to be runnin' some kind of special like the one at the Last Stop Nursin' Home. They usually have great hourly prices that most motels can't match.

Drive down to the part of town where the hookers hang out. Stop and give 'em all Valentine's Day cards. A box of Wet Ones for them to share really shows how much you care about them as well.

Why not pass the love on and give frozen TV dinners to those people out on the streets that hold up those signs that read, "Anything will help." After all, you don't know how long they'll be out there. When they've finished collectin' for the day, the TV dinners should be completely thawed out and ready for them to consume.

### How to Decorate Your Trailer for This Holiday

Cut out hearts from construction paper or paper plates and toss 'em around your trailer home. Tape some of 'em to the walls, chairs, and appliances. Once again, colored glitter is also fun to toss about the trailer. For a real surprise of love, open up the dresser drawer and fill your husband's socks or wife's bras with Red Hots or Hershey Kisses. Don't tell 'em that they're there, but simply let them find 'em on their own.

### Trailer Park Tradition

All the married or spoken-for women in the trailer park wear red articles of clothin' on Valentine's Day. The other gals also wear red clothin', but without bras. A few years back a strong breeze came through, causin' my Me-ma's dress to fly up. Well the sight of her danglin' white breasts blowin' up against her knees was enough to convince all of us at the High Chaparral Trailer Park that widows should be excluded from this particular tradition. To make Me-ma feel part of the community, we have her cut out hearts from red foil and tell her to go and put 'em on all the single gals' front trailer windows. Of course we make her do this while wearin' a bra.

### Somethin' to Bring to a Party

## I LOVE YOU TUNA DIP

*Not only is this good tastin', but when this dish is served, you don't have to worry about how fresh your kissin' breath is.*

*Makes enough for 8 to 12*

16 ounces cream cheese, softened

2 tablespoons brandy

2 (6 ounce) cans water-packed tuna

2 teaspoons lemon juice

4 teaspoons minced green onion

½ cup pecans, chopped into tiny bits

¼ teaspoon salt

⅛ teaspoon pepper

1½ teaspoons dry mustard

½ teaspoon dried thyme

In a bowl, blend the cream cheese and brandy. Add the rest of the ingredients and mix well. Serve with crackers or little pieces of bread that you've cut into heart shapes.

*—JUANITA HIX, LOT #9*

**Dinner Menu**

## BE MY VALENTINE SALAD

*If this don't get your honey happy, then you ain't doin' it right!*

Makes 8 servin's

¼ cup cold water

1½ tablespoons plain gelatin

2 cups crushed pineapple

½ cup sugar

2 tablespoons maraschino cherry juice

2 tablespoons lemon juice

1 (6 ounce) package of cream cheese

1 cup heavy cream, whipped and lightly sweetened

12 maraschino cherries, chopped

Some Valentine's Day candy hearts

Take the cold water and put it in a small bowl. Add the gelatin and let it dissolve.

In a pot, combine your pineapple and sugar and stir well. Put over a medium heat and bring to a boil. Add the dissolved gelatin to the mix, followed by addin' both juices. Take off the heat and let it cool completely.

Mash up the cream cheese real good. Add a little bit at a time to the pineapple mixture. Put it in the fridge and chill until it starts to thicken. Take out of the fridge and add the whipped cream, chopped cherries and candies. Blend real good. Spoon into eight small bowls, cover 'em, and put 'em in the fridge to chill. Once they're set, serve 'em.

*—NELLIE TINKLE, LOT #4*

## MOMMA BOXCAR'S SWEETHEART STUFFED PEPPERS

*Now I know why Daddy has stuck with her for
so long.*

4 pounds hamburger meat

4 large red bell peppers

1 onion, finely chopped

1 teaspoon salt

1 cup barbecue sauce

2 cups bread, torn into small pieces

Ketchup

In a skillet, brown the hamburger meat, makin' sure to break it up into little pieces with a spoon. When the meat is done, drain it and set aside.

Slice the tops off your red bell peppers, take out the insides includin' the seeds, and discard all the inside stuff. Place your gutted peppers in a bakin' pan.

Take your hamburger and mix in the onion, salt, and barbecue sauce. Mix well, then add the bread pieces. Fill the peppers up with the mixture. If you have any left, put it in the bakin' dish around the peppers. Pour a little ketchup over each pepper and some over the extra meat mixture in the bottom of the bakin' dish. Cover loosely with foil. Put it in the oven and bake at 350 degrees F. for 30 minutes. Uncover and bake for an additional 10 minutes. Take out of the oven and let stand for 5 minutes before servin'. This dish is sure to make your husband love you like a dog after dinner.

*—MOMMA BOXCAR, LOT #5*

## LULU BELL'S EASY AS PIE RED VELVET KISS CAKE

*Lulu Bell made this for her boyfriend last Valentine's Day. She forgot he was allergic to chocolate, but so did he. He ate three pieces. By St. Patrick's Day he was up and walkin' again, and last I heard he should have the sight back in both his eyes by year's end.*

*6 to 8 servin's*

Cocoa

1 box fudge marble cake mix

1 teaspoon bakin' soda

2 eggs

1½ cups buttermilk

1-ounce bottle red food colorin'

1 teaspoon vanilla extract

Hershey's Kisses, for decoratin'

Grease up two 9-inch cake pans, and then flour the pans with cocoa.

Get yourself a big bowl and put the cake mix and bakin' soda in it. Stir it real good. Add the rest of the ingredients and blend on low until everything gets moist. Then put the mixer on high speed and beat for 3 minutes. Put the mixture into the pans and bake in the oven for 30 to 35 minutes at 350 degrees F. When the cake is done, take it out and let it cool for 10 minutes before removin' it from the pan. Set aside to cool completely.

In the meantime, make your cake icin' by pullin' out the followin' ingredients from the cupboards and fridge:

1 cup milk

5 tablespoons all-purpose flour

1 cup margarine

1 cup sugar

1 teaspoon vanilla extract

Take a pot and put the milk and flour in it. Put it over low heat and stir constantly until it thickens. Shut off the heat and put your pot aside.

In a bowl, cream the margarine, sugar, and vanilla extract together until fluffy. Next stir in the milk mixture and beat until it gets to the thickness you need so you can ice the cake. Go ahead and ice the cake. Place Hershey's Kisses all over the top and sides of the cake. Serve it to the one you love.

*—LULU BELL BOXCAR, LOT #8*

# *Chapter 3*

Kenny and Donny of lot #15 proudly show off
my Tammy Faye Cake.

# *March*

March is the third month of the year. Way back when they used the Roman calendar, it was known as Martius, for Mars, the god of war, and as we've already learned, it was the first month of the year. Finally the Ancient Romans did all their mumbo jumbo with the dang calendar and added another month and decided to make the first of January the start of the New Year. Can you imagine what them poor Romans were sayin' durin' that first 12-month period? ("Jupiter, Mars, and Quirinus! Will this year never end?")

The one thing about March that's always been true, regardless of where it fell in the year, is that it's always had 31 days. It's also the wake-up call for the entire Northern Hemisphere. It's durin' the month of March, which is said to come in like a lion and go out like a lamb, that the geese fly back to their northern homes; the bears, chipmunks, and hedgehogs come out from hibernation; and us trailer park folk who work at home start gettin' up before noon. Yes, spring is here at last. Now we'll begin to see the green buds appear on our plants. Wildflowers will add a dash of color to the fields. And in the woods we will start to see more and more of those beautiful green pussy willows. Which by the way reminds me: the Blue Whale Strip Club also starts its new season every March.

If February was the month of love, then March would naturally be the month of new beginnin's. It seems like everybody gets a little hot in their unmentionable areas and are ready to find a mate. They played in February and maybe even courted, but now, it's down to business. Of course you'll always have some gals who are on a constant manhunt so they can give their babies a proper last name, and you'll even have those womenfolk who could care less what the fella of the night's first name is. But for the most part, March is the matin' season in the wild and in the trailer park.

We got a couple of big celebrated holidays in the month of March, and let me tell you, they are some humdingers. One of 'em is bound to stuff you while another one is sure to have you wake up the next day tryin' to figure out what your name is. And then there's Tammy Faye's birthday, which will make you realize just how good life is for you, and Reba McEntire's birthday, which will show you just how classy country folk can be. Oh, and of course durin' the rest of the month, you can just celebrate these 31-days-long holidays as well.

# DAYTONA 500
### Traditionally it falls on the first Sunday after St. Valentine's Day.
(Since it falls on a Sunday, it's a prison holiday, but no one would dare
leave the trailer to visit somebody in prison while the race is on.)

"The world's greatest race" better known at the Daytona 500, is to stock-car racin' what the Super Bowl is to football. As any trailer park dweller can tell you, it takes place every year at the "World Center of Racing," the Daytona International Speedway, in Daytona Beach, Florida. This 200-lap granddaddy of all races is the one that NASCAR Winston Cup drivers pray to one day claim for themselves. It's produced such legends in the field of motorsports as Mario Andretti, Dale Jarrett, Buddy Baker, Richard Petty, and the late, great Dale Earnhardt. Speakin' of Dale Earnhardt, it just ain't the same without him out on the track. Old Dale was the type of fella that you either cheered for or booed, but the truth is that no matter how you felt about the man, love him or hate him, you couldn't deny the simple fact that he'd been blessed when it came to his skills behind the wheel. For all of us at the High Chaparral Trailer Park, when we watch the Daytona 500, "The Intimidator" will always be in the back of our minds, drivin' lap after lap in that black Chevrolet, the No. 3 GM Goodwrench Service Plus Monte Carlo. But like they say, the race must go on.

Two years ago, I was proud to be able to buy tickets for the Daytona 500 for Momma and Daddy. It was a dream come true for my folks. My Daddy has always lived and breathed car racin' so when he unwrapped his Christmas present to find tickets good for the admission of two people to the Daytona 500 as well as all the other racin' that took place from Saturday the 12th to the big one on Sunday the 20th, he nearly peed his pants. That was the second time I'd ever seen my Daddy cry (the first time was when he picked up his new Viagra prescription at the Piggly Wiggly). Seein' how it was their first vacation in years, me and my husband, Dew, decided to make a week of it and got 'em a package that included airline tickets, hotel, rental car, and tickets to all the events down at the speedway. Well, they arrived that Friday and checked in to the hotel. Momma said that Daddy was in bed by 7:30 that night just so he would be "fresh" the next mornin' at the speedway. Daddy was like a little boy at Disney World, which by the way is one of my very favorite places, just in case any of y'all happen to be lookin' to get me and my husband, Dew, somethin' special. Daddy and Momma headed over to the hotel restaurant for a big breakfast and then it was off to the racetrack. Now if you've ever been in a car with Daddy, you know full well that the poor man couldn't follow directions if God rode on the hood and pointed out the way. One day he went out to get a pack of smokes for Momma and ended up in Tahlequah, Oklahoma, before he finally stopped and admitted he was lost. Anyways, back to Daytona, two and a half hours later, Daddy finally pulled into the Daytona International Speedway parkin' lot, which I might add was only three blocks from their hotel room. Now, I can't explain exactly how he did it, but Daddy with Momma ridin' shotgun managed to get their rented Kia Sephia on the race track durin' the time trails for "The Greatest American Race." The bad part was Daddy had no idea where the heck he was. All he knew was there was nobody in front of him so he put the pedal to the metal just like he does on the highway. Even when Mike Skinner's Chevrolet shot up behind Daddy's rental, he still didn't get it. He just thought Skinner was some young punk, and he'd be doggoned if that road hog was goin' to pass him. From what I hear, Daddy actually had that poor Kia Sephia's speedometer readin' 125 miles an hour. It seemed as if Skinner didn't have a chance since Daddy was refusin' to give way, but then before you could say, "Don't touch that button," Momma turned on the air conditioner. Well, needless to say, that was the end of that. Daddy's day in the racin' sun was over, but unbeknownst to Daddy and Momma their little Kia rental had been draftin' with Mike Skinner, makin' that little tuna can hit 205 miles an hour. Daddy had won the pole position at Daytona. Needless to say, Mike Skinner was madder than heck, and went like a crybaby to the NASCAR official and filed a complaint. Thanks to his unsportsmanlike attitude and the fact that the Kia didn't have a restricter plate, poor old Daddy was disqualified. And that was the day Dale Earnhardt broke a sweat.

Several hours later, once it became clear that it was all a mistake, they released Momma and Daddy, and the folks at Daytona International moved my folks' seats up to the owners' area for the rest of the week, includin' the big one on Sunday. The car rental company picked up the Kia and gave them an old Dodge Dart to use for the rest of their stay. They had the time of their life, and even today when Mike Skinner shows up on one of the races Daddy happens to be watchin' on TV, he informs everybody in the trailer that he could out drive "that old boy" if he had the right car. Momma chimes in with a "that's right," which leads Daddy to add, "Yep, if I'd had the right car and your momma would've left the darn air off, I coulda been a contender." Momma told me just the other day that Daddy's been talkin' about buyin' a Kia next year. Jeff Gordon, watch your back.

### Things to Get You in the Holiday Mood

Take your car for a spin down an old country road. Remember to make sure you got your auto insurance paid up before tryin' to go faster than 25 on them gravel roads.

Rent and watch *Spinout*. Now I know this ain't about the Daytona 500, but Elvis does play a race car driver. Surely that's close enough!

### Things to Do

Throw a Daytona 500 party! If this idea sounds good to you, check out the section on the Super Bowl Sunday party, 'cause it's goin' to be just like that with the exception that everybody, includin' those in the kitchen, will be watchin' the race. If you ain't throwin' the party, find out who is, and do everything you can to get invited. Come on now, this is the race of the year, and you sure as heck don't want to watch it by yourself!

### How to Decorate Your Trailer for This Holiday

This is not a holiday that you decorate for unless you happen to be throwin' a Daytona 500 party, and if that happens to be the case, then grab a pencil and paper so you can write down all the items you're goin' to need. First off, you've got to get a bunch of white-and-black-checkered fabric or paper. You might even be able to find some of that vinyl stuff at a Paper Warehouse store. Anyways, I like to cover the whole outside of my front door with it. I also have my husband, Dew, paint little checkers on the mailbox flag. And I tie checkered flags to the hands, beaks, or mouths of all my yard statues. All this seems to excite all those guests when they arrive at me and my husband's annual race party. Now, inside your trailer you can cover your dinin' room table with the checkered material. I also tape a big sign on the wall by the table that reads "PIT STOP."

This past year I even cleared off the TV and taped checkered material to both the top and sides. I then put up a framed picture of Dale Earnhardt and some candles along with a Bible back on top the TV. It was very movin', and somethin' I'll be doin' next year as well.

I also placed some black and white balloons around the trailer (I recommend the kind that you blow up since those won't accidentally float in front of the TV set).

If you take old car oil cans and cut the metal tops off, clean 'em out real good, and give the outside a good once over, you can fill 'em up with flowers or candy to create wonderful centerpieces.

A couple of years ago I went to a local junkyard and bought a few old beat-up hubcaps. I cleaned 'em up and use them as individual paper plate holders for my guest to take back to their seats.

I encourage everybody to wear their NASCAR gear or at least the colors of their favorite drivers.

Another fun thing to do is put a yellow flag on the bathroom door. Everybody always seems to get a big kick out of that.

Oh, and another thing that gets a big laugh is to take some poster board and write the words "TIME FOR A PIT STOP" on it with a big marker. Every time I add a new food item to the dinin' room table, I walk over next to the TV, makin' sure I don't get in the way of the viewin', and I hold up the sign. This is a great way to tell the folks who are ready to get up and grab a bite that there is more food on the table without botherin' those who are really into the race at that time. Even those folks get a big chuckle out of that.

### Trailer Park Tradition

Before the race, after church is out, we give each of our next-door neighbors a small plant for them to put in that tire that each of us has spray painted and turned into a front yard planter. Some of us folks who've been around for a while are already on our third or even fourth tire planter.

### Somethin' to Bring to a Party

## TONY STEWART COOKIES

*These taste as good as Tony looks.*
*Makes several dozen*
1 cup margarine
1 cup regular sugar
2 eggs

1 cup confectioner's sugar

1 teaspoon vanilla extract

1 teaspoon cream of tartar

1 teaspoon bakin' soda

1 teaspoon salt

1 cup oil

4½ cups flour

Cream margarine and regular sugar until fluffy. Beat in eggs. Beat in confectioner's sugar, vanilla extract, cream of tartar, bakin' soda, and salt. Alternately beat in oil and flour. Beat until fluffy. Cover and stick in the fridge for 2 hours.

Take tablespoon amounts of dough and roll 'em into balls. Place 2 inches apart on lightly greased bakin' sheets. Flatten each ball with the bottom of a glass that has been lightly oiled. Bake at 350 degrees F. around 10 minutes, or until lightly browned. Take the cookies off the bakin' sheet and let 'em cool.

In a bowl, combine the followin' to make frostin':

1 cup powdered sugar

½ teaspoon imitation vanilla extract

1½ tablespoon half and half

Once you've got it nice and smooth, take half out and put it in another bowl. To one of the bowls add a drop of red food color and a drop of yellow food color (add more of either in order to get a nice orange look). Frost each cookie with both the white and orange frostin's.

—*DOTTIE LAMB, LOT #14*

*Dinner Menu*

## BOBBY ALLISON ARTICHOKE DIP

*Heck, I'd make an extra pit stop for this stuff!*

Feeds 8 to 12

2 cans artichokes

1 can green chilies, chopped

1 (8 ounce) package cream cheese

1 cup Parmesan cheese, shredded

2 cups mozzarella cheese, shredded

1½ cups mayonnaise

½ teaspoon crushed red pepper

1 teaspoon black pepper

½ teaspoon cayenne pepper

Drain and chop up the artichokes. Put 'em in a bowl and add the remainin' ingredients. Stir well and pour into a bakin' dish. Bake at 350 degrees F. for 25 minutes. Serve with your favorite crackers.

*—CONNIE KAY, LOT #13*

## BENNY PARSONS' FAST AS LIGHTNIN' NACHOS

*These are faster than my sister on a Saturday night.*

Serves 8 to 12

1 bag tortilla chips

1 pound hamburger meat

1 pound sausage meat

2 packages of taco meat seasonin'

1 regular can of tomatoes, diced

1 pound government cheese (or your favorite cheese)

1 onion, diced

1 small can jalapeño peppers, chopped and drained

1 small can green chilies, chopped and drained

A jar of your favorite salsa

1 (8 ounce) container sour cream

Cook up the meats and follow the taco seasonin' directions. Take a large plate that will still fit in the microwave and fill it up with tortilla chips. Sprinkle on a good layer of cheese followed by a good helpin' of meat. Add some of the rest of ingredients except for the sour cream. Place in the microwave and cook for 1½ minutes. Top with some sour cream and serve. You should have enough ingredients to make four of five plates of nachos, dependin' on the plate size.

*—LOIS BUNCH, LOT #3*

# DALE EARNHARDT TRIBUTE CAKE

*At the High Chaparral Trailer Park we serve this*
*at the end of the race.*

*Makes one 2-layer cake*

3 ounces semisweet chocolate

1 cup margarine, softened

2 cups sugar

2 eggs

½ cup sour cream

2 cups sifted all-purpose flour

1 cup hot coffee, the stronger the better

1 teaspoon bakin' soda

Turn your oven up to 350 degrees F. Grease and flour two 8-inch cake pans.

Melt the chocolate and set aside. In a bowl cream the margarine and sugar together until fluffy. Add the melted chocolate and beat until it mixes in well. Add the eggs and sour cream, and keep beatin'. Once your batter is smooth, slowly add the flour. Now, don't worry if it is a bit runny. That's OK.

Take your cup of coffee, hold it over the sink, and add the bakin' soda. Now it's gonna look like a science project gone wrong 'cause it will fizz all up and some will go into the sink. Once again, that's OK. Once the soda has dissolved it'll stop overflowin', and you can add it to the batter. Mix well and then divide the batter equally into the two pans. Bake for 30 minutes at 350 degrees, but no peekin'. Openin' the door will spoil the cake, so leave it alone until the 30 minutes are up. Take the cakes out and let 'em cool in the pan for around 10 minutes. After that, take 'em out of the pans to finish coolin' While the cakes are coolin', you can make your icin'. You will need the followin':

4 ounces semisweet chocolate

4 cups confectioner's sugar

4 tablespoons milk

1 tablespoon vanilla extract

Some black food colorin'

Melt the chocolate and then let it cool just a bit. Add the remainin' ingredients. You want a blackish frostin'. When ready, frost the top of one of the cakes. Put the second cake on top of that. Now frost both cakes until they are completely covered. Before servin', place a white wax number 3 candle on the cake. You can light the candle if you want or simply leave it as a decoration only. If you do light it, then before you cut the cake, carefully move it from the cake to a chicken pot pie tin or somethin' about that size, 'cause it's only fittin' that you let it burn until it burns all the way down. Serve the cake alone or with vanilla ice cream.

*—MOMMA BOXCAR, LOT #5*

## WARD BURTON'S FAT CAT CHOCOLATE STRAWBERRY MIX

*Now, this is sure to take the checkered flag wherever it's served.*

*Serves 4 to 6*

1 box frozen strawberries, thawed

½ cup sugar

1 pound semisweet chocolate

Dump the strawberries in a large bowl along with the sugar and stir well.

Put the chocolate in a different bowl and melt in the microwave. Scrape the chocolate in with the strawberry mix. Stir well to make sure that the strawberries are covered.

Lay out wax paper on cookie sheets. Dump the chocolate strawberry mix on the wax paper and spread it out. Cover and put in the fridge for 30 minutes. Take out and cut into sections. Serve with paper plates and forks.

*—LOVIE BIRCH, LOT #20*

## CALE YARBOROUGH JALAPEÑO POPPERS

*Wave that yellow flag, and tell the drivers to pull over, 'cause we got a fire in my mouth!*

*Makes 24 servin's*

24 medium-size fresh jalapeño peppers

1½ cups Cheddar cheese, shredded

3 eggs, well beaten

2 cups bread crumbs
Oil for deep fryin'
Ranch dressin'

The number-one rule when it comes to makin' these babies is to keep your hands away from your face at all times! It takes next to nothin' when it comes to major irritation from jalapeño juice. So make sure you pay attention to your hands at all times. With that in mind, cut off the stem ends of the peppers. Carefully take out all the seeds and the white part. Take the cheese and stuff it in the jalapeños. Take each stuffed pepper and dip it in the beaten eggs, makin' sure that it is totally coated. Now put it in the crumbs and spoon more crumbs on top of it to make sure that it is totally covered. Put the peppers on a bakin' sheet. When you've dipped all the jalapeños, place 'em in the fridge, and give 'em 15 to 20 minutes to dry. Carefully place the peppers into oil in a deep fryer that you've heated to 375 degrees F. Let 'em fry for 2 to 3 minutes then take 'em out and put on paper towels to drain. Continue until all the peppers are cooked. Serve ASAP with the ranch dressin' to dip 'em in.

*—LOIS BUNCH, LOT #3*

March is:
**National Peanut Month**

# CHOCOLATE PEANUT BUTTER BROWNIES

*Heck, I'd miss the bingo bus for these!*

4 to 6 servin's
Butter
1 box of brownie mix
6 ounces peanut butter chips, plus optional extra ones

Line a 13×9-inch bakin' pan with foil. Make sure the foil extends over the handles. Butter the foil and set aside. Turn your oven on to the heat that the brownie box tells you.

Follow the directions for makin' the brownies on the box. Once you've mixed up your batter, pour half of it in the lined bakin' pan. Now sprinkle the peanut butter chips over that batter, makin' sure that it's level. Put in the oven and follow the brownie box's instructions for bakin'. When it's done, take it out. Let the brownies cool for 5 minutes, then take hold of the extra foil and lift the brownies out of the pan. Let them cool. Cut into squares and serve with milk. If you like extra peanut butter, put a layer of chips over the top of the cooked brownies before cuttin' 'em.

*—JUANITA HIX, LOT #9*

### *National Sauce Month*

# EASY PIZZA SAUCE

*If whatever religious order these Kenny and Donny are in allows 'em to marry women, they're goin' to be quite the catch with recipes like this one.*

*Makes enough for 4 pizzas*

¾ cup tomato paste

1 teaspoon confectioners' sugar

1 tablespoon dried sweet basil

¼ cup dried oregano

¼ cup Balsamic vinegar

Combine all the ingredients in a bowl and mix well. Freeze what's left-over in a tightly sealed container for future use.

*—KENNY LYNN, LOT #15*

# NATIONAL PIG DAY
## March 1
### (Unless it falls on a weekend, this is not a prison holiday)

I don't know if my love for these animals is because I use to show 'em or if it's simply that out of all the creatures on God's green earth they're the closest to the average weight of most any member of the Boxcar family. Regardless of the reasonin', I just love pigs, hogs, boars, sows, or piglets for that matter. Call 'em what you will, I just love 'em.

As a little girl growin' up in a trailer park, my access to animals was minimal to say the least. Sure, we lived out in the country, but the ranchers didn't want you messin' with their cows, and the people raisin' sheep felt the same way. There were lots of chicken farms around us, but the smell alone was enough to turn you against poultry. I always thought horses were beautiful, and when I was goin' for my cosmetology license at the Pangburn Academy of Beauty and Horse Shoein', I got to spend a little time with the ones they had around. They were beautiful animals, but by that time in my life, my heart had already been stolen by the round-snouted species. As far as dogs go, I seem to recall that my brother, Jack Daniels, had a dog when I was real little, but we had to give it away because it kept tryin' to hump my sister, Donna Sue. To tell the truth, even to this day, she can't walk past a male dog without it tryin' to hump her. Odd isn't it?

As many of y'all know, when I was just eight years old Daddy brought home a little pig from my Uncle Emmett's farm. He had a pig farm that we'd go and visit from time to time, and once a year right after Easter he'd sell us a hog so we could raise it right there in our yard. Daddy'd build a little fence to hold the hog in and I'd take care of it. It was my job to feed it, make sure it had mud to roll in so it didn't get too hot, and basically to meet any other need it might have. When it'd rain I'd make sure its little converted doghouse was nice and dry inside. And when winter would come, I'd make sure my hog had a blanket and that the hose runnin' directly from our trailer heater to my pig's shelter was pumpin' in warm air. Basically I treated that pig like it was my own child.

When the Arkansas State Fair would come in mid-June, I'd show my pig off in the junior division. It was somethin' I really enjoyed doin'. By that time, me and my pig had grown so close to each other, it was almost like we were of one mind. You might say we had bonded at the brain. Anyways, I was really good at showin' hogs and had several awards to prove it. But the one time that will stand out the most was the year that I was named Miss Feeder Hog (Junior Division). What a thrill that was, and I'll never forget it. There I was in a green evenin' gown standin' smack dab in a mix of mud, pig waste, and urine out in the grand arena gettin' a sash and a crown put on me. It was like I'd died and gone to pig heaven. Even as an adult it's hard for me to think back about that moment in time without sheddin' a tear.

Anyways, I'd continue raisin' that pig and he'd get bigger and bigger each day. It was amazin' how fast they grow. And with every passin' day our love for each other would grow even stronger. Every day after school I'd rush straight home so I could be with him. I'd read my homework assignment to him, or sing him one of my favorite songs, or when it wasn't too cold, I'd just take him on in a one-on-one mud wrestlin' match. Come Thanksgivin', he was more than just my baby, he was my friend. I knew we'd be together forever. I even imagined us goin' old together, but that was not to be. You see, pigs are very smart and clever animals. Given time they figure things out, or so said my Daddy when I came home that Good Friday afternoon only to find that my pig had figured out how to open the gate on its pen. He was gone. I guess the bonds that we shared were not enough to overcome his need to be with his own. Surely he had run off to find out where he'd come from and where his true destiny lay. Even though I understood his need to leave I was still brokenhearted by his rejection. I cried and cried and cried until I couldn't cry anymore. But thank the good Lord for Momma. She understood my pain and did everything she could to help. Why, if it wasn't for that traditional honeybaked ham that she made for Easter Sunday, I probably would've kept right on mournin' my pig's disappearance. But that sweet succulent ham that Momma had taken the time to make was able to snap me out of my depression. And within weeks Daddy would be comin' home with a new pig that I'd grow to love and care for. But it, too, would break my heart just like all the future pigs Daddy would bring home. Regardless of what type of latch I'd put on that dang gate, each one of those pigs in the end would outsmart it. Why, I even had one hog that learnt how to work a combination lock. Yes, every year that we had a pig, when Good Friday would roll around I'd come home to heartache, rejection, and pain. And thank goodness, Momma would come through with that blessed honey-baked ham.

### Things to Get You in the Holiday Mood
Rent and watch the movie *Babe*.
Read the book *Charlotte's Web*.
Watch *Green Acres* reruns.

### Things to Do
Hug a pig or hug your spouse.
Take a pig to work.
Write a letter to your favorite Razorback player.
Go have a mud facial.
When people wish you a good mornin', squeal back at 'em.
When it comes to pigs, there was only one show that truly knew how to treat a pig, and you can find out more about it at www.maggiore.net/greenacres/default.asp.

### How to Decorate Your Trailer for This Holiday
Put out all your blue ribbons that you've won for showin' hogs. If you ain't got any, then go out and buy some at your nearest party-supply store. Scatterin' a little bit of hay around your livin' room will also help to give your place that barnyard feel.

### Trailer Park Tradition
We take a used baby diaper that we've gotten from the nursery at the First Baptist Church of Pangburn and throw it under our neighbor's trailer about two or three days before National Pig Day. By the first of March, that neighbor of yours is goin' to be thinkin' there's a pig somewhere around their trailer.

*Somethin' to Bring to a Party*

# PIGS IN A BLANKET

*Just the name alone takes me back to my childhood.*

*Makes 8 little pigs*

8 hot dogs

8 slices of Government cheese (or your favorite cheese)

1 can of croissant roll dough

Mustard

Ketchup

Take each hot dog and wrap it with a slice of cheese and a piece of croissant roll dough. Place on a lightly greased cookie sheet and bake at 350 degrees F. for 10 minutes, or until the croissant rolls get golden brown. Take out of the oven and cut into four pieces per hot dog. Serve with mustard and ketchup.

*—OLLIE WHITE, LOT #10*

*Dinner Menu*

# TATER PIG

*Boy, we ate a ton of this after Easter!*

*Serves 4 to 6*

½ pound ham, diced

Oil

4 potatoes, cooked and cubed

1 pound Government cheese (or your favorite cheese), shredded

Salt

Put the ham in a large skillet that's been lightly oiled and brown over medium heat. Next add the potatoes, followed by the cheese. (If you can afford it, this tastes even better with Velveeta.) Mash the potatoes with a fork while they are heatin' up in the skillet. Make sure you are mixin' everything up. Once the cheese has melted, dump the mixture out into a bowl. Salt to taste and serve warm.

*—MOMMA BOXCAR, LOT #5*

## LITTLE PIGGY CASSEROLE

*This is what happened to that little piggy that went to town and didn't return.*

*Makes 4 to 6 servin's*

4 cups chopped ham

1½ cups sherry

2 tomatoes, chopped

½ green pepper, chopped

1 onion, chopped

½ cup cream

2 cups cubed cooked potatoes

1 tablespoon dry mustard

1 tablespoon Worcestershire sauce

Salt and pepper to taste

1 cup bread crumbs

½ cup margarine

In a real big bowl, combine the first 10 ingredients and mix well. Put the mixture in a casserole dish. Sprinkle on the bread crumbs. Melt the margarine and spoon it evenly over the top of the casserole. Bake at 350 degrees F. for 1 hour.

*—MOMMA BALLZAK, LOT #16*

## MOMMA BOXCAR'S TWO-DAY HONEY-BAKED HAM

*My Momma's got two really good ham recipes that are in the book. Not only is this one good, but it's sure to fix whatever ails you.*

*10 to 12 servin's*

2 cups packed brown sugar

2 teaspoons ground cinnamon

2 teaspoons grated nutmeg

2 teaspoons ground cloves

⅓ cup cider vinegar

3 cups honey

6 pound bone-in ham

2 cups maple pancake syrup

In a large bowl, mix together the brown sugar, cinnamon, nutmeg, and cloves. Make sure everything is mixed well. Add the vinegar and mix well. Now add 2 cups of the honey and stir until it has a good consistency. Set aside in the fridge for now.

Take your ham and cut little diamond shapes every few inches. Make sure you cut all the way down to the bone. Put the ham in an oven bag and then into a deep roastin' pan. In a bowl, combine the remaining cup of honey with the maple pancake syrup. Stir it all up. Pour the maple mixture over the ham, which means when the excess runs off the ham, it should be fillin' up the oven bag. Usin' clean hands, rub the mixture into the meat, makin' sure it's well covered with the maple/honey syrup. Close the oven bag up. Cover the whole thing with foil and stick it in the fridge to marinate overnight. (If you do this in the daytime, afternoon, or early evenin', just before you go to bed take the ham out of the fridge, carefully take the foil off then, and baste the ham again by turnin' it upside down in the closed oven bag. Re-cover the ham and put it back in the fridge to continue marinatin' for 8 more hours.)

When you're ready to cook the ham, cut a few slits in the top of the bag, re-cover the ham, and put it in a 325-degree F. preheated oven for an hour. Uncover, cut open the bag, and baste the ham with the thick mixture that you had in the fridge. Cook that pig another hour uncovered, bastin' it every 10 minutes with the syrup juices that should be at the bottom of the roastin' pan. After it's cooked, baste it once more from the syrup on the bottom and put it under the broiler to cook on high for an additional 6 minutes. Slice it on up and serve.

*—MOMMA BOXCAR, LOT #5*

# AMAZIN' GRACE GREEN BEAN HAM CASSEROLE

*This dish is very big at Baptist gatherin's.*

*Makes 6 to 8 servin's*

1 regular can of green beans
1½ cups water/green bean juice
3 tablespoons flour
⅔ cup milk
½ teaspoon salt
3 tablespoons margarine
2 cups chopped ham
2 hard-boiled eggs, chopped
¼ onion, chopped
1 cup shredded Cheddar cheese

Over a bowl, drain the juice off the green beans and set the beans aside. Add enough water to make 1½ cups. Put this mixture in a pot and put it on low heat. Slowly add the flour, stirrin' constantly. Add the milk and salt and keep stirrin' until it thickens. Add the margarine and stir for 2 more minutes. Take off the heat. Add all the remainin' ingredients, includin' the beans, except for the cheese. Mix well and pour into a margarine-greased 9 × 12-inch casserole dish. Top with the cheese and cover with foil. Bake at 350 degrees F. for 25 minutes. Uncover and bake for an additional 20 minutes.

*—SISTER BERTHA, LOT #12*

# TAMMY FAYE BAKKER MESSNER'S BIRTHDAY
## March 7
### (Unless it falls on a weekend, this is not a prison holiday)

The good Lord above knows that when it comes to heavy loads, us gals in the trailer park community always seem to have the heaviest ones. If somethin' can possibly go wrong for us it does. If you ever find a lost dog without tags, a stolen car that was made between 1950 and 1979, or a drunken husband, just take 'em to your local trailer park 'cause 20 to 1, they're ours. That's why this day is so special to trailer park women across the world. Regardless of how bad life can get, how downtrodden you might be, or just plain tired you might feel, all you ever have to do is look to Tammy Faye and life will seem so much better. For years we'd watched her and her then husband, Jim Bakker, as they hosted the PTL Club. Tammy Faye's makeup skills as well as her vocal talents inspired us. Thanks to this Mother Teresa of the Protestant faith, many of us found the courage to add that extra bit of Mary Kay and even try out our singin' abilities in church or open-mike night at the local bar and grill. And Tammy Faye showed us that we could love the Lord and Mary Kay at the same time. She also instilled in our hearts the knowledge that it was OK for us to go out and shop. If we were good and honest women, then God wouldn't mind it if every now and then we bought that floral caftan we'd been eyein' at Wal-mart. We weren't goin' to Hell for those new double-knit polyester slacks with the extra durable elastic waistband. But then came the late 1980s, and Tammy Faye's world came crashin' down around her. I don't have to tell you all the hell this poor gal went through. It was somethin' I wouldn't wish on my worst enemy. But still, every time you saw her on TV, she had her makeup on, tears in her eyes, and a song in her heart. It didn't seem like nothin' nobody could throw at her would ever get the best of this dear woman. She was a solid rock, mind you, a weepin' rock, but solid nonetheless, who set a fine example of what it's like to live through the worst life can hand you and still come out on top. Like Tammy Faye says, "If life hands you lemons, make lemonade." That's why we celebrate this day in trailers across the globe. Regardless if our husbands come home at night or not, regardless of how many times our children have been on *Cops,* or regardless if the guy you left your husband for just announced on Jerry Springer that he was really a woman, it could be worse. Just look at Tammy Faye!

Happy Birthday, Darlin'! You know we love you!

### Things to Get You in the Holiday Mood
Rent and watch the videos *The Eyes of Tammy Faye* and *The Crying Game.*
Read the Bible; the book of Job would be a wonderful selection.
Listen to any of Tammy Faye's records, tapes, or CDs.
Visit Tammy Faye's web page at www.tammyfaye.com.

### Things to Do
Throw a Mary Kay or Avon party.

### How to Decorate Your Trailer for This Holiday
This is one of those holidays that's both fun and cheap when it comes to decoratin'. Basically all you'll need is fishin' wire or string, old discarded cosmetic containers, old makeup sponges and powder puffs, tape, and a hot glue gun. Simply cut strands of fishin' wire or string into foot or foot and a half lengths. Place one drop of hot glue on top of a cosmetic container, makeup sponge, or powder puff. Put one end of the wire or string into the glue and hold the other end straight up until the glue dries. Hang these lovely holiday items from your trailer ceilin', doorways, archways, trees, clothesline, birdfeeders, car, or truck rearview mirror. If you want to go all out, you can put a coat of glitter spray on these ornaments as well (I like to put a few of these on my Christmas tree durin' that season of joy).

### Trailer Park Tradition
Tape a brand new tube of mascara and a religious pamphlet on a neighbor's door, knock, and run away.

*Somethin' to Bring to a Party*

## DEEP IN THE VALLEY CRACKER SNACK

*These are so good, you'll wish you were havin'*
*problems just so you could make a batch.*

*Makes a bunch*

1 package Hidden Valley Seasoning and Salad Ranch Dressing Mix Original

1 teaspoon dried dill weed

½ teaspoon garlic salt

1 cup oil

2 (12 ounce) bags of oyster crackers

Put everything but the crackers in a shaker and shake till mixed well.

Put the crackers in a glass gallon jar and pour the mixture over the crackers. Put the lid on the glass jar and turn the jar from end to end until the crackers are completely coated. Then pour everything out on a cookie sheet and leave to dry. You don't need to bake these.

*—JUANITA HIX, LOT #9*

*Dinner Menu*

## WE ARE BLESSED VELVEETA CHEESE SOUP

*Two bowls of this stuff in one settin' and more*
*than your load will be heavy.*

*Serves 6*

¼ cup margarine

¼ cup minced onions

4 cups milk

1 teaspoon salt

¼ cup flour

¼ pound Velveeta, cut into very small cubes

¼ cup diced pimientos

In a saucepan on medium heat melt the margarine. Add the onion and cook clear. Take off of the heat and mix in the milk, salt, and flour. Place back on the heat, stirrin' constantly, until it thickens. Put in the cheese and stir until it all melts. Add the pimientos and stir well. Take off the heat and serve hot. The colder it gets, the harder it gets, so eat quickly.

*—PASTOR IDA MAY BEE, LOT #7*

# ANGEL BISCUITS

*These are almost as angelic as Tammy Faye.*

*Makes 2 to 3 dozen, dependin' on how big you cut 'em*
2 (¼ ounce) packages of active dry yeast
¼ cup warm water
2 cups warm buttermilk
5 cups all-purpose flour
⅓ cup sugar
1 tablespoon bakin' powder
1 teaspoon bakin' soda
2 teaspoons salt
1 cup shortenin'
Little bit of melted margarine

Start off by dissolvin' the yeast in the warm water in a medium bowl. Let it stand for 5 minutes. Stir in the warm buttermilk and set aside.

In a large bowl, mix the flour, sugar, bakin' powder, soda, and salt. Cut in the shortenin' with a pastry blender until the mix resembles coarse meal. Stir in the yeast/buttermilk mixture and mix well. Turn out onto a lightly floured surface. Knead lightly (3 or 4 times). Roll to ½-inch thickness. Cut into round circles with a biscuit cutter or with the floured rim of a small drinkin' glass. Place on a lightly greased bakin' sheet, cover, and let rise in a warm place for an hour and a half. Bake at 450 degrees F. for 8 to 10 minutes or until golden brown. Brush the tops with melted margarine. These babies are as light as air.

*—OPAL LAMB INMAN, LOT #1*

# HAM PIE

*This is so good it'll make you cry.*

*Serves 4 to 6*

1 cup cubed cooked ham

1 cup crumbled government or mozzarella cheese

1 egg, beaten

2 frozen pie shells, partially thawed

In a large bowl, mix together the ham, cheese, and egg. Pour the mixture into one of the pie shells. Cover with the second pie shell and press with your fingers to seal the edges. Bake at 350 degrees F. for 1 hour. Watch it, and cover with foil if it's browning too quickly. Serve with a side of kernel corn.

*—NELLIE TINKLE, LOT #4*

# HOT BUTTERED LEMONADE

*This beverage makes for a heart-warmin' after-dinner drink.*

*Serves 4*

3 cups boiled water

½ cup sugar

2 tablespoons margarine

1 teaspoon grated lemon zest

½ cup lemon juice

Small lemon wedges, for serving

In a large pan over medium heat, mix the water, sugar, margarine, and lemon zest. Stir until the sugar dissolves and the mixture reaches a boil. Take off the heat and add the lemon juice. Stir. Pour into coffee cups and serve with small lemon wedges.

*—WENDY BOTTOM, LOT #4*

# TAMMY FAYE CAKE

*This is one of the reasons I love this time of year.*

*Makes 1 cake*

3 cups flour

2 cups sugar

6 tablespoons cocoa

2 tablespoons bakin' soda

1 teaspoon salt

¾ cup oil

2 tablespoons vinegar

2 teaspoons vanilla extract

2 cups cold water

Combine all the dry ingredients in a large bowl. Add the wet ingredients and stir until smooth. Pour into two 8-inch or 9-inch round cake pans. Bake for 30 minutes at 350 degrees F. Cool on a rack.

To make the frostin':

½ cup creamy peanut butter

2 tablespoons margarine

1½ cups confectioners' sugar

4 tablespoons milk

1 teaspoon vanilla extract

In a small bowl, cream together the peanut butter and margarine. Beat in the other ingredients. Continue beatin' until smooth. Spread some frosting on one cake layer and then put the second layer on top of that. Frost the cake with the remainin' frostin'. If you run out, make some more. Just make sure you got a good thick layer all around.

Take a glass of hot water and put a butter knife in it. Let the knife sit for just a few seconds, then run it over the top of the cake. Continue to dip the knife in the water to clean it and reheat it; the warmth helps the knife to smooth the frostin'. Take a toothpick and lightly draw out Tammy Faye's face (you can get her photo off the Internet). Use green glitter on the eyelids, red glitter for the blush, and Red Hots for the lips. Chocolate chips work great for the eyes and eyebrows. Chocolate chip shavin's make wonderful eyelashes. Finally, take a little water and add one drop of blue food colorin'. Use the knife to drizzle a stream of tears from the outside corners of the eyes. Make sure to say grace before eatin' a piece of this.

*—RUBY ANN BOXCAR, LOT #18*

# ST. PATRICK'S DAY
## March 17
### (Unless it falls on a weekend or the warden is Irish, this is not a prison holiday)

There's an old sayin' about how on St. Patrick's Day everybody's Irish, which is somewhat like my sister's line, "kiss me, I'm drunk." Basically both statements are simply sayin' that everybody's invited with no exceptions. In the United States it doesn't matter if your name is O'Conner or Goldberg, all are welcome to celebrate St. Patrick's Day like they truly were Irish, with the wearin' of green clothin', drinkin' green beer, and even eatin' green eggs and ham.

At the High Chaparral Trailer Park we've tried to capture the luck of the Irish ourselves with an annual St. Patrick's Day party. Since the weather is usually nice this time of year, we try and hold our celebration outside in front of the park's office buildin'. Normally all our trailer park community gatherin' is done out by the park swimmin' pool, but this time of year the water has thawed out and since Ben Beaver hasn't poured in the bottle of Clorox bleach yet, the smell is unbearable. Anyways, we set up card tables and lawn chairs out in front of the office, and everybody brings a covered dish item. Of course the food item and the clothes you wear to the gatherin' have to be green in color. Basically we all have a great time, although the first year of our now traditional St. Patrick's Day get-together was a disaster, to say the least. It all started with an overnight downpour that looked as if it would certainly cancel our shindig. But as luck would have it, with the first sign of mornin', the clouds lifted and the sun came out. When we set up the tables and chairs we all had to wear rubbers on our feet on account of the light floodin' that the rain had left throughout the lower sections of the High Chaparral. But our spirits were high, or at least they were until we took the covers off the food we'd brung. We should've taken the molded somethin' or other that Me-Ma, who was still livin' in lot #16 at the time, had brought for her green food item as an omen for the day. Of course we didn't, and it went downhill from there. Trailer park managers Ben and his now deceased wife, Dora Beaver, had provided the keg of beer as well as the 7-Up for all of us to drink. They'd also brought a large bottle of green food colorin' so we could have green drinks in honor of the day. So they'd put a teaspoon of colorin' in a glass and fill it up with beer or 7-Up. Needless to say, it helped make the gatherin' a real party. That was until we realized that our mouths were green. It wasn't until the next day when our mouths were still green that someone actually read the label on the bottle and found out that it was a concentrate, an industrial-strength concentrate to be exact. The teaspoon of food colorin' that was put in each beverage was actually enough to have easily changed 11 gallons of beer or 7-Up to a nice shade of kelly green. We were sportin' green tongues for three months. The whole thing was a disaster, well, that is, with the exception of seein' Sister Bertha of lot #12 drunker than a skunk. Every time she'd get up from the card table for another helpin' of food, Dora Beaver, who was two sheets to the wind herself, would top off Sister Bertha's green 7-Up with some of the vodka she had in her own glass. By the end of the day, the usually prudish Sister Bertha was sittin' at a table with the top four buttons on the front of her dress undone and her skirt hiked up to her waist, fannin' herself while slurrin', "Damn, it's hot out here." It wasn't pretty, but trust me, I got Polaroids.

### Things to Get You in the Holiday Mood

Visit www.st-patricks-day.com/index.asp.

Watch the streets of Dublin live at www.earthcam.com/ireland/dublin/.

Rent and watch the movie *Leprechaun* (this one will scare more than the gold out of your pants).

Rent and watch the movie *Going My Way,* and sing along with Bing Crosby (every time Bing goes into "Too Ral Loo Ral Loo Ral" my husband, Dew, cries like a woman).

Rent and watch the movie *Darby O'Gil and the Little People* (don't worry, Gary Coleman ain't in this, thank goodness).

Rent and watch the movie *Finian's Rainbow* (I found the story line to be a bit confusin', but the music is good).

### Things to Do

Grab ahold of short men and tell 'em to give you their gold.

Buy and watch the best dang movie ever made about the Irish, *The Quiet Man,* starrin' the Duke.

Drink and eat anything that's green unless my Me-Ma offers it to you.

### How to Decorate Your Trailer for This Holiday

Green is the word. Anything and everything just as long as it's green (the only exception to this in a Razorback fan's home is Notre Dame merchandise).

Another way to decorate your trailer is to hang up shamrocks, pictures of leprechauns, and rainbows. You should see the big rainbow flag that Kenny and Donny fly every year for St. Patrick's Day. I have no idea where they got it. But it sure is nice.

Last year I set out little black plastic pots that I'd bought when they marked the Halloween items way down (witches' caldron and pots are the same thing for all intents and purposes), and I filled 'em up with them gold chocolate coins. I thought they'd be a cute way to decorate and it'd be fun for my husband, Dew, as well as other visitin' guests to go look around the livin' room for the hidden pots of gold. And it would've been fun if our three miniature Schnauzers hadn't found 'em first. Lord, I tell y'all, my sweet girls were so sick it wasn't funny. And my poor carpets told the tale. I finally had to put little diapers on 'em till they got better. But they're better, thanks for askin'.

### Trailer Park Tradition

In keepin' with the spirit of the Irish, everyone hoses down their patio furniture and their gnomes.

### Somethin' to Bring to a Party

## CHEESY GARLIC BROCCOLI SPREAD

*I don't know if it's Irish, but it sure is good.*

*Makes 8 to 12 servin's*

½ pound chopped or diced frozen broccoli

3 tablespoons roasted garlic

8 ounces cream cheese

2 teaspoons chives

Green food coloring

Steam your broccoli for, say, about 4 to 5 minutes. Let it cool down and then put it in the food processor along with garlic, cream cheese, and chives. Add food colorin' until you get a nice green color. Turn that processor on and let it go to town until your mixture is nice and smooth. Pour the mixture out into a greased shamrock Jell-O mold. Cover and put in the fridge to chill for 3 hours. Turn out of the mold and serve as is with butter crackers.

*—ANITA MCBIGGON, LOT #2*

*Dinner Menu*

# CREAMED PEA CASSEROLE

*Rumor has it the Pentecostals make the same casserole, but without the pearl onions. That's like havin' a bark without the dog; it's pointless.*

*Serves 6 to 8*

2½ tablespoons margarine
1 can chopped mushrooms
2½ tablespoons all-purpose flour
3 ounces cream cheese
¾ cup milk
10 ounces frozen peas
1 can pearl onions, drained

Put your margarine in a skillet over medium heat. Add the mushrooms and sauté for 3 minutes. Slowly add the flour. Keep stirrin'. Add the cream cheese. Stir until it gets kind of smooth. Slowly add the milk; stir. Then add the peas. Stir for a few minutes then take off the heat.

In a casserole dish, spread out a layer of pearl onions. Top this with the pea mixture. Cover with foil and bake at 450 degrees F. for 30 minutes.

*—CONNIE O'KAY, LOT #13*

# POTATO SOUP

*The Piggly Wiggly in Searcy carries the Beau Monde seasonin' just for us folks at the High Chaparral Trailer Park.*

*Serves 4 to 6*

4 cups diced potatoes

½ cup finely chopped onion

½ cup margarine

3 tablespoons flour

1 teaspoon Beau Monde Seasoning

2 quarts milk

2 tablespoons chopped parsley

In a big cookin' pot, cook your potatoes and onion until they're real tender. Drain 'em, then mash 'em all together.

In a pot, melt the margarine and add the flour and Beau Monde. Stir and simmer until it gets all bubbly. Add the milk and stir until it thickens and is smooth. Add the potato mixture, followed by the parsley. Stir well and serve hot.

*—LOVIE O'BIRCH, LOT #20*

## CABBAGE ROLL CASSEROLE

*Nothin' says "The top of the mornin' to you" like a good old cabbage roll casserole.*

*This is real good eatin', but after a few servin's of it, whoever shares your bed won't have the luck of the Irish that night, I can tell you.*

Feeds 4–6

1 head cabbage

1 large onion

½ cup margarine

1 pound ground beef

1 cup cooked rice

2 eggs

1 tablespoon dried parsley

Salt and pepper to taste

Pinch of garlic powder

1 can of tomato soup

1½ soup cans of beer

Slice the cabbage and onions up real thin-like. In a large skillet melt the margarine and sauté 'em till they are slightly brown.

In another bowl, mix the beef, rice, eggs, parsley, salt and pepper, and garlic powder.

Grease a casserole dish and layer ½ the cabbage mixture in the dish. Top this with the beef mixture. Put the remainin' cabbage mixture on top of this.

Pour the tomato soup and beer into the bowl that had the beef mixture. Stir it up real good and pour it over the casserole mixture. Bake for 1½ hours at 350 degrees F.

*—KITTY MCCHITWOOD, LOT #11*

## SOMETHIN' GREEN FOR DESSERT PIE

*Strange name, great taste.*

*Makes 1 pie*

1 package of white chocolate instant puddin' mix

½ of a regular container of Cool Whip

Green food color

1 Oreo Cookie piecrust

Green-colored sugar in a shaker

Make the puddin' accordin' to the pie directions on the box. Fold in half the whipped cream. Add a few drops of the food coloring. Stir well until you get a nice light green color. Pour and scrape into the piecrust. Put it in the fridge for 1 hour. Decorate it by sprinklin' on the green sugar. Serve with milk.

*—LULU BELL O'BOXCAR, LOT #8*

# REBA McENTIRE'S BIRTHDAY
## March 28
### (Unless it falls on a weekend, this is not a prison holiday)

Tammy Faye has shown us how to pick ourselves up durin' times of trouble, but when it comes to class, there is only one lady that comes to the mind of us folks in the trailer park world, and her name is Reba McEntire. Reba, who I must admit I've been a fan of since the '80s, is just plain old down-to-earth folk. She doesn't try to be somethin' that she's not, but what she is pure all-American talent.

Born in Oklahoma, she knew what it was like to grow up around simple things. And just like me, she also knew what it was to be blessed with talent at an early age. Unlike me, however, she was able to get up on a horse without it havin' to be hospitalized. And it was at a rodeo that Reba's singin' talents were discovered. The rest of the story for this birthday girl is history.

You know, I've often been told by many people out there that me and Reba are a lot alike, which I guess I can kind of see. We are both show people after all, and we do have larger-than-life personalities. And there are other things that are similar about Reba and me.

Reba can take a song and work it till you feel the true meanin' of the words deep down in your gut. When I sing, it has the same effect on people. Why I've had folks come up to me after I've performed a number just to tell me what my singin' did to their stomachs.

Reba loves her fans and they love her right back. Me and my fans have that same kind of relationship as well. Why, I can walk down a street in most any town and my fans will come up to me. Most of 'em are drunk or needin' a ride, but you can still see the love.

Reba is known to be big-hearted and generous. I, too, am big-hearted. As a matter of fact the doctor says my heart is abnormally big. And when it comes to generous, just ask my neighbors. They'll tell you I always warn 'em before I call the police on their behinds.

She always looks great and her makeup is perfect. The same is true for me. I can't go anywhere without people comin' up to me and askin', "Who in the hell did your makeup?"

Reba is never known to say a bad word about anybody. I also hold to the old code that says if you can't say something good about someone, then don't say nothin' at all unless it's real good gossip.

Reba grew up in a very small town. I'm almost the size of a small town.

In any case, Reba McEntire will always be the gal that we trailer folks look up to and someday hope to be like. With that we wish her a very Happy Birthday.

### Things to Get You in the Holiday Mood
Go visit her web page at www.reba.com.
Rent and watch her movies *Is There Life Out There, Tremors,* or *Buffalo Girls.*

### Things to Do
Hold a Reba-thon showin' episodes of her television show *Reba,* which you been tapin' off just for this occasion.

Play Reba-roundup, where two-people teams race around barrels. The person playin' the rider, regardless of gender, must wear a big red Reba wig durin' the race. If it falls off or gets tangled up in a tree then that team is out of the competition. And let me add that the use of hot glue or even super glue to hold the wig on is not allowed. Just remember that those lighter in weight should never play the part of the horse. My poor husband, Dew, is still havin' back problems.

### How to Decorate Your Trailer for This Holiday
Hang up birthday-greetin' banners as well as some twisted gold and orange crepe paper. Blow up some of Reba's CD covers on a copier and hang those throughout the trailer. And of course decorate the air with the wonderful songs that have made Reba the queen of our hearts.

### Trailer Park Tradition
Anita Biggon closes her Three Cigarettes in the Ashtray Bar and Grill to the general public and allows us folks at the High Chaparral Trailer Park to hold our annual Reba McEntire Karaoke Celebration. All us gals dress up in red; after all, you never know who might get to sing "Fancy." Usually I host the whole night of nothin' but Reba Karaoke tunes. There's good food, and with Momma Ballzak, Donna Sue, Ben Beaver, and the bar's owner, Anita Biggon, you can be sure that

there's good adult drinks on hand as well. And I must admit that in the spirit of the evenin' I, too, usually tend to have a drink or two, but bein' the good Baptist woman that I am, I turn around with my back facin' everyone and sneak a sip. Needless to say, a good time is always had by all.

*Somethin' to Bring to a Party*

# I'M A SURVIVOR SAUSAGE SQUARES

*At the next party you attend, if you show up with*
*a plate of these they won't ask you to take it back.*

*Makes enough for 8 to 12 people*

2 pounds ground sausage meat

1 pound hamburger meat

Salt and pepper

1 tablespoon chili powder

1 pound Velveeta cheese, cubed

1 loaf party rye squares, melba toast, or your favorite crackers

Brown both the sausage and the hamburger together in a skillet. Break up the meat into small pieces while it cooks. When it's all done, drain it, and then add the salt and pepper, and chili powder. Mix well. Then put it in a large microwavable bowl along with your Velveeta and cook for 2½ minutes on High. When done, stir and cook for 2½ additional minutes. If the cheese ain't melted all the way, stir it again and give it another minute or two.

Put a layer of foil on a bakin' sheet and lay out your rye bread, melba toast, or crackers. Take a spoonful of the meat mixture and put it on each one of the breads/crackers. Bake 375 F. for 10 to 12 minutes.

*—LOIS BUNCH, LOT #3*

*Dinner Menu*

## WHEN WHOEVER'S IN NEW ENGLAND CLAM CHOWDER

*Rumor has it that this stuff is just like they eat in
Maine.*

*Makes 6 to 8 servin's*

1 package of bacon
1 can of cream of potato soup
1 can of cream of celery soup
6 cans of chopped clams
½ cup margarine
1 medium onion, diced
2 cups cream or half-and-half
3 cups milk

Chop up your uncooked bacon into small pieces and cook in a skillet. Drain and put the cooked bacon in a big soup pot. Add your two soups, the clams, the juice from three of the cans only, margarine, onion, cream or half and half, and milk. Stir well and put on a low fire so it can simmer for 1½ hours. Serve with oyster crackers.

*—DONNY OWENS, LOT #15*

## IS THERE LIFE OUT THERE ZUCCHINI BREAD

*If you don't like zucchini bread, well then, you can
just walk on.*

*Makes 2 loaves*

2 cups shredded zucchini
3 eggs
1¾ cups sugar
1 cup oil
2 cups flour
¼ teaspoon bakin' powder
2 teaspoons bakin' soda

2 teaspoons ground cinnamon

1 teaspoon salt

2 teaspoons vanilla extract

1 cup chopped nuts

Margarine

Grease and flour two loaf pans and set 'em aside.

Run your zucchini through a strainer, makin' sure to get all the excess juice and water out.

Take a bowl and add the eggs, sugar, and oil. Beat 'em together real good, then add the flour, both the bakin' powder and soda, cinnamon, salt, vanilla extract, and nuts. Usin' a spoon only, mix everything together. Add the zucchini and continue to beat the mixture until everything is mixed well. Put the mix into the bread pans and bake for 1 hour at 350 degrees F. Durin' the last minute, brush a little margarine on the top of the loaves to help give the bread a lovely golden color.

*—PASTOR IDA MAY BEE, LOT #7*

## LITTLE ROCK RANCH BURGERS

*When it comes to these burgers, it's your call.*

4 slices Government cheese (or your favorite cheese)

2 pounds hamburger meat

1 package of dry ranch salad dressin' mix

Margarine

4 hamburger buns

Red onion slices

Cut your cheese up into little bits. Put 'em in a bowl with the meat and dressin' mix. Mix it all together with your hands, makin' sure it get blended thoroughly. Make into four patties and cook. Put margarine on the buns and toast 'em. Put the burgers on the toasted buns and serve with big slices of red onion.

*—JUANITA HIX, LOT #9*

# HERE'S YOUR ONE CHANCE FANCY FRENCH FRIES

*Donna Sue ain't sure which one of her one-night stands gave her this recipe, but she thinks his name was John.*

*Makes 4 to 6 servin's*

1½ cups flour

1 teaspoon salt

1½ cups beer

4 medium bakin' potatoes, peeled

4 tablespoon confectioners' sugar

In a large bowl, mix the flour and salt together. Add the beer and beat the whole thing until it's nice and smooth. Put in the fridge to chill for 3 hours.

Take your potatoes and cut 'em up into good-size sticks about ¼-inch wide. Put 'em in a bowl of cold water to sit for a few hours (this will take out some of the starch). Drain 'em on a paper towel. Take a fresh bowl of water (about 3 cups) and add the sugar, and stir. Add the dried potato fries to the sugar water and let sit for 20 minutes. Take the potato sticks out and drain 'em. Pat 'em dry with a paper towel. Dip 'em in the beer batter that you made earlier in the day and fry 'em in oil that's 375 degrees F. until they're golden brown (4 to 5 minutes). Drain on paper towels and salt. Now, if your fries ain't cooked all the way through, try this trick: After dryin' the potato sticks from their sweet bath, put 'em in oil that's been heated up to 280 degrees F. Cook for 3 minutes only and pull out. Drain well. Then dip 'em in the beer batter and cook for the normal 4 to 5 minutes at 375 degrees F. This should do the trick. And if these ain't the best fancy fries you've ever had, I'll eat a piece of tofu.

*—LOVIE BIRCH, LOT #20*

# WHY HAVEN'T I HEARD FROM YOU BISCUIT PUDDIN'

*This is better than a Sunday kind of love on a Monday.*

1 cup sugar

1 cup milk

1 teaspoon vanilla extract

2 eggs

¼ stick margarine

5 old biscuits

½ cup raisins

½ cup chopped nuts

Cinnamon in a shaker

Put the sugar, milk, vanilla extract, eggs, and margarine in a bowl and cream 'em together. Crumble up the biscuits and add 'em to the creamed mixture. Next add the raisins and nuts. Mix well and pour into a bakin' dish. Sprinkle on the cinnamon and bake for 30 to 40 minutes at 350 degrees F.

*—OPAL WHITE, LOT #10*

# Chapter 4

This is an Easter image the little kiddies and my
slightly dimwitted niece Lulu Bell of Lot #8
will never get out of their minds. We was
cleanin' that fake bunny fur out of our yards
for weeks to come.

# *April*

April is the fourth month in the modern calendar, but if you've been followin' the game you know that in the Roman days it was only the second month of the year. It seems that nobody really knows how April, or Aprilis, as the Romans called it, got its name. Some believe it might have come from the word *open* since it is the time of year when the new season actually does totally open its arms to the old, allowin' it to turn into new growth just like the gals at the Blue Whale Strip Club do. Or possibly the name came from the Greek goddess of love, Aphrodite. But one thing's for sure, it wasn't named for that April Meyers down at the Post Office. Talk about rude. I know you're suppose to respect your elders, but I don't care if she is 67, she's just pure mean-spirited. Every time I walk in, there she sits, all shrunken-down 112 pounds of her, plopped down on a chair with a lip full of chew and a danglin' cigarette hangin' from the corner of her mouth, readin' some trashy supermarket rag or a Victoria's Secret catalog. And she won't look up at you till your standin' right there smack dab in front of her little counter area. Then, after a moment of silence, she finally glares up at you over her brown-framed bifocals, turns and spits into an old glass Coke bottle that's she's obviously been usin' all day long, turns back around, sighs, and utters those immortal words that you won't find in any customer service manual, "I guess you need some help, huh." I tell y'all, if she wasn't an employee of our United States Government and a board member of the First Baptist Church of Pangburn, I'd have knocked the bejesus out of her long ago.

April has 30 days and is known for its rain showers. With the warm temperatures and the rain, by the middle to end of the month, everythin' is just about ready to bloom. This is also the time of year that most farmers plant their seeds. It's also the time of year folks start messin' in their gardens.

There are a number of holidays in this month. For some folks April is a holy month since it contains both Holy Week (Palm Sunday, Maundy Thursday, Good Friday, Easter Saturday, Easter, and Easter Monday) and Passover more times than not. Where there's good, there's evil—or, as we call it in the U.S., Tax Day. We also celebrate the lives of two wonderful gals and pay tribute to our planet and its tree. And if that ain't enough party days for you, we also got our month-long holidays listed below. But first we start the month off with a bang as we celebrate April Fool's Day.

April is:
### *National Alcohol Awareness Month*

## MARTINI SALAD

*You won't find this on the salad bar at the Sizzler.*

1 medium head lettuce

½ cup gin

½ cup dry vermouth

¼ cup vinegar

1 package of Italian dressin' mix

⅔ cup oil

Tear your lettuce up into bite-size pieces and put in a bowl. Add the gin to the bowl, cover with plastic, and shake it up so the lettuce gets a good coatin'. Put it in the fridge and let it sit for 2 days. Now, don't open it up and drink the gin out. Leave it alone.

On the second day, put the vermouth and the vinegar in a cocktail shaker and shake your troubles away. Add the package of dressin' mix and shake it up. Finally add the oil and give it one last good shakin' session. Take the cover off the lettuce and pour the dressin' over the salad. Toss and serve.

*—MOMMA BALLZAK, LOT #16*

*National Florida Tomato Month*

# SPAGHETTI PIE

*Mickey Ray said he used to know some tomatoes in Florida personally back durin' his army days. Connie don't find that kind of talk amusin' at all.*

*6 to 8 servin's*

8 ounces spaghetti

2 tablespoons margarine

2 eggs, beaten

½ cup grated Parmesan cheese

2 regular cans of corn, drained

¾ pound ground beef

¼ teaspoon garlic powder

1½ cups Florida tomato sauce

½ teaspoon dried oregano

16 ounces cottage cheese, drained

8 ounces government cheese (or your favorite cheese), grated

Cook the spaghetti for 10 to 12 minutes, or until tender but still firm; drain well. Stir the margarine into the pasta until almost melted.

In a small bowl, mix together the eggs and Parmesan cheese. Stir in the spaghetti. Brown the ground beef in a fryin' pan. Drain off the excess fat. Add the garlic powder to the meat and stir. Stir in the tomato sauce and oregano and heat until hot. Lightly grease a 9 x 13-inch bakin' dish. Press the spaghetti mixture into the bottom and up the sides of the bakin' dish. Spread the cottage cheese over the crust. Spread the corn over the cottage cheese. Then spread the meat mixture over the corn. Sprinkle with the grated cheese. Bake for 20 to 25 minutes in a 350-degree F. oven, or until hot and bubbly.

*—CONNIE KAY, LOT #13*

# APRIL FOOL'S DAY
## April 1
### (Unless it falls on a weekend, this is not a prison holiday)

I'd have to say that out of all the traditional holidays that are in the calendar year, this one is right up our alley at the High Chaparral Trailer Park. We all enjoy a good practical joke. Well, that's not necessarily true—Sister Bertha hates 'em, which is why she's usually at the top of everyone's April Fool's hit list. Last year me and my sister, Donna Sue, called up the Kingdom Hall over in Searcy pretendin' to be Sister Bertha. We asked if they'd be kind enough to send out a few folks to talk about their wonderful faith. Well, you can only imagine the fireworks that broke loose when these poor Jehovah Witnesses came knockin' on her trailer door. When the sheriff finally arrived, she had one cornered up a tree and was tryin' to baptize the other one in a birdbath. Next year we're callin' the Mormons.

No one really knows how April Fool's started, but many point to the French (shock surprise). Back in 1582, when the calendar changed over to the Gregorian, which we use today, some of the French decided that they weren't goin' to make the change. They continued to celebrate the beginnin' of the New Year on April 1, which is really screwy since everybody else had been celebratin' the New Year in March, but that's the French for you. Anyways, when those pigheaded French would ring in the year on the first of April, the followers of the new calendar would point at the revelers and call 'em fools, thus April Fools. They also played practical jokes on these poor misguided folks. Because of their determination to fight off change even if it was for the good, these people became the butt of all jokes, and were branded with derogatory names. Today we simply call folks like this Republicans.

Now when it comes to the recipes, you'll notice that they are all my Me-Ma's. This will make the old woman happy, but please, please, please, DON'T MAKE THESE! PERIOD!

### *Things to Get You in the Holiday Mood*
Rent and watch the horror movie *April Fool's Day.*
Rent and watch episodes of those British fools *Monty Python's Flyin' Circus.*

### Things to Do

Put "Honk if you're horny" bumper stickers on the cars of the elderly. All the honkin' is sure to motivate even the prudiest senior into eventually pullin' out the old bird.

Go up to occupied port-a-potties and padlock 'em shut. If you want to get the folks in 'em good, shake 'em like you're goin' to tip 'em over. And if you want to get 'em real good, tip 'em.

Go shoppin' with a friend and while they're checkin' out, go up to 'em and say in a loud voice, "Will you come on, Momma's gettin' sick in the car, and I ain't sittin' in the vomit spot this time."

Go car shoppin'. Once a salesperson has spent 30 minutes with you, tell 'em that you really like the car you've been lookin' at, but will have to check with the welfare office to see just how much of the price they'll pay.

Go into public bathrooms and super glue all the toilet seats in the up position. If that's not possible, then super glue the seat to the lid.

If you got kids, short-sheet their beds.

Tell someone how nice they look followed by an "April Fool's."

Put a garden snake in your mailbox and wait for the mailman to arrive.

Go through a fast-food restaurant drive-thru, place a large order, and try to pay with food stamps.

Be creative; come up with your own good pranks.

### How to Decorate Your Trailer for This Holiday

You don't need to buy anything for this holiday. Simply hang your pictures upside down. Change the hot and cold faucets around. Turn your furniture so it faces the wall.

### Trailer Park Tradition

The only tradition we have in the trailer park world when it comes to April Fool's Day is that everyone is fair game.

*Somethin' to Bring to a Party*

# HERE DOGGIE DOGGIES

*Thank y'all for your kind prayers.*
*Serves 12 unless you share with someone else*
12 sweet rolls
Mustard
1 regular can of jalapeños, chopped

Cut the center piece out of each sweet roll and eat it. Put each roll on a piece of wax paper about the size of the roll. Fill the center with mustard. Sprinkle on some of the jalapeños. Place in the freezer for 20 minutes and serve.

*—ME-MA, FORMERLY OF LOT #16*

*Dinner Menu*

# CARROTS ALE ME-MA

*We have her scheduled for an exorcism next week.*
*Serves 4 to 6*
2 regular cans carrots, drained
½ cup half-and-half
2 tablespoons granulated sugar
1 tablespoon brown sugar
Dash of ground cinnamon
Pour the carrots into a bowl.

In a second bowl, mix everything else. Pour this over the carrots. Heat in the microwave on medium-high for 3 minutes and serve. You will get raves on this one.

*—ME-MA, FORMERLY OF LOT #16*

# ME-MA'S CORN PUFF DELIGHT

*How many ways can I say that it's just wrong?*

Serves 4 to 6

1 regular can corn
1 pound hamburger meat
½ onion, chopped
8 pieces of bread
Salt and pepper to taste
Oil

Put everything in a food processor and process for 5 minutes. Put in a blender and pureé for 5 additional minutes. Dump the contents into a skillet with ½ inch of hot oil and cook until the hamburger meat is cooked all the way through, flippin' once. Serve with ketchup or Thousand Island Dressin'. This is loved at the Last Stop Nursing Home.

*—ME-MA, FORMERLY OF LOT #16*

# ME-MA'S COOKIE DESSERT SURPRISE

*She's one track short of a train ride.*

Serves 4 and no more!

1 big box of your favorite cookies
1 box of yellow cake mix
½ gallon ice cream
2 cups milk
Pickle, for garnish

Put the unopened package of cookies on a hard-top table and beat the heck out of 'em with a hammer. Open the package and put the crumbs in a bowl. Sweep up the extras from the floor and add them, too.

Make the yellow cake batter accordin' to the box instructions. Add the cookie crumbs and stir. Put in a big ol' pan and bake accordin' to the directions on the box. Let the cake cool. Crumble it up and put it in a mixer. Add everything else and mix on high speed for 6 minutes. Serve in a bowl and garnish with a pickle.

*—ME-MA, FORMERLY OF LOT #16*

# LORETTA LYNN'S BIRTHDAY
## April 14
(Unless it falls on a weekend, this is not a prison holiday except in Kentucky)

You know, folks, I've known many queens in my life, includin' my dear friend Liz over in England, but none of 'em are as common as our birthday girl. The queen that I speak of is about as common as dirt on a dirt road or water in a river, but that's why we love her. She's one of us—one of the common everyday men or women who make this country what it is today. She was born simple and has remained simple. She never tried to be some flashy top-notch fluff entertainer. No, no, she was always true to herself and her people that she come from. And she never tried to be gracious or kind when it came to her music. She told it like it is. Her songs said what we felt. Her music was and still is as simple as she is, which is why she truly is the people's entertainer, the Queen of Country Music.

Born in Butcher Holler, Kentucky, she would marry Mooney Lynn at the age of thirteen. They stayed together until he went on to meet his maker in 1996. With his passin' Loretta was able to find the strength to make it through this hurtin' time in her life even though she openly grieved just like us trailer folks do. You see, life had never been easy for this Kentucky girl. While other girls were out playin' and wonderin' which boy liked 'em, Loretta was already takin' on the responsible role of motherhood at the tender age of 14. Before she was 21 years of age, she had already birthed four kids, and two more would be on the way. By 29 this girl of ours was officially able to call herself Granny. For some of y'all out there in the trailer park, it's almost as if I'm tellin' your story, ain't it?

Even though Loretta's first big recorded song, which is still one of my sister, Donna Sue's, favorites, "I'm a Honky Tonk Girl," did OK, it wasn't until 1962 that the song "Success" made her a star. She's achieved many awards, honors, distinctions, and trophies, but she's stayed true to her fans, her music, and her roots. She was born in humble conditions and she remains humble even to this day.

Several years back I told Loretta I hope that when I perform, I'm as simple and honest as she is when she does a song. With that she looked me in the eye and said that she was sure I would be. She then made me get in the kitchen and cook somethin' for her (I thought Kenny and Donny in lot #15 had a lot of Crisco in their trailer until I saw her cupboards and pantry).

So if Tammy Faye is our strength, and Reba is our class, then Loretta has to be the true voice that is cryin' out in the wilderness. She is singin' about you and me, about right and wrong, and about the human heart that beats in trailer parks around the world.

Happy Birthday, Loretta. We hope you like these recipes that we've named after you. And thank you for singin' our song!

### Things to Get You in the Holiday Mood
Visit Loretta's web page at www.lorettalynn.com.
With over 100 albums bearin' her golden singin' voice, it can't be hard to get in the holiday spirit.

### Things to Do
Go to Loretta's home state of Kentucky.
If you can't make it to Kentucky, go to Kentucky Fried Chicken.
Rent and watch the movie *Coal Miner's Daughter*.
Visit a coal mine.

### How to Decorate Your Trailer for This Holiday
In honor of the simple men and women that Loretta sings about, there is no decoratin' for this holiday.

### Trailer Park Tradition
Everybody sets an empty Crisco can out on their front porch at sundown on the eve of Loretta Lynn's birthday. Durin' the night, all the members of the trailer park will come by and put a piece of charcoal in your can if you've been good. If you've been bad, then they put somethin' else in there, which I refuse to mention. When you get up in the mornin', you go check your Crisco can. If it's full of charcoal then you've been doin' OK so far this year by your neighbors, and you'll use that come summer for your first barbecue. If you open your trailer door and you've got flies buzzin' around, just put some gloves on, take that can straight to the trash, and change your ways.

*Somethin' to Bring to a Party*

# FIST CITY FRITTERS

*If your squaw is on the warpath, just give her one of these and you're sure to get a peace treaty from her.*

*Makes about 18 to 24 fritters*

1 cup flour
1½ teaspoons bakin' powder
3 tablespoons confectioners' sugar
¼ teaspoon salt
1 egg, well beaten
⅓ cup milk
1 teaspoon vanilla extract
1 can of apple pie fillin'
Oil

Get you a bowl and sift the first 4 items together, makin' sure they mix well.

In a second bowl, beat your egg and milk together, and then add the dry mixture to it. Once you've mixed it well, add the apple pie fillin' and vanilla and keep mixin' until everything comes together. Now drop tablespoon-size portions of the batter into a deep fryer containing clean hot oil that's at 375 degrees F. and fry until they get golden brown on each side.

Next you will need to make the glaze by mixin' the followin' ingredients in a small bowl:

1 cup confectioners' sugar
½ teaspoon vanilla extract
1 tablespoon milk

Pour your glaze into a plastic bowl and add some fritters in it. Put the lid on the bowl and shake for a minute or two. All the fritters should be covered with the glaze. Take 'em out and put on wax paper. Continue this process until all your fritters have been glazed.

*—DICK INMAN, LOT #1*

*Dinner Menu*

# YOU AIN'T WOMAN ENOUGH SALAD DRESSIN'

*You'll swear your tongue is still smolderin' after
the fire is gone.*

*Makes 6 servin's*

⅔ cup lime juice

¼ cup olive oil

¼ cup water

⅓ cup sugar

½ teaspoon minced garlic

¼ teaspoon salt

½ cup jalapeño peppers, chopped up in tiny pieces

Put everything but the peppers in a bowl, cover it, and shake for 2 minutes. When you look at it, there should be no sign of the sugar. Add the peppers, shake for 30 seconds, and place in the fridge overnight. Serve over salads. Be careful; it should be very hot.

*—LOIS BUNCH, LOT #3*

# BLUE KENTUCKY GIRL CHEESE GRITS

*These will make you red, white, and blue.*

*Makes 4 to 6 servin's*

4 cups water

1 cup uncooked quick grits

1 teaspoon salt

½ cup margarine

1 cup grated Cheddar cheese

2 eggs, beaten

1 tablespoon Worcestershire sauce

¼ teaspoon garlic powder

Stir together the water, grits, and salt in a bowl. Put the mixture in a casserole dish and microwave on High for 6 minutes. Stir the mixture and stick it in for another 6 minutes. Now just add your margarine and cheese. Stir it up real good and nuke it for another 2 minutes on High. Stir it again real good.

Put the eggs in a bowl and add the Worcestershire sauce and garlic powder. Mix it up real well and add to the casserole. Stir it up and cook it on High another 12 minutes. Let it rest in the microwave for another 5 minutes before servin'. Now, this is good eatin'.

—*OLLIE WHITE, LOT #10*

## ONE'S ON THE WAY

*This only thing better than this is the pill.*

6 to 8 servin's
2 pounds ground lean beef
½ pound ground pork
2 eggs, slightly beaten
3 tablespoons margarine, melted
¼ teaspoon pepper
1 onion, chopped
1 cup milk
3 tablespoons ketchup
2 teaspoons salt
1 cup bread pieces
6 strips bacon

Put all the ingredients in a large bowl except for the bacon. Mix it all up with your hands and then put it in a loaf pan. Cover it with the bacon strips. Now some of the bacon should vanish into the loaf pan. Bake at 375 degrees F. for 1½ hours.

While it's cookin', take:

1 cup ketchup
3 tablespoons brown sugar
¼ cup diced onions

and mix 'em together. Pour this on the top of the meatloaf after the above cookin' time has ended and cook for an additional 10 minutes.

—*WENDY BOTTOM, LOT #4*

# YOU'RE THE REASON OUR KIDS ARE UGLY DESSERT DIP

*After a bite of this is when the tingle becomes a chill.*

*6 to 8 servin's*

2 cups softened cream cheese

½ cup heavy cream

½ teaspoon vanilla extract

¼ cup packed brown sugar

½ teaspoon ground cinnamon

1 tablespoon lemon juice

½ cup peanut butter chips

½ cup chocolate chips

Graham crackers, for servin'

In a large bowl, beat the cream cheese and the heavy cream until it is nice and smooth. Add the vanilla extract, brown sugar, cinnamon, and lemon juice and blend well. Add all the chips and mix. Pour it into serving bowl and put in the fridge, covered, to chill for an hour. You can either scoop out tablespoon-size portions and spread on graham crackers or you can just serve as is, lettin' folks dip into it with graham crackers. Either way, it's a thrill and a chill for all who partake.

—*JEANNIE JANSSEN, LOT #19*

# TAX DAY
## April 15
### (Unless it falls on a weekend, this is not a prison holiday)

In the High Chaparral Trailer Park, most of us are able to file the EZ form on account of our income, but even that simple-to-follow tax sheet can be a headache. You see, math was not a subject that any of us did real good in. And when it comes to followin' directions, at least the written kind, they might as well be written in Greek if you know what I mean. So as you probably can guess, most of us wait till the last day to do our taxes. By then, we're runnin' from town to town tryin' to find the right state and federal forms that we need. Needless to say, it ain't pretty. You'd think we'd learn our lesson, but of course not, we're just too dang pigheaded for that. So Tax Day is one that we celebrate after we've finally finished, stamped, and sent out those EZ forms.

Now this past year, in an attempt to pick up some extra cash, Harland did some of our taxes. He only charged us 10 percent of the tax return he could get for us, and he even promised that if he couldn't get you some money back, he wouldn't charge a penny. Well you can imagine how excited we all were to find out that we had so much comin'. Harland made $67, so he was happy. Of course our thrill turned into horror when we all started to get these letters in the mail from the state and the IRS informin' us that we all owed money. I don't know what Harland had done wrong, but it was a whopper. After all was said and done, he owed us $697 plus an additional $27 on his own taxes. I have a feelin' Juanita will be doin' their taxes next year. Poor Harland. Now we know why he's a sacker at the Piggly Wiggly and a shoe boy at Great Big Balls Bowlin' Alley.

So good luck to y'all on your taxes. And thank you for buyin' this book, which makes my taxes even harder to figure out. Please feel free to make my life a livin' hell on April 15 by gettin' a book for every member of your family, your friends, and even those you hardly know. Trust me when I tell y'all that I could get used to complicated tax seasons.

### Things to Get You in the Holiday Mood

Hey, they got the tax forms online! No more of those runnin' all over the place to find your right form. Just go to www.irs.gov/formspubs to get those federal forms. And you can get your state tax forms by goin' to the web pages below.

| | |
|---|---|
| Alabama | www.ador.stateincometax/Mainitindex.htm |
| Alaska | *What do you mean they ain't got to pay state tax?* |
| Arizona | www.revenue.state.az.us/#forms |
| Arkansas | www.ark.org/dfa/taxes/index.html.al.us/ |
| California | www.ftb.ca.gov/forms/index.html |
| Colorado | www.state.co.us/gov_dir/revenue_dir/stateforms.html |
| Connecticut | www.drs.state.ct.us/forms/forms.html |
| Delaware | www.state.de.us/revenue/taxforms/99/detax9.htm |
| Florida | *They ain't got to pay state income tax either?* |
| Georgia | www2.state.ga.us/departments/dor/forms.shtml |
| Hawaii | www.state.hi.us/tax/tax.html |
| Idaho | www2.state.id.us/tax/forms.htm |
| Illinois | www.revenue.state.il.us/taxforms/ |
| Indiana | www.in.gov/dor/ |
| Iowa | www.state.ia.us/tax/index.html |
| Kansas | www.ksrevenue.org/taxforms.html |
| Kentucky | revenue.state.ky.us/ |
| Louisiana | www.rev.state.la.u |
| Maine | www.state.me.us/revenue/ |
| Maryland | individuals.marylandtaxes.com/taxforms/ |
| Massachusetts | www.dor.state.ma.us/ |
| Michigan | www.michigan.gov/treasury |
| Minnesota | www.taxes.state.mn.us/index.html |
| Mississippi | www.mstc.state.ms.us/ |
| Missouri | www.dor.state.mo.us/tax/forms/ |
| Montana | www.discoveringmontana.com/revenue/css/default.asp |
| Nebraska | www.revenue.state.ne.us/tax/forms.htm |
| Nevada | *I'm lookin' for a trailer lot and a casino that wants me in Vegas!* |
| New Hampshire | www.state.nh.us/revenue/forms/forms.htm |
| New Jersey | www.state.nj.us/treasury/taxation/index.html?forms.htm-mainFrame |
| New Mexico | www.state.nm.us/tax/trd_form.htm |
| New York | www.tax.state.ny.us/Forms/default.htm |
| North Carolina | www.dor.state.nc.us/ |
| North Dakota | www.state.nd.us/taxdpt/forms/forms.htm |
| Ohio | www.state.oh.us/tax/ |
| Oklahoma | www.oktax.state.ok.us/oktax/incomtax.html |

| | |
|---|---|
| Oregon | www.dor.state.or.us/forms.html |
| Pennsylvania | www.revenue.state.pa.us/revenue/site/default.asp |
| Rhode Island | www.tax.state.ri.us/form/form.htm |
| South Carolina | www.sctax.org/ |
| South Dakota | *Oh, it must be real nice not havin' to pay state tax!* |
| Tennessee | www.state.tn.us/revenue/pubnfrms.htm |
| Texas | *You too, Texas?* |
| Utah | www.tax.ex.state.ut.us/CurrentPackX/currPakX.html |
| Vermont | www.state.vt.us/tax/2001Frm.htm |
| Virginia | www.tax.state.va.us/ |
| Washington | *Well, no wonder Fraiser moved back home!* |
| West Virginia | www.state.wv.us/taxrev/forms.html |
| Wisconsin | www.dor.state.wi.us/html/formpub.html |
| Wyoming | *Well, tie me up and call me state tax free!* |

### Things to Do
Drink heavily and do your taxes.

### How to Decorate Your Trailer for This Holiday
Place bottles of water and aspirin around your house. Trust me, you're goin' to need 'em! Sharpened pencils can be placed in different strategic places in your trailer home as well.

### Trailer Park Tradition
Claim as many people as you can. A new child is not only a blessin', but a write-off as well. We usually take in a needy person on tax day, just so we can write 'em off next year as a dependent.

*Somethin' to Bring to a Party*

# BANKRUPT WHISKEY SOURS

*A pitcher of these and you'll forget your tax troubles.*

*Makes 1 pitcher's worth*

1 package Lemonade Kool-Aid

1 can beer

8 shots Canadian whiskey

1½ cups sugar

Ice

Put everything but the ice in a blender and blend on high for 3 minutes. Strain and pour over ice.

*—FAYE FAYE LARUE, LOT #17*

*Dinner Menu*

# TAXMAN DINNER

*This all-in-one dinner is cheap and easy on your pocketbook.*

*Serves 6 to 8*

6 strips bacon

4 medium potatoes, thinly sliced

1 large onion, chopped

3 large carrots, diced

½ cup chopped celery

1 bunch trimmed and sliced broccoli

1 pound smoked sausage, sliced

¾ cup government cheese (or your favorite cheese)

Salt and pepper to taste

Fry the bacon till it's crisp. Drain the bacon by puttin' it on paper towels. Add the potatoes, onion, carrots, celery, and broccoli to the bacon drippin's, and cook over medium heat till the veggies get nice and tender. Add the sausage slices, but don't stir. Cover the skillet and cook for 12 minutes. Put in a pinch of salt and pepper. Add the cheese and give it another 5 minutes on low heat. Crumble up the bacon slices and sprinkle on top of the entire dish. Serve warm.

*—LOVIE BIRCH, LOT #20*

# 1040EZ PIE

*After a day like today, you need comfort food*
*like this.*

Makes 1 pie

½ pint sour cream

1 14 ounce can Eagle Brand Sweetened Condensed Milk

⅓ cup lemon juice

1 large ripe avocado, mashed

9-inch graham cracker crumb crust

Whipped cream (optional)

Combine the sour cream, milk, lemon juice, and avocado in a bowl. Pour into the crust and chill for 2 hours. Top with whipped cream if you'd like.

*—LOIS BUNCH, LOT #3*

# AUDITOR'S AFTER-DINNER DRINK

*You deserve one of these after you've finished*
*the taxes.*

Makes 1 cup coffee

3 spoonfuls chocolate chips

1 shot Bailey's Irish Cream

Coffee

Take a coffee cup and put in the chocolate chips and Bailey's Irish Cream. Top this off with coffee. Stir until the chips melt. Sip.

*—DONNA SUE BOXCAR, LOT #6*

# EASTER
## Celebrated on a specific Sunday in March or April, so check your calendars.
### (A prison holiday)

Now Easter is just like Christmas in the way that it's celebrated both as a religious holiday amongst Christians and also a secular holiday for everyone else. In our trailer park, we'd all get up and attend sunrise service at the First Baptist Church of Pangburn, unless of course we'd made a $25 donation per household to Pastor Hickey the day before. In that case, he'd say a prayer with us, and then instruct us to dream about Jesus while we slept in. Our new pastor, Ida May Bee, has informed us that as long as we continue to celebrate the Easter Vigil on Holy Saturday, we won't be startin' Easter service until around noon on that Sunday.

When it comes to Easter eggs, I've always liked 'em. As a small girl, I recall that our family didn't have the money to buy food colorin' to dye our eggs. So instead we'd use some of Me-Ma's red hair dye. Those eggs were absolutely vivid and beautiful. Of course we only tried to eat 'em once. Thank goodness they tasted terrible or we might have eaten more than two each. That however was enough to make us kids and Momma and Daddy real sick. I think that's why even to this day I have problems eatin' anything that's red with the exception of cake, frostin', M&Ms, ketchup, Italian sauces, red bell peppers, and Zingers. I even have to have my meat cooked well done or I won't eat it.

The Easter Bunny has always been one of my favorite holiday characters. I've always thought that he was so cute. One year after mornin' services, Harland over in lot #9 decided to surprise all the kids in the trailer park by dressin' up as the Easter Bunny. All week long at the Piggly Wiggly he'd been dressed up as the Easter Bunny for the kids in Searcy to come and see. Well, when he told his manager what he wanted to do, his boss was thrilled with the idea and told him he could borrow the suit for the mornin', and then just bring it back the next afternoon. His good-hearted boss also told him that he could take several bags of candy, which would be discounted on Monday anyways, and pass that out to the kids along with a big stack of Piggly Wiggly business cards for their folks. Well, right after church, Harland drove his car just outside of the High Chaparral Trailer Park entrance, changed into his bunny outfit, and grabbed the candy and cards. No sooner had Harland stepped away from his car when what had to have been a nearsighted hawk swooped down and tried to carry his butt away. That dang hawk would pick poor Harland up a few feet then drop him. It come right back around and dive bombed what it thought was a full year's meal. There was fur, candy, and business cards flyin' everywhere out there on that dirt road. And all poor Harland could do was yell for help, but with that bunny head on, his cries were muffled. Luckily some of us gals were waitin' outside our trailer in hopes to get some of that dang candy. We saw what was goin' on so we went and got Ben Beaver to come out. He had a shotgun and, bein' a war vet, he knew how to use it. Well, his wife, Dora, God rest her soul, pushed Ben's wheelchair out into the road so he could get a good clean shot at the bird, which had now driven Harland a good block from where it had first attacked him. Ben loaded both barrels, took aim, and with one quick motion pulled the trigger. Now let me just insert here that I'm sure if Dora had remembered to have locked the wheel locks on Ben's wheelchair he would have hit that hawk without question. But instead, the buckshot wound up in Harland's bottom, and Ben and his wheelchair took off backwards down Robert E. Lee Lane. God bless him, poor old Ben had gone two and a half miles all downhill before he finally came to a complete stop. Deputy Bobby Wayne, who was on patrol that mornin', clocked Ben and his chair at 37 miles an hour. Needless to say, when we'd finally caught up with Ben, he was a complete mess. He said he saw his life pass right before his eyes three times while he was on that wild ride.

The noise from the shotgun had scared off the hawk, but Harland was now layin' out on the road. Bein' good in emergency situations, I hollered back at Dew to call 911 and then I started to pick up the few pieces of candy that laid out on the road. Most of it had ended up in the ditches, but the high grasses were not somewhere that I'd want to go stickin' my hands on account of all the snakes that call 'em home. Them rattlers could have that free chocolate, but they better watch their backs when they cross the road if I'm drivin'.

Harland was fine, with just a few buckshot to his behind. He wasn't settin' down real soon, but he was still alive. Luckily that bunny suit had slowed down most of the pellets. Of course it was full of bullet holes and the head was nothin' more than a hairless frame, thanks to that dang hawk. Harland had to pay for the suit, plus he almost lost his job on account of the complaints that came in from nearby farmers. They were all upset about the business cards they kept findin' out in their fields. Did I mention that Easter mornin' had been rather windy?

Ben was fine although he was madder than all get out when Sheriff Gentry came knockin' on his door with a handful of tickets. It seemed Sheriff Gentry had heard about what had happened so he charged Ben with speedin', failure to stop at a crossin', drivin' a vehicle that did not meet the state guidelines on a public road, and failure to yield the right of way to another vehicle. Needless to say, Ben beat the tickets in court.

And as for the kids that Harland wanted to surprise, well, most of 'em were traumatized and are still in therapy. God bless 'em, not one of 'em got a piece of that candy, and I can guarantee that.

### Things to Get You in the Holiday Mood

Rent and watch *Easter Parade, The Easter Bunny Is Comin' to Town, Here Comes Peter Cottontail, It's the Easter Beagle, Charlie Brown, Black Hawk Down,* and the rest of them Jesus movies that you ain't finished yet.

View the Holy Land live from the comfort of your own home at www.isra camera.co.il/.

### Things to Do

Clean out your freezer, 'cause you're goin' to need it tomorrow.

Color eggs and hold an egg rollin' contest. Then hide the eggs and let the kids and the elderly look for 'em.

### How to Decorate Your Trailer for This Holiday

I place that fake green plastic grass up on the tables in my livin' room. Be careful if you got small dogs, cause if it falls on the floor, they can get all tangled up in that stuff.

*Trailer Park Tradition*

When you get up, make sure you plug in your Christmas tree lights as well as the Christmas lights outside on your trailer in honor of the risen savior. These will stay on all day, until you get ready for bed. At this point, all good trailer park folk unplug the lights, put the plastic bag on the tree, and roll it into the closet until Thanksgivin'. Under no circumstance will you ever take down the outside lights, and this includes when they wear out. Since the amount of lights you have on your trailer is a sign of monetary worth, this is simply not done in the trailer park community. Just put another strand on top of 'em.

*Somethin' to Bring to a Party*

# BUNNY COTTON TAILS

*These will put a smile on your face and a hop in your walk.*

*Makes around 4 dozen*

2 cups flour

1 cup soft margarine

1 cup ground pecans

½ cup confectioners' sugar, plus more for sprinklin'

⅛ teaspoon salt

1 teaspoon vanilla extract

¼ teaspoon almond extract

Mix the ingredients with your hands in a large bowl until thoroughly blended. Cover and refrigerate for 1 hour.

Preheat the oven to 375 degrees F.

Form into balls that are a little smaller then golf balls and flatten a bit. Place on an ungreased cookie sheet and bake 10 to 12 minutes, until nice and golden. Remove from the oven and sift some confectioners' sugar over the tops.

*—TINA FAYE STOPENBLOTTER, LOT #17*

*Dinner Menu*

## EASTER BANANA DRESSIN'

*Don't ask, I got no idea what banana's got to do
with Easter, but this sure is good.*

*Makes right around 2 to 2½ cups worth*

2 ripe bananas

1 cup sour cream

4 tablespoons brown sugar

1½ teaspoons lemon juice

Blend all the ingredients on the middle speed of your blender until smooth. Either pour the dressin' over a fruit salad or toss it with the fruit salad.

—*DICK INMAN, LOT #1*

## WANDA'S WILD CORN CHOWDER

*Well, it ain't really wild, but neither is Wanda for
that matter.*

*Serves 6*

1 can of cream of potato soup

2 cans of creamed corn

1 can of evaporated milk

1½ cups milk

¼ cup chopped green pepper

1 tablespoon minced onion

1 teaspoon salt

¼ teaspoon pepper

Mix everything together in a microwaveable bowl and heat on High for 19 minutes, stirrin' after 10 minutes. This goes great with cornbread.

—*WANDA KAY, LOT #13*

# TRAILER TATERS

*You have to be able to eat two spoonfuls of these be-*
*fore you're allowed to rent a lot in any trailer park.*

*Serves 6*

3 large potatoes

½ stick margarine

1 regular can corn

¼ cup heavy cream

Salt and pepper

Boil the potatoes with their skins on for 45 minutes; drain. Cut each potato in half. With a fork, take the potato fresh out of the skins and discard the skins. Put the potatoes in a bowl and add the margarine, corn, and cream. Sprinkle on some salt and pepper to taste. Whip with an electric mixer for 2 minutes on medium. Before you serve 'em, put 'em in the microwave for 2 minutes. Add some extra margarine and stir well.

*—BEN BEAVER, LOT #14*

# MOMMA'S TRADITONAL EASTER HONEY HAM

*I can't think of anything that's brought me more joy*
*in my life unless it's my husband, Dew, or my little*
*dogs or watchin' a movie with Mr. Burt Reynolds*
*in it.*

5-pound ready-to-eat ham

¼ cup whole cloves

¼ cup maple syrup

2 cups honey

⅔ cup butter, melted

Preheat oven to 325 degrees F. so it gets all nice and warm.

Score your ham, and stud it with the whole cloves. Place your ham in a foil-lined bakin' pan.

In a bowl, mix the maple syrup, honey, and butter together. Pour it over your ham. Bake for 1 hour and 20 minutes, bastin' the ham every 10 to 15 minutes with the syrupy mixture that's in the bottom of the pan. During the last 4 to 5 minutes of baking, turn on the broiler to caramelize the glaze. Remove from the oven and let sit a few minutes before servin'.

*—MOMMA BOXCAR, LOT #5*

# CHRISTIAN CARROT CAKE

*Yet another staple in the Baptist kitchen.*

*6 to 8 servin's*

1½ cups Mazola oil

2 cups packed brown sugar

2 teaspoons baking soda

1 teaspoon salt

2 teaspoons grounded cinnamon

1 teaspoon vanilla extract

2 cups flour

4 eggs

3 cups grated carrots

1 cup chopped walnuts

In a large bowl, beat the oil and sugar together. Add your soda, salt, cinnamon, and vanilla extract. Add the flour and eggs alternately. Fold in the carrots and walnuts. Bake for 45 minutes at 350 degrees F. Top with one of the best icin's you've ever had pass your lips by mixing the followin':

6 ounces margarine

8 ounces cream cheese

2 cups confectioners' sugar

½ teaspoon vanilla extract

1 teaspoon lemon juice

Cream together the margarine and cream cheese in a bowl. Beat in everything else until it's nice and fluffy.

*—SISTER BERTHA, LOT #12*

# PASSOVER
## Takes place typically in March or April
### (Unless it falls on a weekend, this is not a prison holiday.)

Now let me start right off by tellin' y'all that what you're about to read was not what I'd originally wrote. The original text that I'd put in here was wonderful, or so I'd thought. I have a lot of Jewish friends all across the United States with the exception of Arkansas, and I've always tried to include them in everything when they're here visitin'. Bein' the good Baptist that I am, I've tried to keep up with everyone's religion. So you can understand how disheartened I was when my Jewish friends in Hollywood called me up to share some negative comments on the Passover section I'd sent 'em. It seems that not only had I given wrong facts and information, I'd also used wrong words and had completely twisted the Passover story. Well, I was just in shock. All these years I'd been believin' the wrong thing, not to mention sharin' the incorrect tidbits with my neighbors and friends. Well, long story short, I want to take this part of the book and correct all the falsehoods that I'd been unknowingly passin' on about this wonderful celebration. I'm also goin' to set the record straight on a few other items that my new neighbor, Faye Faye LaRue, who'd dated a Jewish man when she lived in Louisiana, had shared with me for this section of the book. I'm doin' all this 'cause if I could believe these falsehoods to be facts, then who knows who else is unwittingly makin' the same dang mistake. Here we go.

1. Yes, it's correct that Passover is a remembrance of the time in history when the Jewish people were bein' held in slavery in Egypt. And that on the night of Passover, all the Jews in Egypt had marked their doorways with lamb's blood. But the part that I'd been tellin' folks about how the Easter Bunny would leave candy at the houses that had blood, but would go in and kill the firstborn in the houses that didn't, was not correct. That was the Angel of Death and candy was not involved.

2. The story that Faye Faye had shared with me about the reason that those who celebrate Passover eat matzo bread durin' this holiday was wrong. A bad epidemic of yeast infections that was spreadin' across

Egypt at that time had nothin' to do with it at all. The real story was that when Pharaoh finally agreed to let the Jews leave Egypt, the womenfolk didn't have time to let their bread rise so they had to bake it as is.

3. Faye Faye was also incorrect about the little round hats that Jewish men wear. They are not called yamahas, but rather yarmulkes, and they ain't defective beanies whose spinners have fallen off. They are worn on account of a commandment that God gave the Jewish people about how the men should always keep their heads covered in respect for God.

4. I'm sorry folks, but I was wrong. The term *seder dinner* has nothin' to do with keepin' these dishes that they use on Passover in a cedar chest. Seder actually means "order" and refers to the precise order of what is eaten and when the ceremonies takes place.

5. Chag has nothin' to do with that TV show that's on CBS, that's *JAG*. It also was not what was hangin' on them ballots in Florida durin' the Bush–Gore election. Those were chads. Chag is simply a major Jewish holiday that has restrictions on what kind of work those celebratin' it can do. So Passover is a Chag.

6. Another one that I was way wrong on was about the removal of Chametz. This does not require an exterminator or any Raid products. I know, I feel like a dang idiot. Removin' Chametz is to simply get rid of any product that contains fermented grain in it.

7. Do not, I repeat, do not try to wish your Jewish neighbors a "Happy Passover" by given 'em a lovely corn casserole. They ain't supposed to eat corn durin' this time of the year. That especially includes cornbread.

8. The four questions asked durin' a seder meal are not "How much do you weigh?" "So when are you goin' to get married?" "Is George W. really that stupid?" and "Are you goin' to eat that?" The actual four questions are really one question with four different answers. That question is, "Why is this night different from all other nights?" The answers can be found in the Haggadah, which leads us to misconception number 9.

9. Faye Faye was incorrect when she said that Haggadah is a company in Israel that makes ice cream. The Haggadah is a book that contains

the seder. Haagen-Dazs is the ice cream company she was thinkin' about, and their headquarters are in the U.S., not in Israel.

10. And last, but not least, I was confused when I told folks that the empty table settin' for Elijah was for Elijah Woods.

### Things to Get You in the Holiday Mood
Rent and watch *The Ten Commandments.*
Watch the Western Wall at www.kotelcam.tv/.

### Things to Do
Go over to your Jewish friends' house the day before Passover and volunteer to eat all the food products that have Chametz in 'em.

### How to Decorate Your Trailer for This Holiday
I simply blow the dust off our family Bible that we keep on the coffee table and open it to Exodus 12:17. I know Faye Faye says she puts a piece of matzoh out on the table as well for decorations, but I'm sure the roaches probably carry it off before the eight-day holiday is over. Oh, her trailer is just a pit.

### Trailer Park Tradition
Well, since I found out that all my info was wrong, we really ain't got any trailer park traditions that we can do now. We'll just have to come up with some new ones.

### Somethin' to Bring to a Party

## HAPPY PASSOVER CREAM CHEESE BROWNIES

*Even a goyische mama like me can enjoy these babies!*

*6 to 8 servin's*
¼ cup unsalted margarine
⅓ cup soft nonwhipped cream cheese
1 cup sugar
2 eggs, beaten

½ cup matzoh cake flour

2 tablespoons potato starch

3 ounces bittersweet chocolate, melted

1 cup finely chopped nuts

Cream together the margarine and cream cheese in a bowl. Add the sugar and eggs; mix well. Stir in the matzoh flour, potato starch, cooled chocolate, and ¾ cup of the chopped nuts. Spread the batter in a buttered 9 x 9-inch pan. Sprinkle around the remainin' nuts on top. Bake at 325 degrees F. for 30 minutes. Cut into squares while warm.

*—DICK INMAN, LOT #1*

*Dinner Menu*

## TRAILER POTATO LATKES

*Accordin' to Lovie, Senator Lieberman just loved these when he came through town!*

*6 to 8 servin's*

3 cups instant mashed potatoes

1 large onion, diced

2 eggs, beaten

1 teaspoon salt

1/8 teaspoon black pepper

¼ cup matzoh meal

Vegetable oil

Sour cream or applesauce, for serving

Make the potatoes just like the box tells you to. Add the onion. Mix the in eggs, salt, pepper and matzoh meal. Heat the oil over medium heat until it warms up for fryin'. Use a large spoon to scoop the batter; and drop onto the oil and flatten slightly. Fry until crisp. Drain on the paper towel and serve with sour cream or applesauce.

*—LOVIE BIRCH, LOT #20*

## THE HARVEY KORMAN PASSOVER ROAST

*This is Momma's tribute to "the funniest man alive."*

*8 to 10 servin's*

6-pound brisket

1 onion, sliced

2 tablespoons paprika

1 can of tomato soup

If you got a Crock-Pot, stick your brisket in there. Add everything else to the Crock-Pot on top of the brisket and cook on high for 3 to 3½ hours.

*—MOMMA BALLZAK, LOT #5*

## PASSOVER BUTTERBALLS

*I don't know a lot about Jewish balls, but these are dang good.*

*2 or 3 dozen balls*

½ pound margarine

1 cup sugar

2 eggs

1 cup matzoh cake meal

1 teaspoon vanilla extract

In a bowl, cream the margarine and sugar together. Add the remainin' ingredients. Mix well, cover, and put in the fridge overnight. Roll 'em up into small balls and dip 'em in sugar. Put on a bakin' sheet and bake for 20 to 22 minutes at 350 degrees F. Enjoy.

*—FAYE FAYE LARUE, LOT #17*

# *Chapter 5*

After church and a nice dinner, Donna Sue took Momma of lot #5 over to the
Blue Whale Strip Club to watch Vance Poole (second from left) and his
Beef Stick Boys do their tribute to Mother's Day.

# *May*

Personally I think May is the gayest month of the year. All the snow and ice have melted and the summer heat hasn't yet begun. All the flowers have bloomed and the birds have built their nests. Soon we will hear the chirps from the newborn. It's just plain beautiful.

The fifth month of the year used to be the third back when them old Romans played with it. It's always had 31 days, and many folks think it was named after the Roman goddess Maia. It seems that old Maia was the goddess of growth and spring. The good Lord knows that by the end of December, after all the good food I've consumed durin' the holidays, I feel like the goddess of growth. But that's another story.

There is one day in May that will always be tender for many women across the world over the age of 45. It was the day our hearts were first broken. It was the day that our world stood still. It was the day that we learned what men were really like. It was May 1, 1965. Yes, that was the day that Elvis Presley married somebody other than us. I still get teary just thinkin' about it.

We got only a couple of big holidays in May, thank goodness. After the last of April we can all use a little break. One of these holidays is in honor of the woman that brung us into the world while the other remembers those in our military both livin' and dead. And if that don't add up to enough celebratin' for y'all, here are some other reasons durin' May that should suit you just fine.

May is:
*National Asparagus Month*

# THREE CIGARETTES IN THE ASHTRAY BAR AND GRILL FRIED ASPARAGUS SPEARS

*Now, I can eat it if it's cooked this way.*

*Feeds 4*

4 oz. self-risin' flour

1 egg

½ pint milk

Salt

Juice from ½ lemon

Oil

24 asparagus spears

Mayonnaise, for servin'

In a bowl, beat the flour into the egg. Add and beat the milk into this mixture, season with salt to taste, and let stand for 30 minutes.

Add the lemon juice and oil to a large pan of boilin' water. Add the asparagus and cook until tender, drain, and dust with flour, dip in the batter, and deep-fry until golden. Let drain on a paper towel and serve with mayo.

*—ANITA BIGGON, LOT #2*

*National Hamburger Month*

# TRAILER BURGERS

*I like to throw a slab of Velveeta on top of three or four of these.*

*Makes 8 burgers*

2 pounds ground beef

2 tablespoons Worcestershire sauce

½ teaspoon Tabasco sauce

Salt

2 garlic cloves, finely chopped

Mix all the ingredients together in a bowl. Form into eight patties and cook. These are best on the grill.

*—BEN BEAVER, LOT #14*

### National Strawberry Month

# OLLIE WHITE'S STRAWBERRY RHUBARB PIE

*You know May has arrived when Ollie stops by your trailer with a piece of this.*

2½ tablespoons quick cookin' tapioca

1½ tablespoons cornstarch

1 cup sugar

1 cup water

1½ cups strawberries

1½ cups rhubarb

1 tablespoon lemon juice

2 9-inch pie crusts

Heat the tapioca, cornstarch, sugar, and water till thick, but do not bring to a boil. Set aside to cool. Add the fruit and lemon juice to the cooled and thickened juice. Line a 9-inch pie pan with one of the pie crusts and pour in the fillin'. Shape the second crust to make the top, flute the edges, and cut vents. Bake at 425 degrees F. for 20 minutes, or until browned.

*—OLLIE WHITE, LOT #10*

# MOTHER'S DAY
## It falls on the second Sunday in May.
### (A prison holiday)

Mother's Day has never been all that good for my older sister, Donna Sue. One of the reasons for this is that she ain't a mother, regardless of what some folks may have called her in the past. Well, for that matter, neither am I. Both Donna Sue and I chose our careers over motherhood, but I've always been happy with that. After all, I got my little doggies to take the place of the children I might have had. For my sister, well, her babies are her bottles of booze, which means at any given time of the day, she's got more kids then the dang Waltons in that trailer of hers. As she's gettin' closer to the big 6-0, I think she's become more bitter as well as thirsty. Of course I could be wrong on all this. Her dislike could be, and now that I think about it most likely is, on account of the fact that she has to get up early on Sunday mornin' to go to church with Momma and the rest of the family.

The Mother's Day schedule has been a tradition in the Boxcar clan as far back as I can remember. Every year it's pretty much the same thing. Momma, Daddy, Donna Sue, Lulu Bell, me, my husband, Dew, and his momma, Momma Ballzak, all go to church, then we stop by the nursin' home to see Me-Ma. We all give Me-Ma a hug and then Momma asks her if she knows what today is. If she doesn't, we tell her we love her, give her some flowers, and get the heck out of there without sayin' a word about Mother's Day. Y'all might think we're bad, but God bless her, she's been barred from every restaurant in the surroundin' area. If she knows it's Mother's Day, then we got to take her with us, which means we're either eatin' at home or pickin' up an order at the A & W in Searcy. Mind you, I love A & W, but there's nothin' as nasty as seein' Me-Ma tryin' to eat a corn dog with her teeth out unless of course it's the traditional Mother's Day foot massage me and Donna Sue have to perform on Momma. Thank goodness she now lets us wear those work gloves.

### Things to Get You in the Holiday Mood
Watch reruns of *Leave It to Beaver* (Lord, that June Cleaver was such a lady). It was on account of Mrs. Cleaver that I swore never to have children, 'cause I could never live up to bein' that good a mother.

### Things to Do

If you happen to have the kind of money that fame has brought me and my sister Donna Sue, give your momma that special Mother's Day present that says "I love you": Sign her up for a series of healthful yogurt enemas. Just don't make the same mistake we made with Me-Ma for Grandparents' Day. Make sure the guy's licensed.

### How to Decorate Your Trailer for This Holiday

Hang up your favorite photos of your momma. If you ain't got a momma, or hate the one you got, just put my photo up, and feel free to send me a gift.

### Trailer Park Tradition

Even if she's bangin' on the front door, Mother's Day ends at 2:00 P.M. in the trailer park, period.

### Somethin' to Bring to a Party

## SPINACH BALLS OF LOVE

*These are so beautiful, you'd swear a woman had made 'em.*

*Makes 5 to 6 dozen balls*

2 10-ounce packages of frozen spinach
1 onion, finely chopped
6 eggs, well beaten
¾ cup margarine, melted
2 cups stuffing mix
½ cup grated Parmesan cheese
¾ tablespoon cayenne pepper
1½ teaspoons garlic salt

Cook your spinach like the package instructs you to and drain it real good. Mix it with the onion, eggs, margarine, stuffing mix, cheese, cayenne, and garlic salt. Make sure you mix this up real good. With your hands, shape this into little balls and place on a greased bakin' sheet. Bake for 20 minutes at 325 degrees F. Sprinkle these with some more Parmesan cheese.

*—KENNY LYNN, LOT #15*

*Dinner Menu*

# CHICKEN-FRIED FINGERS AND GRAVY

*Yet another reason to stop by Anita's bar.*

*10 to 12 servin's*

1½ cups flour

½ teaspoon salt

½ teaspoon black pepper

¼ teaspoon paprika

¼ teaspoon white pepper

1 egg

1¾ cups milk

1 cup oil

4 good-size beef steaks, cut into strips about 2 inches wide

¾ cup water

Combine the flour, salt, black pepper, paprika, and white pepper all together in a bowl. Make sure you mix it up real good. Set aside.

In another bowl, beat the egg and 1 cup of milk together.

Heat up about ½ inch of oil in a skillet. Once the oil gets hot enough to fry, you can start the dippin' process.

Dip each steak strip into the milk mixture, then dredge in the flour mixture. Dip 'em again in the milk mixture. Carefully put each strip in the oil and cook about 5 minutes on each side. Drain on paper towels and start workin' on the gravy.

Put a coffee filter over a coffee can and pour off all the oil. Your filter should be filled with the battered bits from the strips. Put these back in the pan along with 3 or 4 tablespoons of that oil. Heat it up real hot and sprinkle on the flour mixture (around ¾ cup) you used for the strips. Stir it up till you've browned the flour. For the next portion you're goin' to want to keep stirrin' the entire time. Carefully add the water and the remaining ¾ cup of milk. Turn your heat down and keep stirrin' until it gets nice and thick. If your gravy is too thick, add more oil. Add salt and pepper to taste.

*—ANITA BIGGON, LOT #2*

# MOMMA'S FAVORITE MASHED POTATOES

*Accordin' to Tina Faye, her and her momma, Faye
Faye, lived off of nothin' but these for three months
when they lived in New Orleans. Donna Sue said
knowin' Faye Faye, she most likely lived off of these,
a bottle of gin, and some poor degenerate.*

*Makes 4 to 6 servin's*

4 cups cubed cooked potatoes

2 tablespoons minced garlic

¾ cup milk

1 teaspoon salt

¼ teaspoon pepper

4 tablespoons margarine, melted

4 ounces Velveeta, cubed

Put the potatoes and garlic in a pot and set over medium heat. Add the milk, salt, and pepper. Stir, but don't mash yet. Once the ingredients start to get warm, mash until smooth. Add the margarine and stir. Let sit for a minute, covered. Remove from the heat and add the Velveeta. Stir until it's all melted. Add more salt and pepper to taste.

—*TINA FAYE STOPENBLOTTER, LOT #17*

# RUM CHEESE PIE

*My husband, Dew, always asks me to whip one of these up for his Momma on Mother's Day. I guess in the Ballzak family this is a handed-down recipe from drunk—I mean from mother to daughter.*

*Makes 1 happy pie*

4 8-ounce packages cream cheese, softened

½ cup plus 3 tablespoons sugar

2 eggs, beaten

3½ tablespoons dark rum

Graham cracker pie shell

1 cup sour cream

Mix your cream cheese in a blender, with ½ cup sugar and the eggs. Beat in 2 tablespoons of the rum. Put the mixture in the pie shell and bake for 20 minutes at 350 degrees F.

Put the sour cream and remainin' sugar and rum in a bowl, and beat until it's nice and smooth. Pour this mixture over the pie and put it back in the oven for another 5 minutes. Momma Ballzak says to take a shot of rum and mix it with some confectioners' sugar to make a thin drizzle to decorate it. I like it just the way it is without drizzlin' extra rum on it, but since it's the recipe that she likes to use, I had to mention it.

—*MOMMA BALLZAK, LOT #16*

# MEMORIAL DAY
## May 30
### (A prison holiday)

Bein' the good Americans that we are, we at the High Chaparral Trailer Park treat Memorial Day with respect and honor. If Memorial Day falls on a weekday, just as soon as *The Price Is Right* is over, we all gather outside around the trailer park flagpole for the traditional lowerin' of the flag to half-staff. Nellie Tinkle always makes the event more emotional by accompanyin' this act with a patriotic—yet, as she gets older, breathless—rendition of the "Star Spangled Banner" on her "wind piano." Nellie says the real name for this little keyboard instrument, which she blows to produce music, is melodica, but on Memorial Day, wind piano sounds much more American.

Later on that day we all go out to the cemetery to put flowers on the graves of the soldiers who died to defend this country. We also lay a lovely wreath on the tomb of our very own unknown soldier. Yes, believe it or not, we got an unknown soldier. About six years ago, my sister, Donna Sue, picked up this elderly fella in fatigues at the Blue Whale Strip Club. After she was done dancin' around 2:00 in the mornin', they left the bar and headed straight for her trailer. I guess they had a romantic evenin' together, which I do my best not to picture. Well, the next day this fella wakes up from his drunk and starts goin' ballistic. Now maybe it was because he was havin' flashbacks of bein' in the war, or possibly he was a bit off center to begin with, or it could be that he just saw my sister in the mornin' light. Who knows what caused him to go nuts? But nuts he went. Accordin' to Donna Sue, he started screamin' and pointin' at her feet. When she asked him what was wrong he just slobbered all over himself and said a bunch of mumbo jumbo that she didn't understand and then started screamin' at her feet again. Now my sister's got some ugly feet, with hammertoes like you've never seen before, but they ain't bad enough to scream about. When she finally managed to roll out of her waterbed, which took a while, she tried to calm him down, but it was to no avail. She got on the phone and called Sheriff Gentry to get there as quick as he could, but before she could hang the phone up, this fella cursed at her and dropped dead as a doorknob. Well, long story short, this old man had died without a lick of identification on him. After the coroner had ruled that his death was natural, the sheriff released the old geezer, and Donna Sue paid to have him buried in the cemetery. She claimed that if he hadn't passed, they might have had a future together. She also said that even though she thinks he might have died on top of her for a few minutes, he was the best thing she'd had in her bed since Oreo cookies, and that's high marks from my sister. Donna Sue don't talk about him anymore, but every Memorial Day when we all gather to lay the wreath to that unknown soldier, you can see a little tear in her eye as she looks at his tombstone and then at her feet.

### Things to Get You in the Holiday Mood
Rent and watch the movies *Saving Private Ryan, Pearl Harbor, The Little Colonel,* or any other war movie.
Visit the official page of Arlington National Cemetery at http://www.arlington cemetery.org.

### Things to Do
On Memorial Day we get rid of all the riffraff in the surroundin' area by goin' down to the nearest recruitin' office and pretendin' to enlist usin' their names. You should see their little smug faces when the MPs show up and drag their little Devil-music-listenin'-punk-rock-purple-spiky-haired butts out of their houses. That'll make you proud to be an American.

### How to Decorate Your Trailer for This Holiday
Three simple words: Red, White, and Blue!

### Trailer Park Tradition
When it comes to Memorial Day, flowers and floral wreaths that are placed on the tombstones of our fallen warriors, we usually will go with plastic flowers on account of the weather. You never know if it'll rain or not on Memorial Day, and the last thing you want are wet silk or satin flowers when you go to the cemetery the next day to pick them things up and take them back home to your trailer.

*Somethin' to Bring to a Party*

# CHESS PIE BAR COOKIES

*They ain't got bar cookies like these in them commie countries.*

*Makes 1 pan*

1 box yellow cake mix
½ cup margarine
2 eggs
1 (8 ounce) package of cream cheese
2 eggs
2½ cups confectioners' sugar

Take a mixer and mix the first 3 ingredients together. Press into a 9 × 13-inch pan.

Mix the next 3 ingredients together and pour over the pressed mixture. Bake for 35 minutes at 350 degrees F. Cool and cut into bars.

*—OLLIE WHITE, LOT #10*

*Dinner Menu*

# CHEESEBURGER BREAD BAKE

*This is a traditional Memorial Day trailer park dish.*

*Serves 4 to 6*

1 pound ground beef
1 tablespoon onion powder
1 teaspoon chili powder
8 ounces tomato puree
1 cup water
½ teaspoon Worcestershire sauce
½ teaspoon celery salt
1 loaf frozen bread dough, thawed
½ pound grated Cheddar cheese
Salt

In a skillet, put the first 7 items and cook 'em up real good. Take off the heat and set aside.

Divide the bread into two sections. Be careful not to work the dough more then you need to. Put the first layer in a greased 9 × 13-inch pan. Spread the dough out until it covers the bottom evenly. Put the cooked mixture on top of the dough that's in the pan. Season to taste with salt and top with the Cheddar cheese. Put the second section of dough on top of all this and set aside with a damp cloth on top. Let it rise for 30 minutes and then pop into a 350-degree F. oven for 30 minutes. Serve with your favorite sauce.

*—WANDA KAY, LOT #13*

# DOTTIE LAMB'S UNKNOWN SOLDIER TRIBUTE CAKE

*Dottie made this the first time out of respect for my sister, Donna Sue. Now she makes it every year, and we've nicknamed it the Memorial Day Cake.*

*Makes 1 cake*

½ cup margarine
½ cup shortenin'
2 cups sugar
5 egg yolks
2 cups flour
1 teaspoon bakin' soda
1 cup buttermilk
1 teaspoon vanilla extract
5 egg whites

Put the margarine and the shortenin' in a bowl and cream it together. Add the sugar and beat until it's smooth. Add the yolks and beat.

In a separate bowl, combine the flour and bakin' soda and mix well. Alternate addin' this with the buttermilk to the creamed mixture. Stir in the vanilla.

In a separate bowl, beat the egg whites till stiff. Fold them into the mixture. Pour the batter into three 9-inch cake pans that you already greased and floured. Bake for 25 minutes at 350 degrees F. Give each cake the toothpick test and when they pass, take 'em out and let 'em cool on a rack. Make the frostin' by mixin' the followin' items together:

9 ounces cream cheese
3 tablespoons lemon juice
1 tablespoon grated lemon zest
7½ cups sifted confectioners' sugar

Blend the cream cheese and the lemon juice together in a large bowl. Add the lemon zest and then the confectioners' sugar. Blend till it gets nice and smooth.

*—DOTTIE LAMB, LOT #14*

# Chapter 6

Brother Woody Bee and Pastor Ida May Bee of lot #7 watch
as trailer park manager Ben Beaver kicks off Pride Day by
raisin' the Pride flag.

# *June*

This sixth month of the calendar year is known for roses and weddin's, but not necessarily together. This fact is because more roses bloom durin' the month and more people get married durin' this month than any other month of the year. The latter maybe true on account of June bein' named after Juno, the patron goddess of marriage. This month used to contain only 29 days, but our good friend Julius Caesar decided to go and play with this month as well (in his honor and since it's National Dairy Month, I've included a cheesecake recipe).

There are only two big days that we celebrate in June, which might surprise many of y'all out there, but I'll get to that in a moment. The first holiday is the one when you pay tribute to the most important man in our whole life regardless if you love him or hate him. And the other holiday is a new one that we've just celebrated twice, but I'm sure you'll enjoy it as much as we do. When folks hear that we don't include the first day of summer in our lineup, most of 'em don't get it. Well, it's rather simple. You see, summer means hot days, and the heat and our 100 percent double-knit polyester slacks just don't go together. Lord, thanks to summer I've kept Gold Bond in business. Anyways, enjoy June by makin' merry durin' these month-long holidays as well.

June is:
*National Dairy Month*

# JULIUS CAESAR CHEESECAKE

*This sounds different, but it's real good!*

*Makes about 6 nice-size servin's*

1 regular box orange cake mix

½ cup margarine

1 egg, beaten

8 ounces cream cheese, softened

1 cup pecans, chopped up real good

3 eggs, beaten

In a big bowl, mix the first four items together. Press the mixture into a 13 x 9-inch greased and floured cake pan.

Next clean the bowl and then add the rest of the items. Mix real well and pour it on top of the first layer in that pan. Kick the oven up to 325 degrees F. and bake for 45 minutes. Serve cold with milk or coffee.

—*LOVIE BIRCH, LOT #20*

*National Iced Tea Month*

# LONG ISLAND ICED TEA

*Momma Ballzak can sling these babies back regardless of the month, but durin' June both she and my sister, Donna Sue, declare this their drink of choice. The rest of the year they'll drink anything.*

*1 glass'll get you hammered*

1 ounce vodka

1 ounce gin

1 ounce rum

1 ounce triple sec

1 ounce tequila

2 ounces Sweet and Sour Mix

Splash of Coke

2 lemon wedges for each serving

Mix first 6 ingredients in a pitcher and shake well with ice. Strain into a glass almost filled with ice. Add a splash of Coke for color. Squeeze in the juice from the lemon wedges. Stir. Drink! Repeat from the top.

—*DONNA SUE BOXCAR, LOT #6*

### *National Turkey Lover's Month*

# BEN BEAVER'S BBQED TURKEY SAMICHES

*Boy howdy, these are good!*

*Makes 8*

½ cup margarine

1 cup chopped celery

½ cup chopped onion

¼ cup chopped green pepper

½ cup ketchup

¼ cup firmly packed brown sugar

3 tablespoons Worcestershire sauce

1½ teaspoons chili powder

Dash of pepper

Dash of salt

4 cups chopped cooked turkey

8 buns

Melt your margarine in a pot and add the veggies to sauté for 5 minutes, or till tender. Add the sauces and the seasonin's, stir it up real good, and let it simmer for 8 minutes, makin' sure it don't stick. Throw in your turkey and let it heat for 5 more minutes, or until the meat is hot. Serve on toasted buns with chips and a pickle.

—*BEN BEAVER, LOT #14*

# FATHER'S DAY
## The third Sunday in June.
### (A prison holiday)

Now, Father's Day is handled a little different than Mother's Day. We all still get up and go off to church, which is followed by a nice dinner out, but when it comes to the givin' of cards and gifts, well, that's where the whole holiday practices start to differ. On Father's Day, every male in the park who's at least 12 years older than you gets a Father's Day card on account of how he might just be your real daddy. Don't get me wrong; no one's sayin' that the man you call Daddy ain't your real flesh and blood papa, but well, you never really know, and in some cases, your momma ain't quite sure either. So to avoid any kind of confusion, we've all found this to be the best policy. It also works great for the kids whose daddies have passed on or have moved out of state. It gives them a feelin' of belongin', knowin' that they can give some man a little love and get that bit of love returned. After sayin' that, I guess that's kind of why those kids are here in the first place, ain't it.

Of course there's only one person that actually gets a gift on this special day, and that's the man that you refer to as your daddy. In the case of a deceased father, you give the gift to your granddaddy. If he's passed then you spend the money on yourself. In the very near future I'll be able to get that big screen I've been wantin'.

My niece Lulu Bell has taken this card-givin' thing a bit to the extreme. As I mention back in my *Down Home Trailer Park Cookbook,* Lulu Bell continues to keep the ashes of my late brother, Jack Daniels Boxcar. Well, every year she goes out and hand picks a beautiful card just like she did when he was still kickin'. She spends days writin' exactly what she wants to say to her daddy, and includes it along with the card and some cash for a present in the envelope. She licks it, addresses it to Heaven, and puts a stamp on it. She then takes out a match and while holdin' the envelope over a clean ashtray, she lights the whole dang thing. Once it's burned down to nothin', she empties it in with my brother's ashes and says, "Happy Father's Day, Daddy, I love you." I tell you, it's so touchin' and sweet that it brings us all to tears. Of course, after the first year, we convinced her that only Monopoly money and Argentine pesos are accepted in heaven.

*Things to Get You in the Holiday Mood*

Rent and watch *Life With Father.*

*Things to Do*

Pass out your cards.

*How to Decorate Your Trailer for This Holiday*

Put up pictures of people that you wish were your father. Who knows, they just might be.

*Trailer Park Tradition*

Since eatin' with your parents is a big deal on these days, we all gather together as one big family for a Father's Day potluck. All the men, regardless if they've ever had kids or not, get a large ribbon that they wear, which says "#1 Dad!" It ain't much, but with the exception of my husband, Dew, and my daddy, neither are the men at the High Chaparral Trailer Park.

*Somethin' to Bring to a Party*

# DICK'S HONEY WIENIES

*Just between us, I personally like my SWEET AND SOUR WIENIES recipe, which is in my Down Home Trailer Park Cookbook better, but of course, when it comes to wienies, I'm partial.*

*Makes 3 dozen*

2 cups orange juice

1 cup honey

½ cup mustard

1 pound cocktail wieners

Combine the juice with the honey and mustard in a pot. Simmer for 15 minutes. Add the wieners. Simmer for 5 minutes. Put in a Crock-Pot on low heat and take the whole thing with you to the party.

—*DICK INMAN, LOT #1*

*Dinner Menu*

## DEW'S SWEET NUT LOAF

*Now, I'm not one to get into bread with nuts in it,*
*but Dew's loaf is so good, it's almost as if the nutty*
*taste explodes in your mouth with flavor.*

*Makes 1 loaf*

1 egg, beaten

1 cup sweet milk

3 cups cake flour

1 cup sugar

6 teaspoons bakin' powder

½ teaspoon salt

1 cup chopped pecans

Mix the milk with the egg in a small bowl.

In a larger bowl, mix the dry ingredients, followed by the nuts. Add the milk mixture. Stir well and pour it into a greased bread pan. Turn your oven up to 350 degrees F. and wait 20 minutes to bake (the mixture needs the time). Put it in and let it bake for an hour. Serve with margarine. Make sure you set plenty aside for you since your wife will eat as much of it as she can get her hands on.

*—DEW BALLZAK, LOT #18*

## KYLE'S BIG OLD MEAT PIE

*Kyle ain't jokin': His meat pie really is big.*

*Makes 6 to 8 big servin's*

Piecrust, enough to cover both the bottom and top of a casserole dish

Margarine

1 pound round steak, cut into small pieces

Salt

Pepper

1 can of cream of mushroom soup

4 potatoes, cubed

1 onion, diced

Water

Put a layer of piecrust on the bottom of a casserole dish, makin' sure that the crust comes up the sides so you can pinch it with the top crust. Put several pats of margarine on the bottom crust. Put the meat on the bottom, salt and pepper it, and drizzle on ⅓ of the cream of mushroom soup. Put your potatoes on this and then more salt and pepper, followed by a drizzlin' of ⅓ of the soup. Add your onion. Pour on the rest of the soup. Cover all of this with dough, pinch and seal the edges, and bake for an hour at 350 degrees F.

—*KYLE CHITWOOD, LOT #11*

# PRIDE DAY
### The fourth Sunday in June.
#### (A prison holiday)

Now let me be honest with y'all and tell you that I ain't got the slightest idea as to what this holiday is about, but I can tell y'all, we folks at the High Chaparral sure do have a fun time celebratin' it. Kenny and Donny over in lot #15 were the ones who brought this whole idea of holdin' a party on the last Sunday of the month to our attention. I guess folks all around the world get together on this day and celebrate their pride. Pride in what I really don't know, but as Sister Bertha once said, you should be proud of who you are and who made you (I think she meant bein' Baptist and God), which is why she's one of the biggest supporters of this whole Pride Day that we've been holdin' the past two years.

Since we can't get a permit from the city to hold a parade on account of it not bein' a national holiday, we hold our own right here at the High Chaparral Trailer Park. Sister Bertha pays for the wienies and buns that Harland and Juanita Hix get at an employee discount over at the Piggly Wiggly; Ben Beaver takes care of the beer; Kitty Chitwood supplies the chips from her Gas and Smokes convenience store; Fernando allows us to use his portable CD player with bass boost speakers; Dick Inman lets us use his CD collection; Mickey Ray brings the soda pop; and Kenny and Donny direct and videotape the whole thing. I'm tellin' you, it's somethin' to see! We all drive our cars, which are decorated with rainbow-colored balloons, around the park a few times. Kenny even makes us some signs to hold up about bein' proud and all. Last year Me-Ma rode around the park holdin' a sign that said PFLAG, which I believe is Greek for the word pride.

After the parade, we all wear different-colored handkerchiefs in our back pockets. We spend the next few hours enjoyin' the music that Dick plays for us while we munch down on some wienies and chips. Opal said Dick has really been practicin' for this day. For the past month in the evenin's he'd go in Fernando's room and play his CDs real loud. Of course, bein' as protective as he is about his stuff, Fernando insisted on bein' in the room at the same time. Well, all that practice sure paid off.

Later we play a game called "Anita Bryan Tag You're It." What happens is everyone is divided into 10 teams and given pink triangle and rainbow bumper stickers (these are the official symbols of Pride Day, accordin' to Kenny). The object of the game is to go over to Searcy and put your team's stickers on the back of cars without their drivers knowin' it, and then return to the trailer park before anyone else. The winnin' team gets a whole crate of oranges, while the runners-up get one can of orange juice concentrate. This is lots of fun. The first year Ben was able to get one on the back of every police car in Searcy. There was even a story on the news about it, but they didn't know who had done it.

Kenny and Donny just told me as I was finishin' this section up that we may have to cancel next year's Pride Day on account of some folks in Kansas are threatenin' to picket our celebration next year. I don't know why these people in Kansas can't just stay home and leave everybody else alone. Ain't they got no pride?

### Things to Get You in the Holiday Mood
Rent and watch *The Muppet Movie*. Lift your voice with Kermit when he does his stirrin' rendition of "The Rainbow Connection."

### Things to Do
Make Pride Day signs to carry in the parade. Donny says they should be big, bright, and gay.

### How to Decorate Your Trailer for This Holiday
Bowls of Skittles placed in key locations throughout your house is always a nice touch.

### Trailer Park Tradition
When we've finished the Anita Bryant Tag You're It game, we all go back to our trailers for what the boys call a "disco nap." And then around 6:00 P.M. we get together outside for the High Chaparral's I Will Survive Disco Party. Of course Dick spins his CDs on Fernando's CD player to provide the fun dance music. Kenny and Donny set up a light show includin' a mirror ball that they suspend from the roof of the trailer park office. And what I thought was fun was how we all came dressed as our favorite member of the Village People. You should have seen Me-Ma.

Not only was the outfit that I made for her from an old vinyl couch I found at the Goodwill in Heber Springs beautiful, but after I massacred her old lady mustache, she looked just like that leather man that's in the group. Those boys really know how to throw a party!

*Somethin' to Bring to a Party*

## SWEET PRIDE BREAD

*Accordin' to Kenny, this is eaten at all Pride celebrations.*

*12 to 14 servin's*

6 tablespoons milk

3 teaspoons sugar

6 small containers

Red, yellow, green, and blue food colorin'

12 to 14 slices of white bread

1 small paintbrush

Ground cinnamon (optional)

Mix the milk and sugar together. Divide the milk among the six containers. Put two drops of red food colorin' in one container, two drops of yellow in another container, one drop of green in a third container, one drop of blue in a fourth container, one drop of red and two drops of yellow to make orange, and last but not least, one drop of red and one drop of blue to make purple. Make sure you stir each container each time you use it so the colors mix well with the sugar milk. Take a piece of bread and your paintbrush, and on one side only paint one strip of color on the bread. The order of colors is red, orange, yellow, green, blue, and finally purple. Be careful not to put too much milk on the bread since it will get all soggy. Once you've finished your colors, put the bread in an oven or a toaster oven to bake until it's lightly browned. If you'd like it a bit sweeter, sprinkle a light coatin' of sugar on your bread slices before puttin' 'em in the oven. You can also add just a touch of cinnamon after the bread has toasted, if you like that sort of taste.

*—KENNY LYNN, LOT #15*

*Dinner Menu*

# BBQ BEER BRISKET

*Donny says that this one's "for the girls, 'cause two tablespoons of beer is all you might be able to get away from 'em." I don't know what that means, but this sure is good.*

6 to 8 servin's

1 tablespoon minced garlic

1 tablespoon pepper

2 tablespoons meat tenderizer

1 tablespoon onion salt

4 to 5 pounds brisket

2 tablespoons beer

½ tablespoon liquid smoke

2 tablespoons Worcestershire sauce

Combine the garlic, pepper, tenderizer, and onion salt in a small bowl. Rub it all over your meat. Put your meat fat side up in some aluminum foil. Wrap the meat up tightly and cook in a shallow pan for 1 hour at 325 degrees F.

Mix the beer, liquid smoke, and Worcestershire sauce together in a small bowl. Open just the top of the foil and baste the meat with the mixture (actually baste your meat and then dump the whole mixture on top of it). Wrap the foil back up, lower your heat to 300 degrees F., and cook for another 3 hours. Unwrap and cook for 1 more hour at 275 degrees F. Serve the brisket with your favorite sauce.

*—DONNY OWENS, LOT #15*

# GIANT DING DONG CAKE

*If you like Ding Dongs, you're goin' to love this one.*

Makes 1 great big Ding Dong

1 box moist devil's food cake mix

Mix the cake accordin' to the directions on the box and cook it so that it makes two cakes. Next combine the followin' ingredients in a bowl:

⅔ cup shortenin'

⅓ cup evaporated milk

½ cup sugar

1 teaspoon vanilla extract

Pinch of salt

Beat it until it gets nice and fluffy (about 4 to 6 minutes). Next add

½ cup confectioners' sugar

and beat for another 4 minutes. Set aside.

Take your two cakes and hollow 'em out a bit so that when you set 'em on top of each other, you have a nice empty space between 'em. It should be big enough to hold the fillin'. When you got it that big, add the fillin'. Cover it with store-bought chocolate frostin' and put in the fridge till you're ready to serve.

*—FERNANDO DIAZ, LOT #1*

# Chapter 7

Me and my sister, Donna Sue, are proud to be Americans, where at least we know she's *free*. Shock surprise!

# July

The history of July is an odd one. This seventh month of the year used to be known as Quintilis, which is Greek for fifth. Now, this was all well and good back when it was the fifth month of the year, but when the Romans changed everything around, they didn't change the names. It wasn't until later that the Roman senate officially changed Quintilis to July in honor of a man whose birthday happened to fall in this month, none other than our good friend, old Julius Caesar. (Lord, I feel like Paul Harvey.) It was Julius who, surprise, gave Quintilis a 31st day.

Out of all the months of the year, July has to be my least favorite, with August followin' a close second. I'm sorry, and it might sound unpatriotic, but I hate July on account of that dang-blasted heat! You don't have to be Al Roker to know that July is usually the hottest month in the year. If you don't believe me, just watch the sparks fly from between my thighs when I walk outside durin' the traditional Fourth of July gatherin'. I'm tellin' y'all that fat people and July don't get along. That's why I've only included one holiday for this month and it's a big one.

July is:
*National Beer Month*

## BEER CHEESE SOUP

*Even Sister Bertha enjoys a bowl or two of this*
*tasty treat.*
*Makes 4 to 6 servin's*
4 tablespoons margarine
¼ cup chopped carrot

½ cup chopped onion

5 tablespoons all-purpose flour

½ teaspoon paprika

½ teaspoon dry mustard

1 can beer

1 cup chicken broth

1 pound Cheddar cheese, grated

1 cup evaporated milk

¼ teaspoon hot sauce

Crackers or crushed-up pretzels

Put your margarine in a pan over a medium flame, and sauté your carrot and onion. Reduce heat to low. Stir in flour, and cook for 3 to 4 minutes. Add the paprika, mustard, beer, and chicken broth, and whisk until you got no lumps. Add the cheese and increase the heat. Bring it to a boil. Bring the heat back down and let it simmer for 10 minutes. Shut the heat off and fold in the milk. Add hot sauce to taste. Let each person add the crackers or crushed pretzels. This is also good durin' the colder months.

*—KITTY CHITWOOD, LOT #11*

*National Baked Bean Month*

# WENDY BOTTOM'S BAKED BEANS

*These are best enjoyed outside.*

*8 to 10 servin's*

2 pounds pork and beans

1 cup molasses

1 cup packed brown sugar

1 tablespoon dry mustard

1 tablespoon salt

1 teaspoon pepper

2 cups ketchup

1 onion, sliced

1 bell pepper, chopped

12 uncooked bacon strips, cut up into 2-inch pieces

Pour your beans out into a big roastin' pan. Add the molasses, brown sugar, mustard, salt, pepper, and ketchup. Stir well. Add the onion and bell pepper. Stir and top with the bacon pieces. Bake for 1½ hours at 325 degrees F.

*—WENDY BOTTOM, LOT #4*

### *National Hot Dog Month*

# SURVIVOR WIENIE

*These get their name on account of the Thousand Island dressin'. It was a cross between that and Reuben Wienie.*

*Makes 8*

8 hot dogs

8 slices of Swiss cheese

8 buns

Thousand Island dressin'

Minced pickles or drained relish

Sauerkraut

Cook your hot dogs (on a grill if you can). Put cheese in the buns, followed by the hot dogs, and add some Thousand Island dressin', pickles or relish, and sauerkraut.

*—RUBY ANN BOXCAR, LOT #18*

*National Ice Cream Month*

# OPAL'S SOMETIMES IT AIN'T AS BAD AS YOU THINK VINEGAR ICE CREAM

*THIS AIN'T ONE OF ME-MA'S RECIPES!!*
*This ice cream is as good as Opal is ugly, so get ready for a taste sensation.*

*Serves 4 to 6*

1 cup milk

1 cup heavy cream

½ cup sugar

3 egg yolks

2 tablespoons balsamic vinegar

Put the milk, cream, and sugar in a pan and heat it on a low flame so that it simmers. In a bowl, whisk the egg yolks. Take only a third of the heated milk mixture and add it to the yolks. Whisk them till the yolks get warm. Take the milk mixture off the heat. Then slowly add the yolk mixture into the remainin' milk mixture, whiskin' the entire time. Let cool down and then add the balsamic vinegar. Whisk one last time and put it in your ice cream freezer. Follow your freezer's instructions and enjoy. Just don't tell nobody what it is until they've had a bite! Then watch their faces.

*—OPAL LAMB-INMAN, LOT #1*

# INDEPENDENCE DAY (FOURTH OF JULY)
## July 4
### (A prison holiday)

Say what you want, but there is nothin' like a beautiful Independence Day in rural Arkansas. If you can get around the heat, which is a feat in itself, then there's so much fun to be had on this joyous day. We at the High Chaparral Trailer Park start it off by goin' down to Main Street to attend the annual Pangburn Fourth of July Parade. Five minutes later we're back at the trailer park and in a patriotic mood. We begin our festivities by havin' a midday potluck right out by the pool area. We don't stay there long on account of the flies bein' so attracted to the smell that comes from the pool water. Usually we all move out in front of the office. After getting a belly's full, all us ladies start up the homemade ice cream. You should see the park. Every trailer has an extension cord runnin' out of it with electric ice cream makers attached at the other end. This lets us ladies keep an eye on the ice cream while enjoyin' all the activities as well. We hold our traditional God Bless America Canasta Tournament on the Fourth of July right out in the streets. It's team play, and let me tell y'all it can get vicious and heated. By the time we've got a winner, the ice cream is done and everyone's cooled down.

I remember as a little girl when we'd go over to Granny and Pappy Boxcar's farm house they always make homemade ice cream. Back then they didn't have the electric kind but rather the kind you crank by hand. Well, nobody liked doin' all that so Pappy came up with this device that he'd connect to one end of the crank and the other end to their donkey, Jack. He'd tie a carrot to a pole and Jack would walk around in a circle tryin' to get it. Jack's walkin' was what cranked the handle. It was real brilliant. When Jack got too old to crank the ice cream, Granny would put a Twinkie on the stick, and a teenage Donna Sue in the harness. Oh, those were the days.

After the ice cream, we move into scattered games of horseshoes, checkers, or yard darts. Then around 4:00 P.M. we all lie down and nap for bit in our individual trailers. At 7:00 in the evenin' we regroup with our lawn chairs at the office, where Ben Beaver puts old standbys like "Stars and Strips Forever," "You're a Grand Old Flag," or "America the Beautiful" on the record player and all of us play along on our kazoos. Let me tell you, you've never heard anything as movin' as 30-some odd people kazooin' our national anthem. It'll make you weep.

As the sun sets in the west, we all drive into town for the annual Pangburn fireworks show, and 10 minutes later, unless somethin' catches on fire, we're back in our own front yards settin' off our stash of firecrackers, Roman candles, bottle rockets, and sparklers.

Yes, dear readers, in our little trailer park over in our little part of the world, we celebrate this holiday in the same old-fashioned way that it's always been honored. Of course we've learned to keep a bucket of water close by when Me-Ma handles a sparkler. We ain't stupid.

### Things to Get You in the Holiday Mood
Watch live picture of the Statue of Liberty at www.sccorp.com/cam.
Rent and watch the movies *1776,* and *Independence Day,*

### Things to Do
Set off fireworks.
Sing the "Star Spangled Banner" or at least as much of it as you know. If you put sparklers in your hair for effect, make sure you don't let 'em burn down too far, and give your do a quick once-over with a spray of fire retardant. Warnin': regardless of how good it might look, NEVER stick a Roman candle in your hair!

### How to Decorate Your Trailer for This Holiday
Once again, hang up a flag. This part shouldn't be that dang hard!

### Trailer Park Tradition
What would a Fourth of July be without the traditional throwin' of the firecrackers underneath the trailer of the meanest person in the park? Now, I don't mean just one pack of firecrackers. Oh, no, I'm talkin' the $15 stash! We want to scare the meanness out of that person, not make 'em think they got gas! Just be careful and remember: the only person that's supposed to get hurt is the trailer owner, not you.

*Somethin' to Bring to a Party*

## WANDA'S JUST LIKE DREAM CREAM VANILLA ICE CREAM

*I sure miss the Dream Cream, but thanks to this recipe, the pain isn't so bad.*

6 to 8 servin's

1 cup sugar

1 cup corn syrup

4 eggs

2 quarts half-and-half

1½ teaspoons vanilla extract

In a large bowl, add the sugar and corn syrup together. Usin' an electric mixer, mix 'em real good. Add an egg, and then another, and continue till you've got all of 'em in there. Keep mixin' with that mixer. Add a quart of the half-and-half, followed by the vanilla extract. Mix for another 3 minutes, and then pour into the canister of your ice cream maker. Add the rest of the half-and-half, but don't mix it—it'll get mixed when the machine turns on. Follow your ice cream freezer's instructions for the rest of the steps. When it's done, enjoy.

*—WANDA KAY, LOT #13*

*Dinner Menu*

## CONTINENTAL CONGRESS CUCUMBER DILL DIP

*This is real good with chips, veggies if you can stomach that kind of food, or even on top of a burger.*

8 ounces cream cheese, softened and smooth

1 cup mayonnaise

2 medium cucumbers, peeled, seeded, and chopped

3 tablespoons sliced scallions

1 tablespoon lemon juice

1 teaspoon dill

Dash of cayenne pepper to taste

Put the cream cheese in a bowl. If it ain't smooth, take an electric mixer to it. Add the mayo, cucumbers, scallions, lemon juice, dill, and cayenne pepper. Mix it up real good. If it's too thick, go ahead and add just a touch more mayo. Place it in the fridge so it can chill (about 30 minutes or so). If you use it outside, you might want to keep it covered and settin' in a bowl of ice so it stays cold.

*—JUANITA HIX, LOT #9*

## GOD BLESS AMERICA BURGERS

*If these are cooked any other day, she just calls 'em her St. Matthew Meatloaf Burgers.*

*Makes about 6 burgers*

2 pounds hamburger

1 cup crumbled crackers

1 egg

1 onion, diced

2 tablespoons brown sugar

1 teaspoon salt

½ teaspoon pepper

2 cups ketchup

Oil

Velveeta (if you want cheeseburgers)

Mix the hamburger, crackers, egg, onion, brown sugar, salt, pepper, and ketchup all together in a large bowl. Mix it up real good. Form it into balls, then patties. When you cook it, put a little oil on the grill so that the patties will flip easier. Cook for about 10 minutes on each side, or until completely cooked all the way through. Top with cheese if you want.

*—SISTER BERTHA, LOT #12*

# A MINUTE MAN REFRESHER

*A few of these will help fight the July heat!*

*Makes 4 drinks*

4 cups milk

8 tablespoons chocolate drink mix

20 Oreo cookies, crushed up

8 scoops homemade vanilla ice cream

6 shots of vodka

Get out your blender and put the milk and chocolate drink mix in it and blend. Now add the Oreos and blend. Put in half the ice cream and blend. Once that's smooth, add the rest of the ice cream and blend. Add the vodka. Blend. Pour into glasses and serve. If at any time it looks like you got too much stuff for your blender, dump some of it out into a bowl and use your hand mixer on it. Just make sure the vodka is evenly distributed.

*—DONNA SUE BOXCAR, LOT #6*

# Chapter 8

An aerial photo of me and my husband, Dew's,
weddin', circa 1990.

# *August*

The eighth month of the year was originally named Sextilis since at the time it was the sixth month on the weird Roman calendar. They later changed the calendar as well as the name. And as you already know, they took an entire day from February and put it on the end of August to give it 31 days.

August is known for three things: bein' the peak of summer, the busiest time of the year for vacations, and the continuin' of that dang heat! Needless to say, I count the days till September, when I can once again be that social butterfly without worryin' about gettin' prickly heat. Me and my husband, Dew, don't even take a vacation until the fall months. I love Walt Disney World and Disneyland as well as both them Universal Studios parks, but you won't catch my behind there until the weather's cooled, or the trip is free (I'll just pack the Gold Bond and suffer). I even cut back on my public appearances on account of the summer heat. Regardless of how attractive I might be and how lovely my singin' voice is, nobody wants to see a cow sweat. I looked like one of them dang Italian fountains with sweat just gushin' from every pore. It ain't pretty. But if I do have to go out of the trailer on those days I try to make it late in the evenin' and I spray on my makeup with one of them airbrush machines like they use on them T-shirts at the state fair.

So in the trailer park there is only *one* holiday that we celebrate and it wasn't my weddin' anniversary, I'd be sittin' in front of the TV set enjoy the air conditionin'. Oddly enough there are only two month-long holidays that pertain to food durin' the month of August. I guess that's on account of everyone bein' on vacation. So I've added a third that I think is appropriate. That's the only one I've included here.

August is:
*National State Fair Month*

## CARNY CORN DOGS

*Donna Sue always tells folks that she got this recipe from a carny that she picked up at the fair. What she doesn't mention is how the next mornin' when she woke up he had taken $27 in cash, two cheap flea-market rings, and a massagin' foot soaker. The last item was a surprise since most of her dates, with the exception of the dunk tank clown, don't get near water.*

*Makes 10 corn dogs*

1 cup flour
⅔ cup cornmeal
2 tablespoons sugar
1½ teaspoons bakin' powder
1 teaspoon salt
2 tablespoons shortenin'
1 tablespoon honey
1 egg, beaten
¾ cup milk
10 wieners
Oil for fryin'

Mix the flour, cornmeal, sugar, bakin' powder, and salt together in a bowl. Cut in the shortenin' until it gets crumbly.

In another bowl, combine the honey, egg, and milk; mix well. Pour it into the flour mixture and mix well, makin' sure there are no lumps. Dip your wieners, which now have skewer sticks or chopsticks in 'em, down into the batter. Deep fry 'em in oil at 375 degrees F. until they're nice and brown. Let 'em drain on a paper towel. Serve with mustard or whatever else you like on your corn dog.

*—DONNA SUE BOXCAR, LOT #6*

*National Peach Month*

## GEORGIA ON MY MIND SALAD

*Lovie says Jimmy Carter always asks her to make
a batch of this when he's comin' to town.*

4 to 6 servin's
2 chicken breasts, cooked and diced
½ cup chopped celery
1 (16 ounce) can of peaches, drained and chopped
3 ounces softened cream cheese
¼ cup mayonnaise
¼ teaspoon dried basil
¼ teaspoon salt
Put it all in a big bowl, mix it up, and put it in the fridge to chill.
—*LOVIE BIRCH, LOT #20*

*National Catfish Month*

## BROTHER WOODY'S CATFISH RECIPE

*Personally, if it ain't Long John Silver's or Red
Lobster, I won't eat fish, but everybody just raves
about this dish.*

*The amount this makes depends on how much catfish you done got.*
Catfish fillets
1 egg

1½ cups milk

¼ teaspoon pepper

1½ teaspoons salt

½ teaspoon cayenne pepper

2 cups cornmeal

Beat the egg and pour it into the milk in a bowl. Mix well.

Put everything else in a plastic bag and shake till it's mixed up real good. Dip your fish fillets in the egg/milk mixture and them drop it in the bag. Shake real good. Take each piece out and put it in hot grease to cook until brown. Drain on paper towel or newspaper.

*—BROTHER WOODY BEE, LOT #7*

# RUBY ANN BOXCAR AND DEW BALLZAK'S
## WEDDIN' ANNIVERSARY
### August 24
(Unless it falls on a weekend, this is not a prison holiday)

I know I broke many a heart when I said "I do" on that hot August day in 1990, but I didn't care. Just a month before, I fell in love with my dream weaver. Sure we were both on in our years by then, but no one said you have to marry young. Now don't get me wrong, we were both real good catches, but there had been reasons as to why we had waited to hitch our trailer with someone else. I'd always put my career in the field of cosmetology and then later entertainin' first before my own personal joy, unless of course food was involved. And Dew had never married on account of him bein' so dang shy. I think it's important to also remember that neither one of us had met the person that made our hearts go "zing" either. But by that blessed day when we stood in front of the preacher, our hearts were goin' "zing" and even "zang" with an occasional "zung" from time to time.

Our weddin' was very beautiful. Dew wanted a traditional church weddin', but since neither the First Baptist Church of Pangburn nor the Belcher Baptist Church in Dew's hometown of Belcher was big enough to hold all those who'd want to witness our nuptials, we were forced to go elsewhere. Of course it wouldn't be right to ask a larger church to let us come in with our own preacher so we unfortunately had to go with a non-church venue. We could've been married outside by the spot along the river where we first met, but there was no way I was goin' to stand in that heat. It was August after all, and I was at my wit's end when it came to a place for our weddin'. That's when Jeannie Janssen over in lot #19 came up with a brilliant idea. We could rent out the Dusty Comet Auto Park Drive-In. It was big enough for all the guests, which bein' the star that I was by that point in my life meant there were many, and if it was done just right, I could stay cool. Needless to say, the weddin' was on!

Dusty Comet opened his drive-in at 3:30 and by five minutes to 4:00 all 68 spaces had been filled, which amazed us all since the weddin' wasn't slotted to play until 4:30. Of course this didn't upset old Dusty in the least, especially when the concession stand registers started ringin'. He did almost

$300 and all he had ready was popcorn and sodas. If his Dusty Comet Chilidogs'd been ready, he'd have made a killin'.

Nellie Tinkle, who along with her portable keyboard was in the air-conditioned projection booth, entertained the weddin' guests with a lineup of everyone's favorite oldies. These tunes were broadcast directly to all the cars through the portable drive-in speakers. Right at 4:20, Pastor Hickey arrived in his gold Cadillac and drove right up to the front by the playground. After a few maneuvers, he had his car facin' toward the others. Once Pastor Hickey's car was in place, Dew pulled in, drivin' his beat-up black Ford pickup truck, followed by his best man in a 1972 Pontiac Le Mans. They all parked their cars up by Pastor Hickey's. Then came my bridesmaids in a vivid salmon-colored Ford Pinto. They parked just to the left of the screen by the swing set up front. And as Nellie let into the Weddin' March, I made my way down each of the aisles in a white 1987 Oldsmobile. It was very touchin' for me, especially when all the guests turned their headlights on as I weaved in and out of the each lane, finally parkin' right next to Dew's Ford. He looked over from his truck and winked at me. I was like a lovesick schoolgirl. I winked back and blew him a kiss. When Nellie ended her musical selection, Pastor Hickey pushed the button on his CB radio microphone and said, "Dearly beloved, we are gathered here today in the sight of God to join this here woman and that there man in holy matrimony." As those words blared over my CB in my car as well as Dew's and the portable drive-in car speakers, I still couldn't believe I was finally hearin' those words in reference to me. The whole ceremony was just beautiful. And there was only four or five times when a trucker came over askin' for our "10–20" or if we'd seen any "smokies up ahead." When it came time for the rings, we put our hands out the windows and put 'em on each other's fingers. It was very romantic. The only hitch happened just before Pastor Hickey had announced me and Dew man and wife. My sister, Donna Sue, who'd had to work that night at the Blue Whale Strip Club, came racin' into that drive-in like a bat out of hell in her Dodge Dart. Before you could say "breathalyzer," she'd rear-ended the bridesmaids' car. Their Pinto went up like a ball of fire. Luckily the gals got out in time and there was not much damage done to Donna Sue's car, but all the guests jumped out and started a bucket brigade from the concession stand in order to put out the Pinto. When the excitement was over, and everyone had returned to their cars, Pastor Hickey announced us as man and wife. I leaned out my passenger's side window and Dew leaned out his driver's side and we finally sealed our weddin' vows with a brief but passionate kiss. Of course all the cars started honkin' like crazy as me and Dew drove off with our cars side by side. While Dew and I got situated in the concession stand drive-thru so all the guests could drive up and give us our gifts and their best wishes, Pastor Hickey, with Nellie Tinkle on the keyboard, gave an altar call. I was later told that three cars went down that day and then after the dismissal, followed Pastor Hickey down to the car wash for baptism.

Dew and I spent our honeymoon in Tulsa, Oklahoma, on account of me havin' to emcee a beauty contest that next evenin'. As soon as I get a chance, I'll post on my www.rubyann.org website some of the beautiful aerial weddin' photos that were taken by our weddin' photographer.

### Things to Get You in the Holiday Mood
Rent and watch one of those beach movies that were hits at drive-ins.
Visit www.driveintheater.com/index.htm or www.drive-ins.com.

### Things to Do
Pop some popcorn and think of me and my husband, Dew, while you eat it.
Wash your car.
Go to a drive-in with someone you love.

### How to Decorate Your Trailer for This Holiday
I put out little bowls of Jujubes and Junior Mints.

### Trailer Park Tradition
We traditionally ask that you don't send gifts in honor of our weddin' anniversary, but rather that you just make a monetary donation in the form of cash or a money order to me and my husband, Dew. You can send that along with your anniversary card to Citadel Publishin' and they will be happy to forward it to Pangburn.

*Somethin' to Bring to a Party*

## DUSTY COMET BUTTERED POPCORN

*It only takes a handful of this to know why it sells
so well.*

*Makes 2 servin's*

¼ cup margarine

½ teaspoon salt

2 teaspoons sugar

6 cups popped popcorn

Put the first 3 ingredients in a pot and heat over a medium fire. Stir until the sugar has dissolved. Take off the heat, and let sit for 5 minutes. Pour over freshly popped popcorn and serve.

—*DUSTY COMET AUTO PARK DRIVE-IN*

*Dinner Menu*

## COMET RINGS

*I'd actually paid to get into the drive-in while*
Glitter *was showin' just to get to the concession
stand for an order of these.*

*Makes 4 to 6 great big drive-in-size servin's*

3 cups flour

1 teaspoon bakin' soda

1 teaspoon bakin' powder

1 egg

1 teaspoon celery salt

1 teaspoon garlic salt

1 teaspoon onion salt

1 pint milk

4 onions, peeled and sliced

3 teaspoons seasonin' salt

Oil for fryin'

Ketchup packets, for servin'

Put all the ingredients but the onions and seasonin' salt in a bowl and use an electric mixer to mix up the batter. Now dip the onions in the batter, and, after coatin' 'em, deep-fat fry 'em in some hot oil. Drain on paper towels and sprinkle on the seasonin' salt. Serve with ketchup packets.

—*DUSTY COMET AUTO PARK DRIVE-IN*

## DUSTY COMET CHILI CHEESE DOGS

*People come all the way from Conway to get a bite
of this.*

*Makes 8*

8 wieners

3 teaspoons garlic salt

1 pound ground beef

1 onion, diced real small

½ teaspoon minced garlic

3 tablespoons mustard

1 cup ketchup

2 teaspoons chili powder

1 teaspoon salt

8 buns

Sweet relish

2 cups shredded American cheese

Take a large pan and fill it up to about three quarters full with water. Add your wieners and the garlic salt, and cover. Put it on the stove and bring it to a boil. Let it cook for 15 minutes like that. Reduce the heat and let simmer till you' ready to serve.

Put the ground beef in a skillet and break it up. Add the onion and brown 'em together. Drain. Add the minced garlic, mustard, ketchup, chili powder, and salt. Stir it up and let it simmer for 15 minutes.

Take your wieners out, put 'em on a paper towel, and roll 'em around to get off excess water, then put 'em on buns. Add the sauce from the chili and top each with a tablespoon of relish and 2 tablespoons of cheese. Loosely wrap each one up in foil for 2 minutes. This will get the cheese nice and soft and let the relish and sauce become friends.

*—DUSTY COMET AUTO PARK DRIVE-IN*

## THE COMET'S OUT OF THIS WORLD HOT FUDGE MILKSHAKE

*Now you can enjoy one of these before it gets dark outside.*

*Makes 1 shake*

4 scoops vanilla ice cream

1½ cups milk

4 tablespoons hot fudge sauce

1 teaspoon vanilla extract

Put everything in a blender and let it go to town until it is nice and smooth.

*—DUSTY COMET AUTO PARK DRIVE-IN*

# Chapter 9

While Ben Beaver prepares his pontoon boat, some of the
gals keep an eye on the Labor Day wieners (Bertha Faye,
Wanda, Wendy, Connie, Juanita, Nellie, and Kitty).

# *September*

The ninth month of the year has had 30 days in it since Augustus ruled back in them Roman times. Back then they knew this month as Septem, which as you've guessed by now means seven. Once again, when the Romans played with the calendar they didn't change the names of the months. That's them Italians for you!

I love September. The weather is cool enough for me to come out of my self-imposed hibernation for public viewin'. Plus I know that fall, which is my favorite season of the year, is just around the corner. It also marks harvest time, and the smell of the crops after they've been cut is just wonderful around our trailer area. I'm not sure if it's wheat, barley, or even oats, for that matter. If it don't come ready to eat, I can't tell what the heck it is, but it sure smells good.

This month we'll be doin' three special holidays. The first one originated in New York City and today is celebrated in both the U.S. and Canada. The second is a birthday celebration for both our neighbors in the south and one of the sexiest people around. Third is another holiday that welcomes in a New Year. And of course, as usual, here are the month-long holidays that help you fill in the gaps.

September is:
*National Chicken Month*

## TRAILER PARK CHICKEN BAKE

*This is one of Kitty's specialties.*

*4 to 6 servin's*
2 boxes chicken dressin'
4 chicken breasts, cooked and cut into pieces
¼ cup margarine
¾ cup flour
1 quart chicken broth
1 teaspoon salt
6 eggs, beaten
Bread crumbs

Follow the instructions on the box to make the dressin'. Grease up a casserole dish and put the dressin' along the bottom of it. Top this with the chicken.

In a pan over medium heat, add the margarine. When it melts, whisk in the flour, the chicken broth, and the salt. Whisk constantly until it gets thick, then add the eggs. Once it's stirred well, pour it over the chicken. Sprinkle bread crumbs on top of this, and bake for 45 minutes at 350 degrees F.

*National Honey Month*

## BEN BEAVER'S HONEY MUSTARD DRESSIN'

*This is so good, when you serve it, you'll have bees
knockin' on your door. Refrigerate this, and don't
keep it around for more than a coupla days.*

*Makes about three cups*
1 cup mayonnaise
¾ cup honey
¼ cup mustard
1 teaspoon dried dill weed

¼ teaspoon salt

½ teaspoon garlic powder

Put it all in a bowl and mix until smooth.

—*BEN BEAVER, LOT #14*

*National Rice Month*

## TINA FAYE'S PORCUPINE BALLS

*Donna Sue dated a man with porcupine balls. He was addicted to 'em. Everywhere he went, he always carried a few with him.*

*Makes about a dozen juicy, prickly balls*

1 pound ground beef

½ cup uncooked rice

1 teaspoon salt

1 teaspoon pepper

1½ tablespoons Worcestershire sauce

1 (15 ounce) can of tomato sauce

Mix everything but the tomato sauce together. Shape into little balls and put 'em in a casserole dish. Pour the tomato sauce over 'em and bake for 1 hour at 350 degrees F.

—*TINA FAYE STOPENBLOTTER, LOT #17*

# LABOR DAY
## The first Monday in September.
(Not a prison holiday)

Typically we have a little cookout at the High Chaparral. It's nothin' big, just your everyday BBQ for 60 people. Mind you, we only have 30-some residents, but Lord almighty can we eat! This year, however, Ben Beaver asked us if we'd all like to go down to the lake and ride on his big pontoon boat. It'd most likely be the last time he could use it this year. Of course we all said yes, and grabbed the wieners and other assorted food items and headed down to the water. As luck would have it, Pastor Hickey and his wife as well as their son, little Dick Hickey, were down at the lake enjoyin' Labor Day (it wasn't until the next Sunday that the truth would come out and we'd get rid of him). We couldn't help but ask 'em to join us; after all, he was our preacher for the time bein'. Anyways, we cooked up the wieners on the bank of the lake and before we ate, Sister Bertha asked Pastor Hickey to say a prayer. Well, not only did he pray, but since he was by a body of water, he gave a call for baptism. I don't know if it was the sun or what, but Harland Hix and Lulu Bell both went down to be re-baptized. Harland went in, then under, and back out in record time, but Lulu Bell was a different story all together. Pastor Hickey had the hardest time with her on account of the fact that she won't take off her life preserver for nothin' when she's close to water. Poor old Pastor Hickey did everything but sit on her face in an attempt to get her head under the water. Finally, out of sheer desperation, he went under the water, grabbed her ankles, and turned her over on her head. He said his baptizin' words and then flipped her back over like a teeter totter. Of course we had to put the wieners back on the grill to reheat 'em, but once they were warm, we all filled our plates and loaded up on Ben's pontoon boat. Lulu Bell, who decided she'd had enough water activities for the day, as well as Ben, both decided to stay ashore. We waved goodbye and puttered out toward the middle of the lake. We hadn't gotten 10 feet from the dock when the pontoon boat of fun turned into the ship of fools. You see, Momma saw a dollar floatin' out by the boat. Since Momma uses that 10-10-220, she knows the value of a dollar so she bent over to get it. Well, somehow her less-than-petite figure caused the weight on the boat to shift, makin' the whole front end-dive under the water. Before you could say "man overboard," that thing had noise-dived straight toward the bottom. There were wieners flyin' through the air and people screamin' for their lives. I'm tellin' you, it was like a scene out of that movie *Titanic*. We was all goin' down, or so we thought. But after we'd lost a few brave souls to the murky deep, the weight re-shifted and the boat popped right back up. We was saved, but at what cost. Immediately folks had noticed that loved ones were missin'. "Where's Me-Ma?" Donna Sue yelled. Before I could start to look, some-one said she's over there in that cooler. Somehow she'd managed to get her bottom stuck in the cooler and was safely floatin' back to shore. Thank God she was fine, but what about the others? It was then that all of a sud-den Opal Lamb-Inman came rushin' up out of the water like one of them submarine rockets. That amount of ugly comin' flyin' up out of the water was enough to send all of us scurryin' to the other end of the boat in fright. Of course we once again went under along with the pontoon boat, but this time, on account of the lack of weight on the opposite side, the whole thing flipped over. It was the *Poseidon Adventure* all over again, but without a good theme song. Well, long story short, everybody was fine. Bein' the lady that I am, I managed to get through the whole thing with-out gettin' my hair or makeup wet, thus savin' my Labor Day do from get-tin' water-logged. Donna Sue blew on the rescue whistle that she always keeps with her, and two men who recognized her from the Blue Whale jumped in to save her. She thought one was gettin' all fresh with her, but once they made it to shore, it turned out to be nothin' more than a snap-pin' turtle with no taste. Hubert Bunch and Mickey Ray managed to get Ben's boat back to shore, and with a little maneuverin' got it back on its right side. By then, some of the kids at the lake had managed to get out in the water and rounded up most of the wieners that floated on the surface. We heated 'em back up, and just like the survivors of nautical tragedies gone by, we got back to our lives and our soggy wieners.

*Things to Get You in the Holiday Mood*
Watch videos of your baby bein' born.

*Things to Do*
Go boatin', have a cookout, go to a store and watch people labor.
Pick up employment applications for those deadbeat relatives.

*How to Decorate Your Trailer for This Holiday*
Hey, it's Labor Day. Take it easy.

*Trailer Park Tradition*
Well, it ain't goin' out on a boat, I can tell you that. As long as the horror and mental scars of almost drownin' are still vivid in our minds, we will most likely just BBQ at the trailer park, but not by the pool. But who knows? This time next year we may have completely forgotten about it.

*Somethin' to Bring to a Party*

# BUTTERMILK SALAD

*This is another one of those dishes that I don't think I'd leave out in the hot September sun for very long.*

6 to 8 servin's
1 large can of crushed pineapple
2 small boxes of cherry Jell-O
½ cup nuts
2 cups buttermilk
1 tub of Cool Whip
Put the pineapple, juice and all, in a pan and heat it up. Add the Jell-O. Mix well and let it cool. Add the buttermilk, the nuts, and the Cool Whip. Mix well, cover, and put in the fridge for at least 6 hours so it can set.
—*DOTTIE LAMB, LOT #14*

*Dinner Menu*

## OLLIE WHITE'S OLD-FASHIONED ZUCCHINI CHEESE BAKE

*Just the smell alone takes me back to when I was a little girl askin' the school cooks for more. By the way, I already cut it down for you.*

*Makes 4 to 6 servin's*

1 regular can of crushed tomatoes

2 zucchini, sliced

2 yellow squash, sliced

⅛ teaspoon dried thyme

½ teaspoon dried basil

¼ teaspoon garlic powder

½ cup shredded Cheddar cheese

½ cup grated Parmesan cheese

⅓ cup bread crumbs

1 cup mozzarella cheese

Mix the first 7 ingredients in a bowl. Once it's all mixed up, put it in a casserole dish and top with the next 2 items. Bake at 350 degrees F. for 45 minutes. Pull it out and top it with the mozzarella cheese. Let it set for 5 to 10 minutes so the cheeses can settle.

*—OLLIE WHITE, LOT #10*

## NO-STICK CORN DOG CASSEROLE

*Another way to cook your wieners!*

2 cups thinly sliced celery

2 tablespoons margarine

2 cups chopped onions

1½ pounds wieners

2 eggs

1½ cups milk

¼ teaspoon pepper

2 tablespoons sugar

2 packages of corn bread/muffin mix

2 cups shredded Cheddar cheese

Mustard

Sauté the celery in margarine for 6 minutes. Add the onions and cook for another 5 minutes. Set aside.

Take your wieners and chop 'em up into little bite-size pieces. Put your wieners in a skillet and cook 'em till they're lightly brown. Mix with the veggies.

Stir together the eggs, milk, pepper, and sugar. Add the wieners and veggies and mix well. Stir in the corn bread mix. Add the cheese. Put into a casserole dish and bake for 30 minutes at 400 degrees F. When finished, take out and top with a thin layer of mustard.

—*OPAL LAMB-INMAN, LOT #1*

## FAYE FAYE'S "EASY AS ME" CHOCOLATE PEANUT BUTTER FUDGE

*If the name is true, then a dang monkey could make this fudge.*

*Makes 1 batch*

1 cup semisweet chocolate morsels

½ cup peanut butter

25 marshmallows

Melt your chocolate and peanut butter in the microwave. Follow this by meltin' your marshmallows in a microwave as well. Mix it all together and put in a pan. Throw it in the fridge. When it's hardened, eat it!

—*FAYE FAYE LARUE, LOT #17*

# MEXICAN INDEPENDENCE DAY/
# RUBY ANN'S BIRTHDAY
### September 16
#### (Unless it falls on a weekend, it's not a prison holiday)

Needless to say, this is one of my favorite days of the year as well as one of the favorite days in both the United States and Mexico. Go anywhere in either of those countries and you'll be hard-pressed not to find a party in honor of the Mexican celebration. And of course with my newfound fame, I was told that there were several parties this past September that incorporated both my birthday and Mexican Independence Day all in one, which is exactly what we've been doin' for years at the High Chaparral Trailer Park. Of course this year was a little bit more elaborate since we actually had a full-blooded Mexican amongst us, Opal and Dick's live-in maid, Fernando.

This year Ben Beaver, the manager of the High Chaparral, asked Fernando if he'd mind puttin' together our traditional September 16 festivities. Needless to say he was thrilled. It seems Fernando just loves throwin' parties as well as decoratin' and interior design. Who'd have guessed? All this time I thought he was just a simple maid, but I was wrong. Well, I put a list together in order to help him plan my birthday part of the whole shindig. On it I told him what kind of cake I liked (vanilla), what my favorite frostin' was (butter cream), what kind of ice cream I liked (either cookie dough or peanut-butter cup), as well as other favorite things that I wanted. I took it over to Opal and Dick's trailer, knocked on the door, and Fernando answered. I told him what I'd done, and then handed him the list. He took one look at it, then looked me up and down, said somethin' in Mexican, which I think meant "thank you," and shut the door. He was obviously too busy plannin' the event or doin' maid work to ask me in, and I totally understood. I knew that whatever Fernando did would be just wonderful. And was I ever right!

At 10:00 in the mornin' the High Chaparral Trailer Park was awakened by the loud burst of a trumpet section, which then immediately went into a festive gay Mariachi melody. It quickly became apparent as we came out into the trailer court that the music was bellowin' from the park's PA system. And as we approached the office buildin', we were surprised to see tables decorated in green, yellow, and red, the colors of the Mexican flag. A big white banner hung from the office that read "Viva Mexico! Viva la Revolucion! Viva la Independencia," which Fernando told us meant "Happy Mexican Independence Day." And the next line down below that read "Ruby Ann es una estupida culona," which accordin' to Fernando is Mexican for "Happy Birthday, Ruby Ann." Needless to say, I was just touched. Fernando went on to serve us a real Mexican breakfast, which was followed by games that he'd come up with in honor of my birthday. He'd drawn a picture of what I looked like me from behind and stuck a photo of my head on it. He hung it up on the side of the office and called it "pin the tail on Ruby Ann Boxcar." If you think that was creative, you should have seen how he took some tin cans and pasted little drawin's of me on 'em. He put these over on a bench back by the swimmin' pool, and let folks shoot at 'em. If you got three Rubys, you won a prize. Oh, it was just like goin' to the carnival. He'd even made a kind of dunk tank where you could throw a ball at a target, and if you hit it, a Ruby Ann look-a-like life-size doll with a rope around it's neck would fall off a platform and dangle just above the water. It was really somethin'.

The Taco Tackle Shack catered lunch and dinner. At the end of the day, Fernando brought out a traditional piñata, which had been made to look just like me. Of course, since he had gone to the trouble to make this day special for me, I insisted that he be the one to do the swingin'. He happily agreed and pulled out a baseball bat. Boy did he have a good time, smilin' with each blow to my papier-mâché effigy. After he'd beaten that thing to a pulp, and we'd collected all the candy that had fallen to the ground, it was time for the cake and ice cream. With the Mexican tunes still playin' in the background, Fernando wheeled out a large sheet cake that had a caricature of me surrounded by Mexican soldiers with rifles. Even though there were 30 candles too many on the cake, it was still a wonderful treat, as was the whole day. It will certainly be hard to top this year's celebration, but if anyone can do it, I'm sure it'll be Fernando.

### Things to Get You in the Holiday Mood
Send me a birthday card.
Go get your hair done. Tell 'em you want to look just like Ruby Ann Boxcar.
Visit my web page at www.rubyann.org.

### Things to Do
Buy my books and give them to friends.
Eat at a Mexican restaurant.

### How to Decorate Your Trailer for This Holiday
Put up photos of me all over your house.

### Trailer Park Tradition
At the High Chaparral our Avon lady and Mary Kay consultant is one and the same, but that is rare in trailer parks around the world. In those parks they invite the separate Avon lady and Mary Kay to throw parties at the same trailer as well as at the same time in my honor. What eventually happens is that the two gals will go at each others throat before the night is over, givin' you and your guests plenty of time to take at least several cosmetic samples without anyone knowin'.

### Somethin' to Bring to a Party

## TACO TACKLE SHACK TACO DIP

*You should see me try to say this tongue-twister when I order it.*

*Makes about 5 cups*

16 ounces sour cream
1 package of taco mix
Three packets of taco sauce that you got from one of them fast-food places
Shredded lettuce
1 regular can of diced tomatoes
2 cups shredded Cheddar cheese
1 small onion, chopped
Tortilla chips

Combine the sour cream, taco mix, and the taco sauce together in a bowl, and let it chill, covered for 1½ hours. Spread this in the bottom of a bakin' dish. Startin' with the lettuce, top it with other ingredients one at a time. Serve with tortilla chips.

*—LOIS BUNCH, LOT #12*

*Dinner Menu*

# SEXY SENORITA CHEESE SPREAD

*Fernando actually called this the Old Cheese
Cow Spread, but I think the new name is more
appetizin'.*

*10 to 12 servin's*

2 cups Velveeta (get the Mexican kind), sliced and diced into thin
    pieces

8 ounces cream cheese, softened

1 can of deviled-ham spread

2 tablespoons chopped green onions

2 tablespoons milk

½ teaspoon Worcestershire sauce

Mix it all together and chill for 6 hours. Serve with corn chips.

*—FERNANDO DIAZ, LOT #1*

# RUBY ANN'S BIG OLD BIRTHDAY BURRITOS

*These are so good I ate four at one time and
passed out for a few minutes. I did notice that the
burritos Fernando gave me had an almond smell
to 'em, but there ain't no almonds in this recipe.*

*Makes 8 burritos*

2 pounds hamburger meat

1½ tablespoons chili powder

½ teaspoon ground cumin

½ teaspoon salt

¼ teaspoon pepper

1 package frozen chopped spinach, thawed and drained

1¼ cups salsa

2 cups shredded Cheddar cheese

8 flour tortillas, warmed

Fry the meat in a pan, stirrin' now and then to get out the lumps. Add the
chili powder, cumin, salt, and pepper to your cooked meat. Mix well. Add

the spinach and salsa. Turn on the heat and cook for a few minutes more, makin' sure that everything is nice and hot. Add the cheese and stir. Put an equal amount of the mixture on each tortilla, and fold, then serve.

*—FERNANDO DIAZ, LOT #1*

# J. LO SWEET BUNS

*I think little old Fernando has a crush on this gal. Opal says he's got his bedroom covered with pictures of her, and every time one of her songs comes on, he always pretends that he's singin' it.*

*Makes 18 warm buns*

1 package of active dry yeast

¾ cup warm water

1¾ cups sugar

3 tablespoons margarine, melted

2 eggs, beaten

Salt

4½ cups all-purpose flour

1 teaspoon ground cinnamon

½ cup margarine

1 egg yolk

In a large bowl, dissolve the yeast in the warm water. Give it around 5 minutes, then add ¾ cup sugar, the melted margarine, the eggs, and ½ teaspoon salt. Usin' an electric mixer, mix at medium speed until well blended. Add 3½ cups of the flour. Place the sticky dough into a greased bowl. Turn it so the dough gets greased, then cover it and put it in a warm place to rise for 1½ hours.

In a bowl, mix 1 cup sugar, the remaining cup of flour, the cinnamon, and ⅛ teaspoon salt together. Then cut in the margarine. Add the egg yolk and mix. Divide this into eighteen sections and set aside.

Punch the covered dough down and put it on a floured countertop so you can knead it for 2 minutes. Divide it into eighteen equal pieces and shape 'em into balls. Take two greased cookie sheets and put balls about 2 inches apart. Lightly squash each ball down just a bit. Take each of the 18 little sugar pieces you set aside earlier and roll 'em into balls. Flatten those out and place 'em on top of each dough piece, makin' sure they cover the entire top of the dough section. Take a sharp kitchen knife and cut a cross halfway through the whole thing. Cover the pans and put them in a warm place for 35 minutes. Uncover and bake for 10 minutes at 400 degrees F. Serve with milk and margarine.

*—FERNANDO DIAZ, LOT #1*

# ROSH HASHANAH
## It falls sometime in September.
### (Unless it falls on a weekend, it is not a prison holiday)

Happy Rosh Hashanah to all my friends out there. This special day marks the Jewish New Year all across the world. Now, what in the heck happened to their calendar, I really don't know. I thought them Chinese were crazy for celebratin' their New Year's as late as they did, but, God bless 'em, some folks just ain't real good with keepin' track of time. Take my momma for instance. If we're all goin' out to the Sizzler at 6:00 in the evenin', you've got to tell Momma that it's at 3:00 if you want her ready in time. I swear, if she wasn't good conversation, sometimes I'd just as soon leave her when she ain't ready.

Anyways, from what I hear, Rosh Hashanah is a real big thing in the lives of the Jewish people, and is followed by a whole series of holidays until they get to what's called Yom Kippur or the Day of Atonement. On Rosh Hashanah, a person of the Jewish faith will ask for forgiveness and pray that God grants them a good year. Now although I am a good Baptist woman and have never been to one of these celebrations, I do keep up with other faiths includin' Judaism. Plus Donna Sue dated this fella who was a world traveler and had been to the Holy Land many times. Actually you couldn't mention a place or a name without him sayin' that he'd been there or met 'em. And he'd done so many kinds of different jobs like brain surgeon to rocket scientist that the fella could've written a book about his life if the U.S. Government hadn't sworn him to secrecy. Anyways, accordin' to him, the celebration actually starts on Rosh Hashanah Eve. Since the days go from sunset to sunset in the Jewish faith, that means that Rosh Hashanah Eve would be durin' the day right around 6:00, 7:00, or 8:00 P.M. in the evenin'.

I guess this is quite the party. Accordin' to Donna Sue's date at the time, all the Jews in Jerusalem gather at the Wailing Wall in observance of this comin' holiday. I guess it's just jam-packed. And on the TV they got live coverage with a fella named Dick Clarkberg who entertains the viewers that could not make it to the Wailing Wall. As the sun starts to set, this Dick Clarkberg and all in attendance count down the remainin' seconds. And then, right at that moment, durin' the last few seconds, a giant matzoh ball starts to descend down this long pole, and when it hits the bottom of the pole, everyone yells "Happy Rosh Hashanah!" They drink a glass of Mogen David Concord Wine, give that special loved one a big Rosh Hashanah kiss, and blow on their ram's horns. From what that fella said, it's quite the deal. People are singin' and dancin' out in the streets. It sounds like a good time is had by all.

You know I just found out while I was writin' this section that Mickey Ray over in lot #13 is a big Rams fan and has told me that if I ever get a chance to attend the Jewish New Year in the Holy Land, he'll loan me his official Rams' horn. He says the only thing is you have to be careful not to blow it at anyone cause it could make 'em deaf. It is just a boat horn with a fancy cover on it, after all. Watch out Jerusalem. This party girl may be comin' your way next year!

### Things to Get You in the Holiday Mood
Rent and watch the movie *Exodus.*
Read the creation story in Genesis so you can get a feel of what the first Rosh
    Hashanah was like.

### Things to Do
Light the menorah. Hey, why not use it twice a year?

### How to Decorate Your Trailer for This Holiday
Remember all them matzohs you bought but can't stomach to eat. Attach 'em to fishin' wire and hang 'em from the ceilin'.

Carefully punch holes in matzoh balls and put 'em on a sting of Christmas lights. You can hang these throughout the trailer, but be advised that burnt matzoh balls don't smell all that good. Don't hang 'em outside, 'cause when I did that last year, it was like a scene out of the movie *The Birds* with them winged bastards dive-bombin' me for them matzoh balls like some crazed kamikaze pilots. It was terrible. Who knew hummingbirds could be so vicious or suicidal?

### Trailer Park Tradition
As soon as we can find somebody in the county that is Jewish, we're goin' to take 'em a big pot of Hoppin' John with the black-eyed peas in 'em. We don't want 'em to miss out on good luck in the comin' year.

*Somethin' to Bring to a Party*

## APPLE SOUR CREAM COFFEE CAKE

*With good food like this, who cares how late in
the year New Year's might come?*

6 to 8 servin's

1 cup margarine

1 cup granulated sugar

3 eggs

1 cup sour cream

1 teaspoon vanilla extract

2½ cups sifted all-purpose flour

2 teaspoons bakin' powder

1 teaspoon bakin' soda

½ teaspoon salt

1 regular can of apple pie fillin'

⅓ cup raisins

1¼ teaspoon grounded cinnamon

½ cup packed brown sugar

⅓ cup finely chopped nuts

Cream your margarine and sugar in a bowl, then add the eggs individually, mixin' after each egg. Add the sour cream and vanilla extract and stir.

In a separate bowl, combine your flour, bakin' powder, soda, and salt. Make sure it's mixed well. Fold it into the egg mixture.

Grease up and flour a casserole dish, then take half the mixture and put it in this dish. Spread it till it's even. Add the pie fillin' and spread it too. Toss your raisins over this followed by the rest of the mixture.

In a small bowl, combine the cinnamon, brown sugar, and nuts. Sprinkle this mixture over the top and bake for 30 minutes at 375 degrees F.

*—FAYE FAYE LARUE, LOT 17*

*Dinner Menu*

# CHICKEN FRICASSEE

*Nobody here at the High Chaparral Trailer Park*
*knows what "fricassee" means.*

*Feeds 4 to 8*

½ cup flour

⅔ cup oil

2½ pounds chicken breast, diced

2 tablespoons minced garlic

½ cup chopped celery

2 tablespoons sugar

Salt and pepper

2 quarts warm water

½ cup chopped bell pepper

2 tablespoons parsley flakes

1 small can of mushrooms

Take a big pot and put the flour and oil in it. Put it over medium heat and stir until the mixture becomes brown. Add the chicken and stir it, makin' sure it all gets covered real good. Now add your garlic, celery, sugar, salt and pepper to taste and the water. Cover and let it cook on that medium heat for 40 minutes. Take off the cover and put in the bell pepper, parsley flakes, and mushrooms. Cook for 15 more minutes.

*—NELLIE TINKLE, LOT #4*

# FAYE FAYE LARUE'S
# "COME AND GET IT HONEY" CAKE

*After one of these I now know why so many men go*
*out with a woman who can tie her breast in a knot.*

6 to 8 servin's

6 eggs

½ cup sugar

¾ cup oil

1 pound honey

6 cups sifted flour

4 teaspoons bakin' powder

2 teaspoons bakin' soda

1 cup coffee

⅓ cup whiskey

½ teaspoon grated nutmeg

1 teaspoon allspice

Ground cinnamon

In a bowl, combine the eggs, sugar, and oil. Mix well, then add the honey. In a separate bowl, combine all the dry ingredients and spices.

Add the coffee and whiskey to the egg mixture, alternatin' with the dry ingredients. Mix well.

Pour into a greased bakin' dish. Bake at 350 degrees F. for 1 hour. Give it the old toothpick test.

*—FAYE FAYE LARUE, LOT #17*

# Chapter 10

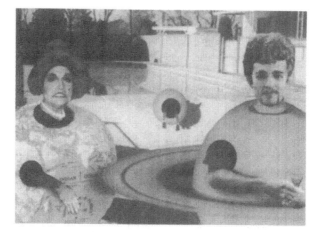

From lots #14 and #1 are Dottie Lamb as Earth with her son-in-law,
Dick Inman, as Saturn and a fallen Fernando Diaz as Uranus.

# *October*

Originally the eighth month of the year, October was named after its position in the early Roman calendar. As we all know, it got moved around, but kept its initial name even though it no longer made sense. It also kept all of its 31 days as well.

I start to do a lot less reachin' for the Gold Bond come October. With the beautiful weather that goes from nice sunny days to cool evenin's, October is one of the nicest months temperature-wise for most people. It's almost like an omen or forwarnin' that old Jack Frost and his frozen fingers are just around the corner. But of course, before he can make his glorious entrance all dressed up in white, the leaves must first do their dyin' dance of color that I find to be so beautiful. Even though the leaves in Arkansas aren't to be believed, I someday hope to make it to the East Coast to view what I've been told is as close to Heaven in fall as you can get without passin' on.

We actually celebrate a combination of two holidays to form one great big one around the end of this month. And we've got a few month-long celebrations in the meantime.

October is:
*National Country Music Month*

# STAND BY YOUR MANICOTTI

*Sometimes it's hard to be a woman, especially when you're tryin' to stuff your manicotti.*

*Feeds 4*

1 pound hamburger meat, browned
1 pound sausage meat, browned
¼ cup chopped onion
1 tablespoon minced garlic
1½ cups cottage cheese
Salt and pepper
2 eggs, beaten
1 box of frozen spinach, thawed, drained and cut into little tiny pieces
1 box cooked manicotti shells
1 can or jar of spaghetti sauce
½ cup grated Parmesan cheese
2 cups shredded mozzarella cheese

Take the same skillet that you browned your meat in and sauté your onion and garlic for 5 minutes, then take it off the heat. Put the meats, cottage cheese, salt and pepper, eggs, and finally the spinach into the skillet and mix well. Stuff each of your manicotti shells with this mixture and put 'em in a greased casserole dish. If you got any of the mixture left over, pour the spaghetti sauce in the skillet and mix it all together. Then pour the sauce mixture over the stuffed manicotti. If you ain't got any of the mixture left, then simply pour the spaghetti sauce over the stuffed manicotti. Put your Parmesan and mozzarella cheeses over top of this. Put it in the oven and bake for 30 minutes at 350 degrees F.

*—JUANITA HIX, LOT #9*

*National Pork Month*

# SNAP CRACKLE POP PORK CHOPS

*This recipe is just like Tina Faye, plain and simple.*

*6 servin's*
1 egg
1 tablespoon milk
3 cups Kellogg's Rice Krispies
1 tablespoon pepper
1 teaspoon garlic powder
1 teaspoon salt
6 pork chops
6 pats margarine

In a bowl, beat the egg. Next add the milk. Mix this up real good. Set aside. Put your cereal, pepper, garlic powder, and salt in a plastic bag or a paper bag. Crush it all up real good, bein' careful not to poke a hole in your bag, and then shake it to mix everything up. Take your pork chops and dip 'em in the egg/milk mixture. Put it in the bag with the cereal mix and shake it up real good. Put your chops in a lightly greased casserole or bakin' dish. Put a pat of margarine on each chop and bake for about 1 hour, checkin' for doneness durin' that time, at 350 degrees F.
— *TINA FAYE STOPENBLOTTER, LOT #17*

Oh, and one last thing, as a retired cosmetologist, let me remind y'all that October is National Cosmetology Month, so make sure you buy your favorite hairdresser a real nice gift. If you ain't got a favorite hairdresser, then, and I say this as a retired cosmetologist, send that gift to me at:

Ruby Ann Boxcar (Retired Cosmetologist)
c/o Kensington Publishing Group
850 Third Avenue
New York, NY, 10022

# MOTHER-IN-LAW'S DAY/HALLOWEEN
## Mother-in-Law's Day is actually on October 27, while Halloween is on October 31.
### (Not a prison holiday)

Two years ago all of us at the High Chaparral Trailer Park decided to try somethin' new, which turned out to be a big success for the most part. What we did was we combined Mother-in-Law's Day with Halloween on account of the fact that they're so close together. It was just amazin' how the traditions and practices of these two separate holidays were able to fit together so well. For example, both the children, who were dressed in their favorite costumes, and the mothers-in-law would go from trailer to trailer, knockin' on each flimsy door. When the door is opened by the resident, the kids would yell, "Trick or treat," and hold out a bag, while the mothers-in-law would recite their traditional "Hello, I hate to be a bother, but what the hell," and hold out their purses. At this point they'd push their way into the trailer, set down in the most comfortable chairs in the place, and complain about how you keep house. The children would be given pieces of wrapped candy while the mothers-in-law would be tempted back outside with tubes of ointment, medical ID bracelets, denture cream, videotapes of *Diagnosis Murder,* or apples with razor blades in 'em (the razor blades are taken out when they get back home and are later used to shave their back hair and chin whiskers).

Jack-o'-lanterns are also big on this special day. At the High Chaparral, we always have a pumpkin-carvin' contest that anyone in attendance can enter. Not only is it a big hit with the kids, but the mothers get a kick out of it as well. And the best part is that when all the carvin's done, the mothers-in-law will proudly think that their baby based the three-toothed funky-eyed jack-o'-lantern creation on them. You can feel the love that night.

Those of you who've read *Ruby Ann's Down Home Trailer Park Cookbook* will recall that in an attempt to cure the evilness that he felt was in Halloween, Pastor Hickey held a "Holy Wiener Roast" at the First Baptist Church of Pangburn. That was also the first year that we at the High Chaparral Trailer Park started combinin' the two holidays together. Well, now that he's gone, our new pastor, Ida May Bee, has decided to allow us all to go back to our traditional Halloween/Mother-in-Law's Day practices and do away with the whole church thing. I think it's a wise decision on her part, especially when you consider some of the mothers-in-law who were stopped at the church door by Pastor Hickey last year and told they could not attend the festivities on account of them bein' dressed up as witches and demons. God bless 'em, they were in their street clothes. I could be wrong, but I really do think Pastor Hickey's demise started that evenin'.

Happy Mother-in-Law's Day/Halloween!

### Things to Get You in the Holiday Mood
Rent and watch *Throw Momma from the Train.*
Rent and watch *It's the Great Pumpkin, Charlie Brown.*

### Things to Do
In the spirit of the holidays, tip over a port-a-potty that has your mother-in-law in it.
Leave a flamin' bag of dog doo on your mother-in-law's porch. Ring the doorbell and run, but not too far.
Let your mother-in-law bob for apples. Give her a lovin' hand by holdin' her head under the water till she gets an apple or becomes very still.

### How to Decorate Your Trailer for This Holiday
Don't bother, she won't have nothin' good to say about it anyway.

### Trailer Park Tradition
If you have kids, encourage them to dress up like your mother-in-law. It'll thrill her, and it might win them a prize at a costume contest. Also remember, warn your kids not to eat any unwrapped casserole a stranger might give 'em until you've checked it.

*Somethin' to Bring to a Party*

## SPOOKY JELL-O POPCORN BALLS

*The kids call 'em Jiggler Balls!*

*Makes lots of balls*

1 small package of orange-flavored Jell-O

1 cup sugar

1 cup corn syrup

8 or 10 cups of popped popcorn

Follow your directions on the Jell-O box to make Jell-O. And the sugar and stir till it dissolves. Add the corn syrup and stir. Pour this over the popcorn, stir, and then shape into balls. Wrap up in wax paper.

*—JUANITA HIX, LOT #9*

*Dinner Menu*

## MOTHER-IN-LAW MONSTER CASSEROLE

*The color alone is enough to frighten small children!*

*4 to 6 servin's*

2 regular cans of cream of mushroom soup

Green food colorin'

1 (12 ounce) package of egg noodles, cooked and drained

Red food colorin'

Yellow food colorin'

1 regular can of Spam, cubed

1 can corn, drained

1 small package of Velveeta, cubed

Salt and pepper

Mix the soup with a few drops of green food colorin' until you get a nice swamp color. Put the egg noodles in a bowl and add some red and yellow food colorin'. Stir until you get orange noodles. Add everything but the soup to that bowl and stir. Place this on the bottom of a casserole dish. Put the mushroom soup on top of this and bake for 30 minutes at 350 degrees F.

*—PASTOR IDA MAY BEE, LOT #7*

# PUMPKIN BARS

*The price she charges for these at the Lamb's De-
partment Store will make you scream!*

*About 1 dozen bars*

4 eggs

1 cup oil

2 cups sugar

1 can of pumpkin pie fillin'

2 cups flour

2 teaspoons bakin' powder

1 teaspoon soda

½ teaspoon salt

2 teaspoons ground cinnamon

½ teaspoon ground ginger

½ teaspoon ground cloves

½ teaspoon ground nutmeg

Take the first 4 ingredients and mix 'em in a bowl. Set aside. Mix the rest
of the ingredients together, then add them to the pumpkin mixture. Mix
well and pour into a greased and floured 9×12-inch pan. Bake at 350 degrees F. for 20 to 25 minutes. Let cool. Make a frostin' by mixin' the followin':

6 ounces cream cheese

¾ cup margarine

1 tablespoon heavy cream

2 drops green food colorin'

1 teaspoon vanilla extract

4 cups confectioners' sugar

In a bowl, cream the first 4 items together, followed by the vanilla extract. Add the confectioners' sugar and mix well. Spread on the pumpkin
mixture and cut into bars.

*—DOTTIE LAMB, LOT #14*

# *Chapter 11*

Me and my husband, Dew, along with our dogs,
Shady Lady, Trixy, and Silver Fox, celebrate Turkey Day
with Anita Biggon; Ben Beaver; Daddy; Dew's momma,
Momma Ballzak; Ollie White; Mickey Ray;
and my niece Lulu Bell.

# *November*

All right kids, get them thinkin' caps on, 'cause it's time for a quiz. Are you ready? The eleventh month of the year, better known as November, takes it's name from the Latin word *novem,* which mean's what? OK, pencils down. If you said "nine" then you were correct. Yes, once again them wacky Romans didn't change the name of the month after movin' it from the ninth position in the calendar to the eleventh spot. Now, in all fairness they were goin' to change the name in honor of the then Roman Emperor Tibu-rious Caesar. Luckily he turned it down or we would be celebratin' Thanks-givin' in Tiber rather than November. As far as length goes, November went from originally havin' 30 days to 29 days, then 28 days, only to be brought back to the 30-day-long month that we know and love so well.

It's durin' the month of November, which the Anglo-Saxons used to refer to as "the wind month," that we start spendin' more quality time together with the family members that reside in the park as well as those who live outside the High Chaparral like Me-Ma, who herself has been referred to as "the wind machine."

Durin' November we celebrate one major holiday that's American as American can be. And of course that's Thanksgivin'. It's also the official start of the happiest dang time of the year. We've got lots to do over these next 30 days, but if you're lookin' for more fun, then take a look at this here month-long celebration.

November is:
*National Raisin Bread Month*

# OPAL'S CINNAMON CARROT RAISIN BREAD

*Makes 2 loaves*

2⅔ cups sugar

⅔ cup shortenin'

4 eggs

⅔ cup water

2 cups shredded carrots

3½ cups all-purpose flour

¼ teaspoon ground cloves

1 teaspoon ground cinnamon

1 teaspoon bakin' powder

2 teaspoons bakin' soda

1 teaspoon salt

1 cup raisins

Grease 2 loaf pans.

Cream the sugar and shortenin' together in a large bowl, beat in the eggs and water and add the carrots. Sift together the flour, cloves, cinnamon, bakin' powder, bakin' soda, and salt. Add to the batter. Add the raisins and mix well. Divide the batter into the loaf pans and bake for 45 minutes at 325 degrees F.

*—OPAL LAMB-INMAN, LOT #1*

# THANKSGIVIN'
## The fourth Thursday in November.
### (A prison holiday)

Thanksgivin' is the longest holiday in the whole darn trailer park year. Sure, the Christmas season is longer day-wise, but when it comes to the actual amount of time spent with family members or people you may not want to be around, it wins hands down. Now, I don't want y'all to think that us trailer park people hate our families, 'cause that just ain't so. I love my family. However, when it comes to spendin' long periods of time with 'em, well, let's just say the odds are that someone is likely to get hurt. I kid you not! And this statement isn't only true for my family. Around 99.9 percent of all trailer dwellers are likely to admit their undyin' love for members of their clan, but they are also likely to admit that they can't be with the whole family for more than two hours at a time without feelin' the urge to put some of 'em out of their misery. To better understand this love-hate relationship that goes on, let's take a look at a typical trailer park Thanksgivin'.

First, you arrive at the home that's been designated as the holiday trailer with your immediate family and a few covered dishes, and then you and your husband and kids, if you got 'em, stand around waitin' until all the food is done and ready to be served. Then y'all argue over who sits where and why you ain't sittin' where you were told to sit, as well as which channel the TV should be tuned to. Then somebody is goin' to complain about the chair they're sittin' on or the size of the glass that they got in front of 'em or how their plate is smaller or even bigger than everyone else's at the table. Once that gets settled, then comes the problem of who will say grace. Should it be the owner of the trailer? Or maybe the eldest should ask God's blessin' on this family and the food? Or how about the person who goes to church most often? Or better yet, maybe the person who brought the most food should do the honors? Anyways, this goes on till the sweet potatoes have cooled down to nothin', leavin' those once-encitin' little browned marshmallows that set on top dry and hard like a dang rock. Once we've asked the Lord's grace, the fun really starts.

Nobody, and I do mean nobody, outside of a trailer family can eat larger amounts of food while talkin' at the same time, and still manage to understand what every person at the table is sayin' word per word! When it comes to a personal conversation or good gossip, my family members are able to pick up decibels that would put the Bionic Man's hearin' capability to shame. Even my dear old Me-Ma, who couldn't hear a train if she was standin' right there on the track, is able to make out words like *pregnant, prison, erotic, hooker, 69,* and *Catholic* from 50 feet away. I tell you, it just ain't natural!

Once the meal is over and everyone's complained about how no one hardly touched what they brought and next year they might as well just bring somethin' from the store instead of spendin' hours over the hot stove, we all beach ourselves in front of the TV. We want to just get up and walk out of the trailer door, but the large amount of food we've consumed has made this utterly impossible. The fact that we're able to actually rise out of our chairs without the use of a mechanical device is a feat that could legally qualify us for a mention in the *Guinness Book of World Records.* We are lucky to make it to the livin' room let alone to the front door and down the steps. That's why we are forced to listen and, yes, even take part in the discussion that is soon to follow. Someone, in what has to resemble a small herd of walruses assembled on a collection of rocks out in the noonday sun, has to say somethin' negative about some issue that is sure to start yet another family argument. And everybody has an opinion, and the good Lord above knows we have to share it. Let me tell you, when we are finally able to get up off the floor, couch, or chair, we'd march right out of that trailer and back home if it weren't for the fact that there's leftovers and somebody has to stick around and eat 'em!

Another way of celebratin' turkey day in the trailer park is as a community. That's what we folks at the High Chaparral Trailer Park have been doin' for the past five years. Personally, I think it makes Thanksgivin' much more enjoyable. Although I have to be honest, that first one was one that went down in the books.

Somebody had seen them fryin' turkeys on some cookin' show and told us all about it. I think it was Dora Beaver, may she rest in peace, but don't quote me on that. Anyways, everybody thought it'd be great if we turned our first Thanksgivin' as a community into somethin' that we'd all remember. So all us ladies as well as Kenny and Donny from lot #15 started savin' our bacon drippin's every mornin'. We'd put 'em in spare coffee cans and then, once they were full, we'd take 'em out to this old washin' machine that my husband, Dew, and Mickey Ray from lot #13 had salvaged from the dump. They'd cleaned it all up and scrubbed out the inside. Since it was one of them old metal ones, they didn't have to remove hardly any plastic parts or other items that might've melted durin' the cookin'. Anyways, everything had gone smooth durin' the rest of November, all of December, January, and even most of February. We'd all take our coffee cans of bacon drippin's and dump 'em in the washin' machine just like we'd all planned. But when the days started to grow a little warmer, and the flies started to come around a little bit more often, we all started to notice a little change goin' on in that washtub. That half-full tank of bacon drippin's was startin' to take on a life and smell of its own. The Bunches over in lot #3 were the first to wonder if maybe this collectin' of perishable animal fats was the best idea that had ever come out of the High Chaparral Trailer Park. Even my mother-in-law, Momma Ballzak, questioned our judgment. So we did what rural people do when they need information on this kind of subject, we asked our local FFA instructor. LeRoy Dobbs had been headin' up our local chapter for now on 40 some odd years, which is why we took his word when he assured us that the drippins would be just fine once they'd gotten hot enough to purify. He also told us not to worry about that terrible smell, it was just nature doin' its duty. So durin' the hot summer months of June, July, and August we simply held our noses and continued to do our part. By the time Thanksgivin' had rolled around, the cold weather and a good freeze had chased off some of those more unattractive odors. Dottie Lamb and her daughter, Opal, of lot #14, had been thoughtful enough to donate three big frozen turkeys for the fryin' while the menfolk had gone out and collected enough wood for the fire, which they started underneath the washin' tub itself. Well, it took a few hours before the old drippin's started to heat up, and as it grew hotter, the stench grew stronger. It got so bad that we were shovin' damp towels in the bottom of our front and back doors in an attempt to keep the smell out of the trailer. I can't tell you how many cans of Glade I went through that day.

Anyways, it was my daddy who ended up fryin' the birds that day. His lack of bein' able to smell most foul odors made him the most likely candidate for the job. And like Doris had told us, those turkeys came out nice and brown. So with that all done, we put out the fire so the grease could cool down, moved into the trailer park office, and with our covered dishes settin' at the makeshift buffet table, we thanked God for this day of peace, brotherhood, and good neighbors. With that, we all formed a line and dug in. I believe it was Nellie Tinkle of lot #4 who first made a comment about how juicy her turkey slices were. And if I recall correctly, I also think it was Nellie who was the first to go down. Originally I thought she'd made the mistake of samplin' my Me-Ma's lima beans in a Pine-Sol sauce (we warned everybody not to eat the lima beans, Me-Ma had made 'em). I don't remember much more of that day except that we were droppin' like flies. And accordin' to the doctors, if it hadn't been for Donny and Kenny of lot #15, we all might have been goners. You see, neither one of the boys would touch the turkey on account of the smell, and because of that, they were able to call 911 for help.

Sheriff Gentry, who came out with some of his men after gettin' the 911 call, couldn't believe his eyes. There were people lyin' unconscious everywhere. The first problem they faced was how to get us all to the hospital in nearby Searcy. There had never been a need for more than one ambulance in this neck of the woods in the past. So while the sheriff and his men pondered this question, they helped themselves to a few plates of our Thanksgivin' feast—minus the turkey, of course. Finally, with a full stomach, Sheriff Gentry came up with the idea of borrowin' old man Keener's great big manure truck. That would hold all of us, and luckily it was empty, well sort of. Anyways, accordin' to Kenny, the sheriff and his boys loaded us all in the truck bed and sent it along with a sample of the turkey on to the hospital. Meanwhile Sheriff Gentry had his men dump out the contents of the washin' machine straight into the trailer park's main septic tank, and then locked it up in a shed by the police station for evidence.

Thank the good Lord above none of us was seriously hurt. We'd all come down with a bad case of food poisonin' and had weak stomachs and diarrhea for a week, but we were OK and released the next day. But that bacon grease ended up cloggin' up our sewer and, well, it was just a mess. We had to wear gas masks around the trailer park for almost a week and a half. But things eventually got back to normal.

Needless to say, we haven't deep-fried a turkey since. As for LeRoy

Dobbs, shortly after the incident, he resigned his position with the local chapter of the FFA, and on that same day he and his wife moved out of town to an undisclosed location. Mind you, they didn't have much to move since they lost everything in that mysterious house fire that claimed their home just the night before. The Sheriff didn't do much investigatin' on the cause of the blaze on account of his attempt to recuperate from his own bout of poisonin'. It seems he had eaten a good helpin' of Me-Ma's lima beans on that tragic day.

As you might expect, there will be no recipes for fried turkey in the followin' section, but don't be surprised by the variations on salad, stuffin', and pie. Remember, we love to eat!

### Things to Get You in the Holiday Mood

Rent and watch the videos *A Charlie Brown Thanksgiving, Avalon* (that Thanksgivin' scene makes me think the screenwriters must have lived in a trailer one time in their life), *Home for the Holidays,* and *Miracle on 34th Street* (this one we watch on Thanksgivin' Day).

Read *The Berenstain Bears' Thanksgiving* (Lulu Bell and I always read this one together a week before Thanksgivin').

Listen to any recordin's by the Gaithers, the Happy Goodmans, the Cathedrals, or any other good old southern gospel music group (these wonderful songs of hope about leavin' this world for a better place that's far away from those damn neighbors of yours and them bill collectors who won't stop callin' you at all hours of the day are sure to put you in a thankful mood).

Visit the followin' web pages: *www.wildturkeybourbon.com, www.ny.com/holiday/ thanksgiving/parade.html,* and *www.thanksgiving-traditions.com/.*

### Things to Do

Grin and bear it! Remember, it's only once a year, and as soon as Me-Ma passes, you won't have to do it with the rest of the family ever again.

Watch the Macy's Thanksgivin' Day Parade.

Eat!

Rest.

Eat again!

## How to Decorate Your Trailer for This Holiday

Decoratin' for Thanksgivin' is simply done by puttin' up a few more items, but mostly by addin' to the Halloween decorations that you already have up. For example, put some dried-out leaves around those jack-o'-lanterns and add pilgrim hats that you've crafted from black construction paper, a paper plate, some black paint, and tape. A little headband with a feather in the back is all that's needed to turn that frightenin' skeleton into a pilgrim-friendly Indian.

You can use those same apples you had left over from the Halloween classic bobbin'-for-apples game to create fun little turkeys. With the stem away from you, insert a toothpick deep into the portion of the apple that is close to you (there should be just a tiny bit of toothpick comin' out of the top of the apple). Next, impale a kernel of candy corn onto the toothpick. This will be the head and beak of the turkey. Now put seven or eight toothpicks slightly into the back stem side of the turkey. These toothpicks will make the brace for the turkey's feathers. Take some miniature marshmallows and carefully put them on each toothpick until they are completely full (assorted colored marshmallows look the best). Take a toothpick and break it in half. Put the two pieces into the back of the apple so they face down. These should help to hold your turkey apple straight up. You can also take a magic marker and draw on a few wing feathers on the sides of the apples for a more realistic look.

A real simple holiday look for your trailer can be achieved by just addin' a pile of dead leaves to those corn stalks that I had you put in the corner of your trailer for Halloween. We are goin' to play with these corners all the way up to Christmas.

## Trailer Park Tradition

The relative with the biggest trailer hosts the festivities regardless if they're Jehovah's Witnesses or not.

*Somethin' to Bring to a Party*

## DONNA SUE'S HARVEST CHEESE DIP

*My sister the stripper is always welcomed to any Thanksgivin' party as long as she brings a big bowl of this dip. So what if her date happens to pocket a few of your valuables and family treasures. As long as you can serve your guests this crowd-pleasin' cheese dish nothin' else matters.*

1 onion, chopped up
3 celery ribs, chopped up real good
2 tablespoons margarine
1 package of frozen broccoli, thawed, chopped, cooked, and drained
1 can of cream of mushroom soup
1 pound Velveeta
Tabasco sauce
Worcestershire sauce

In a saucepan sauté your onion and celery in the margarine over medium heat. Add the broccoli, soup, and Velveeta and stir till the cheese melts. Add the Tabasco and Worcestershire to taste and mix well. Serve warm with corn chips.

*—DONNA SUE BOXCAR, LOT #6*

*Dinner Menu*

## PILGRIM POTATO SALAD

*One bite of this and you'll know why the Indians stayed around for dinner.*

*Serves 6*
12 medium potatoes
⅔ cup diced bacon
¼ cup chopped onion
1 teaspoon flour

2 teaspoons salt

¼ cup sugar

¼ teaspoon pepper

⅔ cup cider vinegar

⅓ cup water

½ teaspoon celery seed

3 tablespoons chopped parsley

In a big pot of boilin' water, cook your potatoes in their skin till tender. Drain, cool, peel, and slice thin. While your potatoes are cookin', bake the bacon till it's good and crisp. Add the onion and cook for just 1 minute. Blend in the flour, salt, sugar, and pepper. Stir in the cider vinegar and water. Cook for an additional 5 minutes, makin' sure that you stir well.

Once your potatoes are done and ready to go, put 'em in a nice bowl. Pour the above mixture over 'em, add the celery seed and parsley. Mix it up and serve.

*—WENDY BOTTOM, LOT #4*

## CAIN AND ABEL COLESLAW

*This stuff is so good, you'd kill you your brother
for a second helpin'.*

Serves 6

1 head cabbage, shredded

1 small carrot, peeled and shredded

⅔ cup mayonnaise

¼ cup sugar

2 tablespoons milk

2 tablespoons vinegar

½ teaspoon salt

¼ teaspoon pepper

Toss the cabbage and the carrot in a medium bowl. In a small bowl, combine the remainin' ingredients and pour over the cabbage mixture. Mix it all up real good, then cover and refrigerate overnight for the best flavor.

*—SISTER BERTHA, LOT #12*

# THE ORIGINAL THANKSGIVIN' DRESSIN'

*Lois might be right, and this just might be the
dressin' they served at the first Thanksgivin'. So
where'd they get the Swanson's Chicken Broth?*

*Serves 6*

1 cup chopped celery

1 cup chopped onion

⅓ cup margarine

1 teaspoon poultry seasonin'

¼ teaspoon pepper

½ teaspoon salt

8 cups dry bread crumbs

¾ cup Swanson's Chicken Broth

In a medium saucepan, cook the celery and onion in the margarine until tender but not brown. Remove from the heat. Stir in poultry seasonin', pepper, and salt. Place the dry breadcrumbs in a large mixin' bowl and add the onion mixture. Drizzle with enough broth to moisten, and toss lightly.

—*LOIS BUNCH, LOT #3*

# OYSTER STUFFIN'

*Now, this here is some fancy stuffin'.*

*Serves 6*

1 loaf white bread, unsliced

½ pound margarine

1 small onion, chopped

1 celery rib, chopped

3 tablespoons minced parsley

1 teaspoon fresh thyme leaves

2 teaspoons salt

Freshly ground black pepper

1 pint oysters in liquor

Crumble the bread into small pieces. Melt the margarine in a saucepan. Add the onion and celery. Cook until the onion is soft. Stir in the bread pieces. Add the parsley, thyme, salt, and pepper to taste. Drain the oysters, reservin' the liquor. Heat the liquor to the boiling point. If the oysters are large, cut them in half. Add them to the liquor and cook until the edges start to curl. Drain promptly and stir the oysters into the bread mixture.

*—KENNY LYNN, LOT #15*

## CORNBREAD DRESSIN'

*One bite of this, and my husband thanks God
that he got me.*

*Serves 6*

1 bunch celery, chopped
2 green peppers, chopped
2 medium onions, chopped
1 bunch green onions, chopped
¼ cup oil
8 cups sweet cornbread, crumbled
1 (14 ounce) can chicken broth
2 cans of cream of chicken soup
3 eggs, beaten
1 teaspoon garlic powder
1 teaspoon sage
¼ teaspoon pepper

In a skillet over medium heat, cook the celery, green peppers, and all the onions in the oil for 5 minutes.

In a large bowl, mix the cornbread, broth, cream of chicken soup, eggs, garlic powder, sage, and pepper. Add the above mixture and mix well. Put it in a greased 13 × 9-inch bakin' pan and bake for 1½ hours at 325 degrees F.

*—RUBY ANN BOXCAR, LOT #18*

# TAMMY'S GREEN BEAN BAKE

*She may be gone on the road with her new husband and kids, but she sure ain't forgotten, thanks to this dish.*

*Serves 6*

1 can of cream of mushroom soup

¾ cup milk

⅛ teaspoon pepper

2 cans of green beans, drained

1 can of French-fried onions

In a good-size bowl, mix all the ingredients minus the onions together. Put in a casserole dish and bake for 30 minutes. Stir it up and top with the French-fried onions. Bake at 350 degrees F. for 5 minutes.

*—TAMMY CANTRELL, FORMERLY OF LOT #1*

# PERFECT MASHED POTATOES

*That Dick sure has got some high-dollar taste.*

*Serves 6*

2 pounds Yukon Gold potatoes

2 tablespoons butter

½ cup heavy cream

1 (8 ounce) package of cream cheese

2 tablespoons chives

Salt and freshly ground pepper to taste

Chopped parsley for garnish

Cook the potatoes in boilin' salted water until they are tender. Drain the potatoes and return to the pot. Usin' a ricer, mash the potatoes slightly and set aside.

Heat 1 tablespoon of butter and half the cream in a saucepan. Simmer for 1 minute. Add the mixture to the potatoes and stir well. Put the pan on low heat and add the rest of the cream; and stir well. Add the cream cheese and stir well. Add the chives and salt and pepper and stir well. Take off the heat. Sprinkle with parsley.

*—DICK INMAN, LOT #1*

## DOTTIE'S DANDY CANDIED YAMS

*These are a tradition in the Lamb household and thanks to an unlocked front trailer door, now they can be a tradition in your household.*

Serves 6

6 sweet potatoes

1 cup brown sugar

¼ cup water

½ cup margarine

2 tablespoons vanilla extract

Miniature marshmallows

Preheat the oven to 350 degrees F. Boil the potatoes in their skins until about halfway done. Drain the water from the potatoes, remove the skins, and cut into lengthwise slices. Place the slices in a greased bakin' dish and dot with half of the margarine. Mix the brown sugar, water, and vanilla extract together. Pour it over the yams. Dot remainin' margarine on the sliced yams and bake for 45 minutes. Baste the yams with the syrup water from the bottom of the pan. Add the marshmallows and bake until they are melted. Rebaste. The total cooking time should be 1 hour.

*—DOTTIE LAMB, LOT #14*

## MOMMA BALLZAK'S SWEET POTATO CASSEROLE

*I dare you to have two servin's of this and then walk a straight line.*

Serves 6

3 cups sweet potatoes, cooked and mashed

1 cup sugar

2 eggs

1 teaspoon vanilla extract

⅓ cup milk

½ cup margarine

1 cup packed brown sugar

⅓ cup flour

⅓ cup margarine

2 cups Kahlúa liqueur

1 cup chopped pecans

Combine the sweet potatoes, sugar, eggs, vanilla, milk, and ½ cup margarine. Beat with an electric mixer until smooth. Put into a greased shallow casserole.

In a large bowl, combine the brown sugar, flour, ⅓ cup margarine, 1 cup of the Kahlúa, and pecans. Sprinkle over top of the casserole, and bake at 350 degrees F. for 25 minutes. Pour the remainin' Kahlúa over the casserole and cook for 5 more minutes.

*—MOMMA BALLZAK, LOT #16*

## BAPTIST CARROT RAISIN SALAD

*Every good Baptist that is worth their weight knows how to make this one.*

*Serves 6*

3 cups shredded carrots

½ cup flaked coconut

½ cup raisins

⅓ cup mayonnaise

¼ cup pineapple juice

⅓ cup salted peanuts

Lettuce leaves

Combine all the ingredients except the lettuce in a salad bowl. Stir well, cover, and chill for 2 to 3 hours. Serve on lettuce leaves.

*—SISTER BERTHA, LOT #12*

## GOOD OLD GIBLET GRAVY

*This'll make your plate dance!*

*Serves 6*

¼ cup pan drippin's

¼ cup flour

1 cup water

2 cups turkey stock

Turkey giblets, cooked and chopped

Salt and pepper

Pour off all turkey fat from the roastin' pan into a glass measurin' cup. Measure and return ¼ cup to pan. Sprinkle the flour into the fat. Cook and stir for 2 or 3 minutes over low heat. Add the water and the turkey stock. Cook, stirrin' and scrapin' up the browned bits in the pan, until the gravy thickens. Strain the gravy into a saucepan. Add the chopped giblets. Season with salt and pepper to taste.

*—JEANNIE JANSSEN, LOT #19*

# THE TURKEY

*This is the same turkey recipe that Ollie served to us kids back when I was in Pangburn High School.*

Serves 8 to 10

1 (18-to-20-pound) turkey

2 cans of chicken broth

1 can of beef broth

Margarine

Poultry seasonin'

Remove the giblets and any other items from inside the bird. Place the bird in the middle of a roastin' pan, and fill the pan with the chicken and beef broth. Lightly grease the bird with margarine and poultry seasonin'. Cover with aluminum foil and bake at 350° degrees F. for 20 minutes per pound. The state says you can't cook the turkey with the stuffin' inside. It can be a health risk, since the stuffin' does not cook thoroughly enough to kill all the bacteria.

*—OLLIE WHITE, LOT #10*

# MOMMA BALLZAK'S AMBROSIA SALAD

*This is about the only ambrosia salad I know of that'll make you tipsy.*

Serves 6

2 (6 ounce) packages of apricot-flavored gelatin

2 cups boilin' water

1 cup dry white wine, chilled

¾ cup cold water

1 (10 ounce) package of frozen sliced strawberries; thawed and undrained

1 regular can of crushed pineapple, undrained

2 bananas, peeled and sliced

1 cup sour cream

2 tablespoons brown sugar

2 tablespoons coconut, toasted

Combine the gelatin and boilin' water in a large bowl. Stir 2 minutes, or until the gelatin dissolves. Add the wine and cold water; chill until the consistency of unbeaten egg white. Stir in the strawberries, pineapple, and bananas; pour into a lightly greased 6-cup mold. Cover and chill 8 hours.

In a small bowl, combine the sour cream and brown sugar; spoon into a servin' dish. Sprinkle with toasted coconut. Unmold the salad onto a plate and serve with the sour cream mixture.

*—MOMMA BALLZAK, LOT #16*

## VERMONT PUMPKIN PIE

*Kenny and Donny brought this recipe back with
'em after a recent visit to Vermont.*

*Makes 1 pie*

2 eggs

¾ cup light cream

½ cup maple syrup

3 cups cooked pumpkin

1 teaspoon ground cinnamon

½ teaspoon ground ginger

¼ teaspoon grated nutmeg

1 9-inch pastry shell

Heat your oven to 425 degrees F., and then lightly beat the eggs in a bowl and blend in everything else. Put in the pie shell and bake for 15 minutes. Reduce heat to 350 degrees F. and bake an additional 40 minutes. Remove it from the oven and let it cool.

Make the toppin' by combinin' the followin' in a bowl:

1 cup chopped pecans

½ cup packed brown sugar

½ cup margarine, melted

Mix well and spoon it over the top of the cooled pie. Put it in the oven and broil it about half a foot from the top of the oven for 2 minutes. Let it cool and serve with ice cream.

*—KENNY LYNN, LOT #15*

## OPAL'S GINGERSNAP PUMPKIN PIE

*She may be uglier than sin, but the gal can cook!*

*Makes 1 pie*

1½ cups cold half-and-half

3½ ounces Cool Whip

1 cup pecans, crushed

1 cup crumbled gingersnaps

½ can of pumpkin, combined with 1½ tablespoons pumpkin pie spice

1 graham cracker crumb pie shell

Beat the half-and-half and pie fillin' in a large mixin' bowl with a wire whisk for 1 minute. Let stand 5 minutes. Fold in the toppin' and remainin' ingredients, then spoon into the crust. Freeze until firm. Let stand at room temperature for 10 minutes before servin' to soften. Store leftovers in the freezer.

*—OPAL LAMB-INMAN, LOT #1*

## PERFECT PECAN PIE

*This is one of the reasons even the sinners were happy to have Pastor Ida May Bee move into the trailer park!*

*Makes 1 perfect pie*

3 eggs

2 tablespoons margarine, melted

1½ cups pancake syrup

⅛ teaspoon salt

½ cup sugar

3 tablespoons flour

¼ teaspoon vanilla extract

⅔ cup chopped pecans

1 unbaked 9-inch pie shell

Take them eggs and put 'em in a bowl. Add the margarine, syrup, salt, sugar, flour, and vanilla. Blend it all together real well and then drop in the pecans. Stir it up and dump it in the pie shell. Stick it a hot oven and cook at 425 degrees F. for 12 minutes. Turn that heat down to 325 degrees and bake for another 45 minutes. This will make you the talk of the table.

*—PASTOR IDA MAY BEE, LOT #7*

## NANNA STOPENBLOTTER'S PECAN RAISIN PIE

*Well, I guess this proves that despite what my sister,*
*Donna Sue, says, Faye Faye did have a mother.*

*Makes 1 pie*

1½ cups raisins

½ cup margarine, softened

1¼ cups sugar

2 eggs

1 cup pecan pieces

1 teaspoon grated nutmeg

1 teaspoon ground cinnamon

1 teaspoon vanilla

1 unbaked 9-inch piecrust

Put your raisins in some boilin' water and let 'em cook for 10 to 12 minutes. They should get big and plump. Once they've reached that state, drain 'em and set aside to cool down.

Take a bowl and add the margarine and sugar; cream 'em together. Add the eggs, nutmeg, cinnamon, and vanilla. Mix well and add both the raisins and pecans. Stir it up and put it in the pie shell. Bake it in a preheated oven at 350 degrees F. for 40 to 45 minutes.

*—TINA FAYE STOPENBLOTTER, LOT #17*

# Chapter 12

Even though we are good old trailer park Baptists, me and my husband, Dew, and our girls Trixy, Silver Fox, and Shady Lady, like to incorporate both Christmas and Chanukah (even though we ain't got the slightest idea of what it is, for the most part). Happy Holidays to y'all!

# December

The word Decem is Latin for, you guessed it, 10, which is what the name of the 12th month is based on. December used to only have 29 days, but our dear friend Julius Caesar added not one but two days to the month.

Winter is finally here accordin' to our calendar, which means that all that other butt-freezin' weather you've been livin' through durin' the later part of November was actually spring. Call it what you want, it's still colder and whiter than my Me-Ma's creamy white thighs.

The holiday spirit, which hit us upside the head just last month, continues to build with more and more enthusiasm and excitement. Yes, the happiest month of the year is finally upon us with two religious holidays, one special day that is only rivaled in the shoppin' world by last month's Day After Thanksgivin' sale, and the final conclusion to our year.

December is:
***Bingo's Birthday Month***

## O-69 CAKE

*One bite of this and you'll be yellin' "BINGO!"*

*6 to 8 servin's*
2 packages of unflavored gelatin
4 tablespoons cold water
1 cup boilin' water
1 cup sugar
3 tablespoons lemon juice
1 regular can of crushed pineapple

1½ cups strawberries, pureéd

2 (8 ounce) containers of Cool Whip

1 box of yellow cake mix

1 cup coconut

3 ounces maraschino cherries

1 (8 ounce) container of Cool Whip

In a large bowl, put your gelatin in the cold water. Add the boilin' water and stir. Add your sugar, lemon juice, pineapple, and strawberries that you already pureéd in the blender to this mix and stir. Cover and put in the fridge for 20 minutes. Pull out and fold in the 2 containers of Cool Whip.

Make your cake as directed on the box, but divide the batter among four lightly greased cake pans. Bake accordin' to the box. Let the cakes cool on a rack. Take a platter and put one cake on it. Top this with a thick layer of the Cool Whip mixture. Put another cake on top of this and then another layer of the mixture. Do this again, but when you put the fourth cake on, stop. Take wax paper and tightly wrap it around the tower of cakes and fillin', tapin' it together. This will hold the cakes together. Put in the fridge and chill overnight. The next day frost your cake with Cool Whip and sprinkle on the coconut. Take your cherries and place 'em on the top of the cake so they spell out "O-69". Serve.

*—OLLIE WHITE, LOT #10*

# CHANUKAH/HANUKKAH
### Celebrated in November or December.
#### (A prison holiday)

Regardless of how you spell it, this Festival of Lights is very interestin'. It's a celebration that even our Savior practiced before he became a Baptist. Basically the story goes somethin' like this. There was this Syrian king named Antiochus III who insisted that all the people, regardless of their backgrounds or race, be united into one culture. This was called "hellenization," which basically means that everyone includin' the menfolk would all put on a set of pearls and a blue dress and call themselves Helen. Well, the Jewish people at the time didn't go for that kind of stuff, although it did get a bit lax when Milton Berle had his show on TV. In any case, an elderly priest, who refused to join in on this one-culture thing with the Syrians, and his five sons formed resistance army that they called the Maccabees. Well, the Temple in Jerusalem, where the Jews had always been allowed to practice their faith freely, was overtaken by the Syrian army. This really made the Maccabees mad so they went into action, and after just four very brutal battles, they had regained both Jerusalem and the Temple. Quickly they cleaned up the Temple and disposed of all the statues and such that the Syrians had put up. The Jews had to rededicate the house of worship but could find only enough holy oil, which had been hid away, to light the menorah for one night. But miraculously the lamp remained lit for eight days and eight nights. Not only was the Temple cleansed, but thanks to the light from the menorah, Santa Claus was able to locate the Maccabees and leave 'em presents.

Happy Chanukah, y'all!

### *Things to Get You in the Holiday Mood*
Stare at your drippin' oil statue.
Rent and watch *A Rugrats Chanukah* or *Shalom Sesame* Show #6: *Chanukah*.
Go to Dunkin' Donuts.
Visit www.caryn.com/holiday/holiday-chan.html.

### *Things to Do*
Each day durin' Chanukah go to a different neighbor and wish 'em a Happy Chanukah. Bring 'em an inexpensive gift. When they say "Thank you, but I'm

afraid I don't have a present for you," tell 'em, "That's OK, I'll just take this," and pick out a picture frame, ashtray, or any other item that they got in their trailer that you've wanted for the longest time.

### How to Decorate Your Trailer for This Holiday

Even though my trailer is decorated for Christmas at this time of year, I still make sure to keep it Chanukah-ready in case one of my Jewish friends from out of state happens to stop by. For example, I hang up potato latkes with mistletoe attached to 'em; I put stars of David up on my tree; I make little yarmulkes that I put on all my lawn statues; I hang dreidels in my Christmas wreaths; and last but not least, I burn both the menorah that a friend gave me and one that I made out of fruit cakes.

### Trailer Park Tradition

Since we ain't got no Chanukah cards in these parts, we simply take old Christmas cards and white out words like "Merry Christmas," "Christ," "round young virgin," "Santa Claus," "savior," and "Holly Jolly Christmas." We leave the elves in since they can easily be explained away as Maccabees. You can make any nativity scene Chanukah-acceptable by simply drawin' a tiny little dreidel in our savior's infant hand.

### Somethin' to Bring to a Party

## MACCABEE DONUTS

*These are a good reason for a Baptist to celebrate Chanukah!*

*Makes about 2 dozen*

2 packages of active dry yeast

¼ cup warm water

1 teaspoon salt

½ cup sugar

1½ cups milk, scalded and cooled

2 eggs

⅓ cup shortenin'

1 teaspoon grated nutmeg

4½ cups flour

⅓ cup margarine

2 cups confectioners' sugar

1½ teaspoons vanilla extract

4½ tablespoons water

Oil for deep frying

In a large bowl, dissolve your yeast in the warm water. Add your salt, granulated sugar, milk, eggs, shortenin', nutmeg, and 2 cups of flour. Blend lightly for a minute, then add 2½ more cups of flour. Stir it all up real good, cover, and set aside for 1 hour.

Sprinkle some flour on a clean surface and put your dough there. Roll out your dough to a ½-inch thickness. Cut the dough with a drinkin' glass. This will make your donut shape. Take a thimble and cut out a little hole in the middle of each piece. Save those tiny pieces to make donut holes. Put each donut and the holes on a greased cookie sheet. Cover and let sit for 30 minutes.

Make a glaze for your donuts by blendin' the margarine, confectioners' sugar, and vanilla extract together. Add the water and keep mixin' until you get a consistency of glaze that you like.

Fry the donuts and holes at 400 degrees F. for 3 minutes. Drain on paper towels, and cover with glaze. Set the donuts and the holes on waxed paper.

*—LOVIE BIRCH, LOT #19*


*Dinner Menu*


# HAPPY CHANUKAH BRISKET

*Faye Faye says that one year after that Jewish fella she was datin' dumped her, and who can blame him, she made this and was able to feed both her and Tina Faye on it for eight days.*

*6 to 8 servin's*

1 tablespoon oil

4 to 6 pounds beef brisket

2 cups grapefruit juice

1 (6 ounce) can of tomato paste

8 ounces ketchup

2 onions, sliced

1 garlic clove

2 teaspoons salt

¼ teaspoon hot sauce

3 carrots, cut into pieces

3 celery ribs, cut into pieces

¼ cup packed brown sugar

3 tablespoons molasses

12 ounces beer

1 cup water

4 potatoes, cut into pieces

Put your oil in a skillet and put it over medium-high heat. Add your brisket, fat side up, and sear it on all sides. Now place your brisket in a Crock-Pot that you've set on low or automatic. Add all the ingredients, stir, and cover. Let it cook for 8 hours, checkin' occasionally to make sure it has enough liquid in it. If not, add some water. Remove the brisket and veggies and serve.

*—FAYE FAYE LARUE, LOT #17*

# CHRISTMAS
## December 25
### (A prison holiday)

My favorite time of year has always been the days from Thanksgivin' to Christmas. Even now, as I look back on my life as an adult, I find that the majority of my warmest memories seem to fall durin' those 30 some odd days. A close second in warm memories would be the ones I got from the month me and my husband, Dew, courted as well as those from our honeymoon, but I can't write a book about them in fear of it windin' up as a late-night feature on Cinemax. But enough about that, let's get back to Christmas and the memories that season of cheer holds for me.

My earliest recollection of Christmas was when I was just a pup at the tender age of two goin' on three. Now I know that might sound a bit odd for a person to recall somethin' from such a young age, but my daddy really went all out on Christmas. As a matter of fact he'd involve the whole Boxcar family when it came time to decorate our trailer. Everybody had a specific job and he'd hold you to it. My older brother, Jack Daniels, would be in charge of untanglin' the strings of outside Christmas lights, my older sister, Donna Sue, would brace the ladder when Daddy climbed up onto the roof, and Momma would help pass the strings up to Daddy as well as be his eyes on the ground by tellin' him which areas of the trailer needed more or less lights. But as a small child, I had the special job that no one else in the family could do. My brother was too tall and my sister weighed too much, but God bless her heart, isn't that the way it's always been for her. As a small toddler, I was just the right size for the job. I remember Daddy carryin' me in his strong arms up the ladder onto the roof. Even though he was born without index fingers, I always felt so secure when he'd hold me. It was as if nothin' bad could ever get to me as long as I was wrapped in his arms and freakish hands. I also recall lookin' up into the clear blue sky watchin' birds fly overhead as I lay on my back up on top the roof of our home. I can still hear Daddy's voice tellin' me that I was such a "pretty baby" and a "big girl" while he tied a short rope around my head. I'd giggle all the while as he continued to fill my ears with praise and love. Then he'd go on to ask if "Daddy's princess was ready to help." With that he'd grab a hold of my legs, turn me upside down, and hang me head first over the trailer. With me facin' toward the trailer, Daddy would swing me out away from the trailer and then quickly back toward it. Each time I'd stop just inches from the wall. He'd do this repeatedly, stop, walk over a few steps, and begin the swingin' motion once again. For me this was just a game I was playin' with my kind and carin' Daddy. I loved it and felt special. It wasn't until I'd grown older and saw the pictures that Momma had taken of us "playin' our game" that I realized what it was he'd tied around my head. My dear old lovin', carin' Daddy had strapped a hammer to my forehead and used me as a human nail driver for those hard-to-reach tacks and nails. All this time that I thought I was a special girl, I was simply a poor man's Black and Decker–type apparatus. Accordin' to Momma, after me and Daddy had done our hammerin' duties he'd lower me down to her waitin' arms, she'd untie the hammer from my forehead, and he'd string out the lights along those tacks and nails that I'd driven in. Mind you, I don't remember any of that part, but that could be on account of a slight concussion I might have gotten. No matter, though, I'm fine and smart as a whip. Still, I can't help but wonder if sometime in my life some suppressed memory will spring up out of my head, and I'll vividly recall some Christmas when my Daddy loaned me out to the neighbors like some common tool in the shed.

Momma, Daddy, and us kids would start our Christmas season off on Thanksgivin' Day. As soon as we could all manage to get up off the couch after restin' from the fine Thanksgivin' dinner Momma had prepared for us, we'd all load up into the pickup truck and head out into the country. Mind you, the country was less than half a block from our trailer home, but we'd drive around the local roads lookin' for what would later be the Boxcar family Christmas tree for that year. Whenever Momma and Daddy would spot the one they thought was just right, they'd ask us kids for our input. I never understood why they did this, 'cause regardless of what me and my siblin's said, my parents would go with the tree they liked. Once the tree had been finalized, Donna Sue would jump out of the pickup truck, tie a pair of her panties to the fence, climb back in, and we'd head back home to put a dent in those Thanksgivin' leftovers.

Later that day, Me-Ma and Pa-Pa would show up with an assortment of unusual Christmas cookies for us all to enjoy. Me-Ma was a fantastic cook, but due to her vanity and refusal to wear glasses, her cookies rarely were the correct shape for the season. She couldn't tell the difference between the cookie cutters so we'd end up with jack-o'-lanterns, Easter bunnies, four-leaf clovers, or God knows what else. But they sure tasted good (after eatin' a large bite of mashed potatoes accidentally salted with sugar, Pa-Pa made sure all the canisters and bottles in their trailer had been clearly marked with large letters that Me-Ma could easily read). Us kids never said nothin' directly to Me-Ma about her strange Christmas cookies, we just ate 'em. Besides, we knew sometime durin' the remainder of the day Pa-Pa would stop mid-sentence durin' one of his speeches on the ways of the world, take a second look at the cookie he'd just picked up from the tray, and utter the words that would start the traditional Boxcar Christmas banter, "Dang it, woman, what in the heck are you tryin' to doggone feed me?"

Me-Ma would innocently look toward the object Pa-Pa was holdin' up in her face and without a beat answer right back with "Well, Pa-Pa, it's a Christmas cookie."

"A Christmas cookie," Pa-Pa would exclaim. "What the heck kind of dang Christmas cookie is shaped like doggone George dang Washington's doggone head?" Pa-Pa was a God-fearin' Baptist through and through, but he was also a sailor who'd proudly served his country durin' World War II. Well, actually he only served his country for six months before his left big toe was crushed by a loose industrial-size can of pineapple cubes that fell off a counter while his ship was engaged in battle. In any case, he was still a sailor deep down inside the very depths of his heart. Yes, a sailor who'd never quite mastered the fine seaworthy skill of swearin'.

"Chester," Me-Ma would scold, "shut up and eat the cookie or put it back on the plate." Even Pa-Pa knew that when Me-Ma called you by your middle name, you'd better just shut up or risk her wrath or even worse, the wrath of the other people sittin' around you. When Me-Ma would get mad, she'd start swingin', and everyone sittin' in your area was a potential target since she couldn't see who you were till she was right up on you and had already clobbered you one. And trust me when I say that back in those days Me-Ma had a mean right hook.

"Do you know who the heck I think is a dang commie?" Pa-Pa would ask before takin' a bite out of the cookie he was still holdin'. He'd go on, attemptin' to change the subject and save face at the same time, to name some local person he'd branded a communist because he felt they'd overcharged him for somethin' or other. Needless to say, Pa-Pa had once again made his jab about Me-Ma's need for eyeglasses, and luckily no one in the room had gotten hurt.

By nine in the evenin', after the old folks had headed back over to their trailer with an empty tray, we'd all pile into the pickup truck and head out into the dark country roads to claim our Christmas tree. Daddy would drive to the area where Donna Sue had left her marker, passin' it up till he got to the crossroad. He'd then turn the truck around and shut his headlights off. Slowly he'd head back down the road as we all kept a watchful eye out for Donna Sue's white panties blowin' in the cool moonlit November night from a barbed-wire fence. The truck cab was filled with silence as we drove further down the dark dirt road until finally one of us would shout out, "There they are!" Thanks to my sister's large behind, her white panties were always easy to spot even durin' pitch-black, foggy, overcast nights. Daddy would shift the truck into neutral, killin' the engine, and coast the quarter mile up to the fence. Quietly we'd all get out of the truck and climb under the fence, and Daddy would saw down the tree by hand, being careful to make as little noise as possible. Then we'd make our way back to the truck with the tree in hand, while Donna Sue quickly retrieved her hefty underwear. With all of us in, Daddy would start up the truck and floor it down the dirt road with the lights still off. Us kids yelled out and cheered with joy as Momma and Daddy laughed at our excitement. These were times I'd never forget, and as I grew older, I'd hold each memory of our tree-pickin' nights close to my heart.

The next day, we kids would help Momma make decorations for the tree, and then on Saturday, with Daddy's precise directions, we'd hang 'em up with thoughts of Christmas racin' through our heads. With lovin' care Daddy would thoughtfully instruct us where to place each handmade ornament. But when it came time for the tinsel, well, where it went was for us kids to decide. As you can guess, before we were done there was tinsel all over that tree and us. As a matter of fact, that next day when we went to church, we had the sparkliest hair in the whole place. Even Pastor Pickles, who has long ago gone to meet his maker and claim his bounty, would end his sermons on those Sundays by mentionin' how nice it was to see the "heavenly glow that the Boxcar family was bestowin' upon us durin' this season of joy, goodwill, and celebration of our Lord's birth." At that time a young Nellie Tinkle would kick the organ into a heart-wrenchin' rendition of the tried-and-true Baptist hymn "Just as I Am" while Pastor Pickles would give his altar call, tellin' everyone that they too can have that "glow" if they just come on down.

For most of my early years in life we were pretty much poor, but us kids didn't know it. Momma and Daddy did their best and really worked hard to provide for us. But it seemed like when they were just about to make ends meet; someone would up and move the ends. But Momma really knew how to give the impression that we had a lot more gifts durin' Christmas than we actually did. By the looks of packages and the way they were strategically placed, it looked like rich city folks lived in our humble trailer home. One of the ways she was able to create this illusion was by wrappin' up items that we already had. My sister, Donna Sue, got the same toothbrush eight years in a row. My brother, Jack Daniels, got it on the ninth year. So what if one of my presents was a half-used box of corn pads? The fun and thrill for us kids was not always what was inside the packages, but rather just the simple pleasure of unwrappin' 'em. In later years there've been times I wish I hadn't given those corn pads back to Momma after all.

### Things to Get You in the Holiday Mood
Rent and watch any movie that was ever made about Christmas. I'm sure there are hundreds of 'em. Unfortunately, there ain't no trailer park Christmas movies, but I'm workin' on that.

### Things to Do
Get up and unwrap presents.

### How to Decorate Your Trailer for This Holiday
The more the better as I always say. Of course we roll out the Christmas tree from the closet, take off the garbage bag that kept it from the dust, and plug it in. One thing Momma always did was wrap all the photos and works of art that hung on the walls in wrappin' paper. She'd also put bows or ribbons on 'em. And she'd put a

birthday hat on the pictures of Jesus. I always thought that was classy. When it comes to the outside of the trailer, we keep our lights strung up all year round so all you got to do is plug 'em in. Now if you can afford to add more, by all means do so.

### Trailer Park Tradition

We hold the traditional Christmas cake bake-off between all the trailers each year. Every trailer can enter a cake that looks like a Christmas tree and the best-tastin' one wins two free months of lot rent. The last year Me-Ma was livin' in the park, she made a cake out of real pieces of tree, which, needless to say made all of us sick, but she did not win. This year we'll all enter, but we have a feelin' Dottie Lamb will be the winner, cake or no cake, if you know what I mean.

### Somethin' to Bring to a Party

## DONNA SUE'S MEATY BALLS

*My sister puts the "Ho" in "Ho-Ho-Ho" with these little babies.*

*Serves 4 to 5*

3 pounds hamburger meat
¼ pound cracker crumbs
2 eggs
1 big onion, chopped
1 green pepper, chopped
2 teaspoons chili powder

Put all the ingredients in a big bowl and mix with your hands. Mix well and form into nice-size balls. Place 'em in an oiled skillet and brown 'em on all sides.

Preheat the oven to 325 degrees F.

In a new bowl, combine:

½ chopped onion
2 (20 ounce) cans of tomato sauce
2 tablespoons hot sauce
Salt and pepper to taste
This is your sauce.

Put the balls in a large oven dish, pour the sauce over 'em, and cover. Cook for 2 hours at 325 degrees F. Goes great with mashed taters.

—*DONNA SUE BOXCAR, LOT #6*

*Dinner Menu*

# AWAY IN THE MANGER ZUCCHINI SQUARES

*I'd have slept in a barn with a camel and an ass,
too, if these had been in there.*

*Makes 4 dozen*

3 cups sliced thinly zucchini

¼ cup minced onion

2 tablespoons chopped parsley

½ teaspoon dried oregano

¾ teaspoon salt

1 clove garlic, minced

½ cup grated Parmesan cheese

4 eggs, slightly beaten

2 tablespoons milk

1 cup flour

½ teaspoon seasonin' salt

⅛ teaspoon pepper

1½ teaspoons bakin' powder

1 tablespoon margarine, melted

½ cup vegetable oil

Preheat the oven to 350 degrees F.

Take a large bowl and mix together the zucchini, onion, parsley, oregano, salt, garlic, and cheese. Stir in the eggs and milk, mixin' well.

In a small bowl, combine the flour, seasonin' salt, pepper, and bakin' powder. Add this to the first mixture, followed by the melted margarine and the oil. Pour it all into a greased casserole dish and bake for 25 to 30 minutes, or until nice and brown. When you pull it out, cut it into little squares and serve it warm.

—*SISTER BERTHA, LOT #12*

# MOMMA BALLZAK'S DOWN-HOME-STYLE EGGNOG

*A couple cups of this and you'll forget what holi-*
*day it is you're celebratin'!*

*4 to 6 servin's*

6 eggs, separated

2 cups heavy cream

1 cup milk

¾ cup sugar

½ cup rum

½ cup whiskey

½ cup brandy

1 tablespoon grated nutmeg

Get out two bowls. In one put all the egg whites and in the other put the yolks. Mix the yolks well, slowly and gradually addin' the heavy cream, milk, and sugar.

Whip the egg whites until they form into soft peaks. Fold the whites into the yolk mixture and add the rum, whiskey, and brandy gradually. Put it uncovered in a fridge for 2 hours. When you serve it, sprinkle the nutmeg on top.

—*MOMMA BALLZAK, LOT #16*

# PASTOR IDA MAY BEE'S BLESSED BAPTIST EGGNOG

*Its kick comes from the good Lord above . . . and*
*all that sugar.*

*8 to 10 servin's*

12 eggs

3½ cups sugar

1 quart heavy cream

1 teaspoon vanilla extract

Grated nutmeg

Separate the eggs. Take the yolks and beat 'em real good and cream with 1 cup of the sugar.

Now take the whites and beat 'em till they peak. Add the rest of the sugar and cream and beat it until stiff. Fold both mixtures together. Add the vanilla extract. Mix well. Put it in pitchers and keep it in the fridge overnight. Top with nutmeg. Serve with a prayer.

*—PASTOR IDA MAY BEE, LOT #7*

# DOTTIE LAMB'S LITTLE LAMB LEMON BREAD

*If this stuff don't make you want to deck your halls,*
*nothin' will!*

*Makes 1 loaf*

½ cup margarine

2 cups sugar

2 eggs, beaten

Grated zest of 1 large lemon

1½ cups flour

1 teaspoon bakin' powder

½ teaspoon salt

½ cup milk

½ cup chopped nuts

Juice of 2 medium lemons

Cream the margarine and 1 cup of sugar in a bowl. Add the eggs and lemon zest.

In a bowl sift the flour, bakin' powder, and salt. Add the dry mix to the other, alternatin' with the milk. Add the nuts. Pour the mixture into a greased and floured 9×5-inch loaf pan and bake for 30 to 40 minutes at 350 degrees F. Take out of the oven and cool for 15 minutes. Carefully remove from the pan.

To make a glaze, mix the remaining cup of sugar with the lemon juice in a small bowl. Glaze the loaf with this mixture. Cover and store in the fridge.

*—DOTTIE LAMB, LOT #14*

# SING CHOIRS OF ANGELS AMBROSIA SALAD

*Oh, look! Another ambrosia salad recipe!*

Serves 6

1 can fruit cocktail, well drained

1 (15 ounce) can of mandarin oranges, well drained

1 banana, sliced

2 tablespoons almonds, sliced

½ cup flaked coconut

2 cups whipped toppin'

½ teaspoon almond extract

Combine the canned fruits, banana, almonds, and coconut.

In a medium bowl mix the whipped toppin' with the almond extract. Stir the whipped toppin' into the fruit mixture. Serve chilled.

—*SISTER BERTHA, LOT #12*

# FIVE BUSY ELVES CAKE

*Even if there was no Santa Claus, I'd make this cake.*

6 to 8 servin's

2 sticks margarine

3 cups sugar

½ cup shortenin'

3 cups flour

½ teaspoon bakin' powder

5 eggs, well beaten

1 cup milk

1 teaspoon coconut flavorin'

1 teaspoon rum flavorin'

1 teaspoon butter flavorin'

1 teaspoon lemon extract

1 teaspoon vanilla extract

In a large bowl, cream the margarine, sugar, and shortenin' until light and fluffy. Stir together the flour and bakin' powder. Beat the eggs until they look kind of like a lemon and then add 'em, alternatin' with the flour mixture and the milk. Stir in the flavorin's. Carefully spoon the mixture into a greased and floured bundt pan. Bake at 325 degrees F. for 1½ hours. Meanwhile, make the glaze:

2 cups sugar
½ cup water
1 teaspoon coconut flavorin'
1 teaspoon rum flavorin'
1 teaspoon butter flavorin'
1 teaspoon lemon extract
1 teaspoon vanilla extract

Mix the above ingredients in a saucepan and bring it to a boil. Stir until all the sugar is dissolved. Pour half of the glaze over the cake while it is still in the pan. Let it cool for 10 minutes and then remove from the pan. Pour the rest of the glaze on the cake. Serve with milk.

*—RUBY ANN BOXCAR, LOT #18*

# NEW YEAR'S EVE
## December 31
### (Not a prison holiday)

We've made it! The year is just about over, and we're still kickin' like don-keys at a basketball game. Now most of y'all know the routine for New Year's Eve on account of it not bein' all that different from the non–trailer park one. Of course, there are two ways to correctly bring in the New Year, and one of 'em is to attend a New Year's Eve party where everyone drinks a toast at midnight and kisses the one they come with. The other may not be as familiar to the rest of you.

What happens is that you take a covered dish, typically a casserole or dessert, to church with you at about eight in the evenin' for a rite that is known worldwide as Watch Night Service. All the food is set up down in the church basement, while upstairs the preacher welcomes everyone and tells 'em to get ready 'cause tonight we're goin' to welcome in the new year "with praises and singin'." That is basically the startin' gun for the vocal part of our holiday. Now, if your church has a choir, they'll sing a bit, followed by a guest singin' group or two. Actually, in some churches there's a whole lineup of gospel vocal groups who come up and sing. But at the First Bap-tist Church of Pangburn, the 31st of December is Karaoke night. That's right, if you can sing, think you can sing, or couldn't sing if a dang songbird flew down your throat, you get your chance on the mike tonight. And of course, dear Nellie Tinkle, who has napped all day long to prepare for this special night, will do everything she can to accompany you on the organ. Back when Pastor Hickey was with us, he'd always choose this event to bring in his drum set. Now, sayin' that Pastor Hickey was bad on the drums is like sayin' the ocean is wet. It's just the way it is, but God bless him, he had no idea of just how bad he was. I'm tellin' y'all I've seen corpses with more rhythm than Pastor Hickey had. Watch Night Service at the First Baptist Church of Pangburn became better known throughout the county as the Night of the Deaf. It was terrible. I know people who actually took the bat-teries out of their hearin' aids before church started just so they wouldn't have to hear Pastor Hickey on the drums. The only thing worse than him was his wife's singin', and on that night, she had six numbers prepared. Oh,

Lord have mercy, she was just terrible. That gal's voice could have turned lifelong Baptists into Catholics. It sounded like somebody was beatin' cats. Imagine bein' tied to a chair and havin' 60 people run their fingernails simultaneously down a chalkboard, and you've basically got her rendition of "Because He Lives."

Anyways, this would go on all night long with a break around 10 P.M. for all of us to go downstairs for the potluck. We'd eat and socialize for an hour and then return for Pastor Hickey's sermon. On that night he'd end right at a minute till midnight and then as we bowed our heads in prayer, he'd give us a countdown. And right as he got to the number "1," Sister Bertha would drop a mirror ball into the baptismal tank, which would be followed by a loud "Happy New Year!" from all in attendance. After we'd all greeted each other with a warm handshake or a Christian hug, Pastor Hickey would give a quick altar call, pass the plate, and send us and our dirty dishes on our way out into the new year to bless the Lord and spread the good news.

I love our new preacher, Pastor Ida May Bee, but the truth be told, I think I just might miss Pastor Hickey and his tone-deaf wife. If only his penis had been larger. Oh, well, Happy New Year to all of you out there!

### Things to Get You in the Holiday Mood
Rent and watch the movie *Duets*.
Ring in the New Year at www.earthcam.com/usa/newyork/timessquare.

### Things to Do
Practice puttin' enough cotton in your ears so that you can't hear, but not so much that people can see that you got it in. And remember to pack a pair of tweezers in your purse so you can easily get it out after the singin' is done.

### How to Decorate Your Trailer for This Holiday
There are no decorations.

### Trailer Park Tradition
Now, this is the day that you clean up all the decorations in your trailer corners. Get out that broom, vacuum, mop, and wet-vac and start cleanin'. Just remem-

ber, it's bad luck if come midnight you have any of last year's decorations still in your trailer. So get busy, you got a whole year's worth of cleanin' to do in only one day's time.

*Somethin' to Bring to a Party*

# RUBY ANN'S CHILI CHEESE DOG BAKE

*Your wieners will thank you for this.*

*Makes 8 servin's*

1 package of frozen tater tots
1 package wieners
2 regular cans of chili
2 cups grated cheese

Put the tater tots on the bottom of a casserole dish and bake at 350 degrees F. for 20 to 25 minutes.

Chop up your wieners into bite-size pieces. Take out the casserole dish and put your chili and wiener pieces in it. Cover these with the cheese and pop in the oven for 20 to 25 minutes more.

—*RUBY ANN BOXCAR, LOT #18*

*Dinner Menu*

# TRAILER PARK LASAGNE

*This will get you ready for the New Year, wherever you spend it!*

1 pound hamburger meat, browned and drained
½ cup water
1 regular bottle or can spaghetti sauce
1 teaspoon salt
8 ounces lasagne noodles, cooked and drained
1 cup small-curd cottage cheese
4 cups sliced or grated mozzarella cheese
½ cup grated Parmesan cheese

Keep your meat in the skillet that it was browned in and add the water, sauce, and salt. Get it to a boil and stir.

Put your noodles in a bakin' dish, followed by the cottage cheese and mozzarella. Put some of the sauce on top of this. Repeat until you've run out of either dish or sauce. Top with the Parmesan. Cover the dish with foil and bake at 375 degrees F. for 1 hour.

*—PASTOR IDA MAY BEE, LOT #7*

## MIDNIGHT CHOCOLATE CHIP COOKIES

*Happy trailer park New Year to you and yours!*

*Makes 3 to 4 dozen cookies*

½ cup margarine

¼ cup granulated sugar

½ cup brown sugar

1 egg

1 teaspoon vanilla extract

1 cup flour

1 cup chocolate chips

½ teaspoon bakin' soda

½ teaspoon salt

In a bowl, cream your margarine and sugars until fluffy. Put your egg and vanilla extract in another bowl. Beat it until it gets nice and smooth. Stir in the flour, soda, and salt and mix real good. Add your chips and mix. Put tablespoon-size balls of dough on a greased cookie sheet and bake for 10 minutes at 350 degrees F. Repeat and eat!

*—KITTY CHITWOOD, LOT #11*

# Helpful Holiday Hints

I've included this chapter in this book on account of all the wonderful and positive comments I got from folks about the "Helpful Hints" section in the *Down Home Trailer Park Cookbook*. From the way people were actin' you'd have thought none of 'em had neighbors who share their secrets to an easier life with 'em. When people come up to me in the streets and say how much the tips from me and the folks at the High Chaparral Trailer Park have helped 'em in their everyday chores in the kitchen, all I could do is to promise 'em even more in my next books. So, with that in mind, here you folks go. Me and the rest of the gang at the High Chaparral hope they help make your holidays as well as the rest of the year easier and a little less stressful.

Now, I want to start off with a list that I find very helpful. If y'all recall, in my first book, *Ruby Ann's Down Home Trailer Park Cookbook*, I had a list for y'all that gave you some measurin' tips. Well, this time around I wanted to start off with this wonderful list that everyone in the High Chaparral Trailer Park helped to put together. It'll help you with the recipes in many ways. For example, if a recipe calls for 1 pack of yeast, but you've only got the big can of yeast, it'll tell you how much out of that can will equal 1 pack. Ain't that nice? Anyways, I hope it's as helpful for you as it has been for me.

**Beans**
    Kidney 1 lb. = 2½ cups dry = 7 cups cooked
    Navy 1 lb. = 2½ cups dry = 7 cups cooked
    Split Peas lb. = 2 cups dried = 5 cups cooked
**Bakin' powder** 1 cup = 5½ oz.
**Bread** 1 slice = ¼ to ⅓ cup dry crumbs
**Butter/Margarine** 1 lb. = 2 cups; ½ lb. = 2 sticks; 1 stick = ½ cup or 8 tablespoons
**Cabbage** 1 medium head = 3 lbs.; 1 lb. = 4 cups shredded

**Cheese**
  ¼ lb. grated = 1 cup
  1 lb = 2⅔ cup
  Cheddar 1 lb. = 4 cups grated
  Cottage cheese 1 lb. = 2 cups
  Cream cheese 3-oz. package = 6 tablespoons; 6-oz. package = 1 cup
**Chocolate** 1 square = 1 oz. = 3 tablespoons grated = 3 tablespoons melted
**Chocolate chips** 6-oz. package = 1 scant cup; 12-oz. package = 1⅛ cup
**Cocoa** 1 lb. = 4 cups
**Coconut** 1 lb. = 5 cups shredded and lightly packed
**Coffee** 1 lb. = 5 cups = 40 to 50 cups of brewed
**Cornmeal** 1 lb. = 3 cups; 1 cup = 4 cups cooked
**Cornstarch** 1 lb. = 3 cups
**Crab meat** 1 lb. = 2 cups
**Crackers**
  Graham crackers 1 cup crumbs = 12 to 15 crackers
  Soda crackers 1 cup crumbs = 20 to 23 crackers
**Cream** ½ pint heavy = 2 cups whipped
**Dates** 1 lb. pitted = 2 cups = 2½ cups chopped
**Eggs** (large)
  1 = ¼ cup
  4 to 5 = 1 cup
  9 = 1 lb.
  7 to 9 whites = 1 cup
  12 to 15 yolks = 1 cup
**Figs** 1 lb. = 3 cups chopped
**Flour**
  All-purpose 1 lb. = 4 cups sifted
  Cake flour 1 lb. = 4½ cups sifted
  Graham flour 1 lb. = 3½ cups
  Whole wheat 1 lb. = 3½ cups
**Fruit**
  Apples 1 lb. (3 medium) = 2 to 2½ cups pared and sliced; 2 quarts = 3 lbs.
  Apricots 1 lb. = 3 cups dried = 6 cups cooked
  Bananas 1 lb. = 3 large with skins off = 2 to 2½ cups sliced
  Fruit peels ½ lb. = 1½ cups cut up
  Lemon or lime 1 medium = 3 tablespoons juice; 5 to 8 = 1 cup juice; 1 rind = 1 tablespoons grated

Oranges 1 medium = 2 to 3 tablespoons juice; 3 to 4 = 1 cup juice; 1 rind = 2 tablespoons grated

**Fruit, candied** ½ lb. = 1½ cups cut up

**Gelatin, plain** 1 envelope = 1 tablespoon dry

**Herbs** 1 teaspoon dry = 1 tablespoon fresh

**Marshmallows**

1 large = 10 miniatures

10 large = 1 cup miniature (lightly packed)

100 mini = 1 cup (lightly packed)

½ lb. = 16 regular

1 lb. = 8 cups miniature = 75 to 80 regular

10-oz. bag = 6 cups miniature

**Milk, canned**

Evaporated 5-oz. can = ⅔ cup; 14½-oz can = 1⅔ cups

Sweetened Condensed 14-oz. can = 1¼ cup

**Mustard, prepared** 1 tablespoon = 1 teaspoon dry

**Nuts**

1 lb. nutmeats, chopped = 4 cups

Almonds 1 lb. (in shell) = 1¾ cups nutmeats

Almonds 1 lb. blanched and whole = 3½ cups

Pecans 1 lb. (in shell) = 2¼ cups shelled; 1 lb. already shelled = 4 cups

Peanuts 1 lb. (in shell) = 2¼ cups shelled; 1 lb. already shelled = 3 cups

Walnuts 1 lb. (in shell) = 1⅔ cups shelled; 1 lb. already shelled = 4 cups

Walnuts, raw 1 lb. = 5 cups raw = 8 cups cooked

**Oatmeal** 1 lb. raw = 5 cups = 9 cups cooked

**Onion** 1 medium = ½ cup chopped

**Pasta**

Macaroni 1 lb. = 4 cups raw = 8 cups cooked

Noodles 1 lb. = 6 cups raw = 9 cups cooked; 1 cup = 1½ cups cooked

Spaghetti 1 lb. = 4 cups raw = 6 to 8 cups cooked

**Peas** 1 lb. (in pod) = 1 cup shelled

**Pepper, green or red** 1 large = 1 cup diced

**Popcorn** 1 cup raw = 5 quarts popped

**Potato**

White 1 lb. = 3 to 4 medium = 2 cups cooked and mashed

Sweet 1 lb. = 3 medium = 2 cups cooked and mashed

**Rice** 1 lb. = 2 cups dried = 4 cups cooked

**Rice, instant** 1 cup = 2 cups cooked

**Shortenin'** 1 lb. = 2 cups
**Stuffin's**
  Herb-seasoned 8-oz. bag = 4½ cups seasoned dry bread cubes
  Croutons 11-oz. bag = 10 cups (if large-sized cubes)
**Sugar**
  Granulated 1 lb. = 2 cups
  Brown 1 lb. = 2¼ cups
  Confectioner's 1 lb. = 3½ cups sifted
  Cubes 1 lb. = 96 to 160 cubes
**Tomato** 1 lb. = 3 to 4 medium
**Wafers, Vanilla** 24 wafers = 1 cup crumbs
**Whipped toppin's**, frozen 9-oz. container = 3 cups; 12-oz. container = 4 cups
**Yeast** 2-oz. cake = 3 packages dry yeast
**Yeast, dry** 1 envelope = 1 tablespoon

Several people provided the followin' candy cookin' menu, so a big thanks goes out to 'em all.

| Consistency | Temperature (F) | Test | Uses |
|---|---|---|---|
| Soft ball | 234° to 240° | Syrup forms a soft ball when dropped into cold water; ball flattens when removed | Fudge |
| Firm ball | 244° to 248° | Syrup forms a ball when dropped into cold water; ball does not flatten when removed | Caramels |
| Hard ball | 250° to 266° | Syrup forms a ball when dropped into cold water; hard enough to hold its shape, yet still plastic | Popcorn balls divinity |
| Soft Crack | 270° to 290° | Syrup separates into threads when dropped into cold water; threads are hard but not brittle | Butterscotch, taffy |
| Hard crack | °300 to 310° | Syrup separates into threads that are hard and brittle when dropped into cold water | Peanut Brittle |
| Caramel | 338° | Barley sugar becomes brown | Flavor and color |

### *And now, on to the HELPFUL HINTS!*

- To squeeze juice from a lemon, place it in the microwave for 40 seconds on high. You won't believe how much more juice you'll get from it.
- If a recipe calls for only a tablespoon or a teaspoon of juice from a lemon, follow the directions above, but then simply poke a small hole in it the size of a skewer or the tip of a knittin' needle. Take out the needed amount of juice and put the fruit back in the fridge. Your fruit will last and can be used later.
- Simmer beans, don't boil 'em. Boilin' can cause the liquid to overflow and hurt your beans.

*—OPAL LAMB-INMAN, LOT #1*
*—DICK INMAN, LOT #1*
*—FERNANDO DIAZ, LOT #1*

- Put hot water in a pan that has stuck-on food in it. Put it back on the burner and bring it to a low boil. Usin' a wooden or plastic spoon, push on the stuck-on food. It should eventually float up to the top of the water. Wash with soap and water.
- For really resistant stuck-on food, sprinkle a layer of bakin' soda over the bottom of the pan and add enough water to form a paste. Cover and let it sit overnight. By the next day, it should come off with a wipe.

*—ANITA BIGGON, LOT #2*

- A potato peeler is wonderful for cuttin' nice even slices on a block of cheese. You can even cut little pieces for tacos if you use it on a corner of the block.
- I dice up onion and keep in ice cube trays, which, once frozen, can be put into little freezer bags for future use in soups and sauces.

*—LOIS BUNCH, LOT #3*

- To avoid cryin' when peelin' onions, put 'em in the fridge for a while or put 'em in ice water.
- If your hands smell like onions, garlic, fish, or whatever, put a few shakes of salt on your palms and rub briskly. Wash with soap and water now. Be careful, you don't want to get this all over the organ when you go to play.

*—NELLIE TINKLE, LOT #4*
*—WENDY BOTTOM, LOT #4*

- I find this tip to be very useful and time-savin'. Measurin' shortenin' or margarine into measurin' cups can be quite messy. I hated washin' the measurin' cup afterwards. But if you place Saran Wrap into the measurin' cup beforehand, then all you have to do is lift the plastic wrap and shake out the shortenin' or margarine! And the best part is you don't have a dirty greasy measurin' cup!

- Use cream-style corn instead of oil in your cornbread recipes.

*—MOMMA BOXCAR, LOT #5*

- Corn should never be husked before it's cooked. Put it in the microwave for 4–5 minutes with the husks intact. The results are fantastic. You can take the husks off after the cookin'. And no pots of water to boil and clean up afterward. You can just eat your corn and have a drink.
- To give your frostin' a more enhanced taste, use vodka or gin instead of water.

*—DONNA SUE BOXCAR, LOT #6*

- Dental floss is an excellent way to slice cake, especially when you have a lot of cake!
- Candles will burn slower, and last longer, if you refrigerate them for one day before using. Be careful not to crack them when they're cold.

*—PASTOR IDA MAY BEE, LOT #7*

- Before puttin' a bag of microwave popcorn into the oven, knead it until the lumps are broken. This way, all the kernels will pop. Save the kernels that don't pop and string 'em to make beautiful jewelry.
- Try refreshin' stale chips and crackers by puttin' 'em on a plate and microwavin' 'em for 30 to 45 seconds. Let 'em stand one minute to crisp.

*—LULU BELL BOXCAR, LOT #8*

- Add some spice to your homemade pizza sauce by addin' medium or hot salsa to it.
- To make measurin' honey easier, spray spoon or measurin' cup with Pam cooking spray and the honey will fall out of the measurin' device without a lot of mess.
- Place tablespoons of leftover tomato paste on squares of plastic wrap on a bakin' sheet. Put the bakin' sheet in the freezer and when the individual portions are frozen solid, wrap 'em tightly and store in the freezer in a plastic bag for future cookin'.

*—JUANITA HIX, LOT #9*

- I keep a solution of ammonia and water in small pump bottle on my kitchen sink. I use it on my sponge or a paper towel to wipe my stove top. Dried with a paper towel, it leaves a nongreasy, nonstreaky surface with no rinsin' and without a lot of trouble.

- Put flour in a large salt shaker and keep it in the freezer. When you need to flour a pan or make homemade gravy, give it a shake. It helps prevent lumpy gravy and messy counters.

*—OLLIE WHITE, LOT #10*

- To reduce the strong taste of onions in a salad, dice them and put in refrigerator overnight.
- Saltin' the cookin' liquid for dried peas and beans tends to slow cookin' and toughen the beans. Salt should be added after they're cooked.

*—KITTY CHITWOOD, LOT #11*

- Keep an empty 18-ounce plastic peanut butter jar handy to mix dry ingredients. Just measure dry ingredients into the jar, screw the lid on, and shake to combine. No lumps, no dust, no mess, and a lot more thorough than mixin' them in a bowl with a spoon.
- Keep your nuts in airtight containers in the refrigerator. They'll stay fresher longer.

*—SISTER BERTHA FAY, LOT #12*

- Large tuna fish cans can be used to bake small pumpkin breads for gifts. Great size, great shape.
- Sprinkle a little flour on potatoes before fryin' 'em and they will be extra crispy and crunchy.

*—CONNIE KAY, LOT #13*
*—WANDA KAY, LOT #13*

- For a cheap tenderizer, add lemon juice or vinegar to liquid in which meat is bein' cooked.
- Try gratin' a raw potato after you've grated cheese. The potato clears the cheese out of the holes.

*—DOTTIE LAMB, LOT #14*

- To clean small-neck bottles or vases, place a little rice and warm soapy water inside and shake well. Rinse out and let drip dry.
- Don't throw away that egg you just accidentally cracked. Just wrap it up in foil, twist both ends, and boil it like that.

*—DONNY OWENS, LOT #15*
*—KENNY LYNN, LOT #15*

- Put some red wine in the water when cookin' rice. It gives it a real special taste.
- To make soft bread crumbs for a recipe, tear soft bread with fingers into small pieces. A glass of rum with ice helps to make this task easier.

*—MOMMA BALLZAK, LOT #16*

- As soon as you get your lettuce home from the Piggly Wiggly, immediately wrap it in a couple paper towels, turn the plastic bag it came in inside-out, and put the wrapped lettuce back in there, and put it in the fridge. This will make your lettuce last longer.
- For softer beans, cover the cookin' pot.

*—FAYE FAYE LARUE, LOT #17*
*—TINA FAYE STOPENBLOTTER, LOT #17*

- Place a damp dishcloth under your bowl when beatin' somethin' to keep the bowl from bouncin' around.
- If you want to keep your yolk in the center of an egg while you're boilin' it, stir the water.

*—RUBY ANN BOXCAR, LOT #18*

- Store a tongue depressor in your sugar and flour canisters for a quick means of levelin' off your dry measures.
- If you cut a thin slice off both ends of your taters when you cook 'em, they'll bake much faster.

*—JEANNIE JANSSEN, LOT #19*

- Use an apple corer to core tomatoes.
- To make cleanup easier, tear off a piece of wax paper and place it on your kitchen counter. Then measure all your ingredients over the wax paper. Cleanup is a breeze since all you have to do is toss the wax paper away.

*—LOVIE BIRCH, LOT #20*

---

Thanks to the whole gang at Citadel/Kensington: Bruce Bender, Margaret Wolf, Carol Cady, Laurie Parkin, Joan Schulhafer and Mary Pomponio, Doug Mendini, Laura Shatzkin, and Kris Noble.

# Index

# COMIN' IN 2003:

## More Trailer Park Entertainin' from Ruby Ann Boxcar—AND somethin' else to shake your tail feathers, from her sister Donna Sue:

If you liked this book, just wait, 'cause come May 2003, me and the gang down at the High Chaparral Trailer Park are at it again! That's right, we've pulled our favorite recipes together as well as our cookin' secrets and helpful hints to present *Ruby Ann's Down Home Trailer Park BBQin' Cookbook*. Not only do we give you fantastic food items like Kelly Ripa's Tribute Hot Links (Lulu Bell just loves her), Billy Bob's Kabobs, Pastor Ida May Bee's Bible Belt Brisket, Nellie Tinkle's Tender Ribs, Harland Hix's Shriveled Wienie Bake, Momma Ballzak's Slap Me Silly Sauce, and Sister Bertha's Born Again Baked Beans, but we even help you select the best kind of BBQ grill that will meet your needs. And what would one of my books be without a gossip-filled up-date on all the fine folks at the High Chaparral Trailer Park? Yes, dear friends, *Ruby Ann's Down Home Trailer Park BBQin' Cookbook* is sure to be as much fun as a cool breezy summer night in Pangburn with a bottle of Lulu Bell's Simple Sauce and a plate full of Donna Sue's Pork Rump Delight.

Speakin' of my sister Donna Sue, she's actually found time in between drinks and her busy schedule as the headliner at the Blue Whale Strip Club to put pen to paper and write her own collection of recipes (who knew she could write, too?). Comin' June 2003 is *Donna Sue's Down Home Trailer Park Bartender's Guide*. My sister assures me that this ain't your momma and daddy's cocktail makin' guide, and with drinks like the Storm Cellar Door (after one of these you'll feel like a twister done hit you), the Pole Dancer, the Bionic Beaver (the late Dora Beaver of Beaver Liquors just loved this one), Viagra Please (after one of these you'll need somethin' to get you up off the floor), Ruby Ann's Cosmopolitan (two of these and you'll think you're back in the 70s), or a Flamin' Dr Pepper, she might just be right. Of course she'll also include the mixin' styles for icy sweet drinks for coolin' summertime fun as well as for standard screwdrivers, whiskey sours, maitais, martinis, and other traditional adult beverages. Plus, keepin' in the who's who tradition of the Down Home Trailer Park series, Donna Sue also introduces you to and provides all the lowdown on her fellow dancers and coworkers down at the Blue Whale Strip club. She's even snuck back into the kitchen and got several recipes from Chef Bernie D. Toast just so you can enjoy the same kind of food that the Blue Whale patrons try to keep down while they watch my sister dance.

So keep your eye out, 'cause with *Ruby Ann's Down Home Trailer Park BBQin' Cookbook* and *Donna Sue's Down Home Trailer Park Bartender's Guide*, you ain't got no reason *not* to throw a party or two this summer.